IT WAS SAID TO BE THE WAR FOUGHT BY THE UNWILLING, LED BY THE UNQUALIFIED, TO DO THE UNNECESSARY FOR THE UNGRATEFUL.

In every person's life there are special times that are never forgotten. Vietnam offered a year of triumph, despair, horror, and other emotions burned into my memory so strongly that I can never forget them. It all happened when I was so young, inexperienced, and naive that I did not thoroughly realize the impact on the rest of my life at the time.

When I had left my wife back in the spring of 1969, I could hardly wait to get to Vietnam. I had looked forward with anticipation to the adventure and excitement of being part of the war. Leaving my R&R in Hawaii was different. This time I knew exactly what I was going back to....

Also by Lt. Col. Michael Lee Lanning
Published by Ivy Books:

A COMPANY COMMANDER'S JOURNAL

INSIDE THE LRRPS: RANGERS IN VIETNAM

With Ray William Stubbe:
**INSIDE FORCE RECON: RECON MARINES IN
VIETNAM**

With Dan Cragg:
INSIDE THE VC AND THE NVA

THE ONLY WAR WE HAD

A PLATOON LEADER'S JOURNAL OF VIETNAM

Michael Lee Lanning

IVY BOOKS • NEW YORK

...for Linda

Ivy Books
Published by Ballantine Books
Copyright © 1987 by Michael Lee Lanning

Grateful acknowledgment is made to the following for permission to reprint previously published material:

Alkatraz Corner Music Co.: excerpt from the lyrics to "Feels
Like I'm Fixin' to Die, Rag," words and music by Joe
McDonald. Copyright © 1965 by Alkatraz Corner Music Co.
Used by permission.

Playboy Magazine: excerpt from an article entitled "The Risk
Takers" by Robert Daley in the June 1969 issue of *Playboy*.
Originally published in *Playboy*. Copyright © 1969 by PLAY-
BOY.

Reader's Digest and *Farm Journal*: excerpt from an article
entitled "Signs of Life" from the June 1969 issue of *Reader's
Digest*. Reprinted with permission from *Reader's Digest* and
Farm Journal.

Library of Congress Catalog Card Number: 87-90918

ISBN 0-8041-0005-5

Printed in Canada

First Edition: November 1987

20 19 18 17 16 15 14 13 12

CONTENTS

AUTHOR'S NOTE

This book focuses on the actions of a United States Army infantry platoon in Vietnam. A basic explanation of that organization and where it fit into the "big picture" of the war may be beneficial to the reader.

The official organization of an infantry platoon consisted of four squads. Each squad was composed of a squad leader and two fire teams of four and five men. A platoon headquarters containing a platoon leader, a platoon sergeant, and a radio-telephone operator brought the total strength up to 43 men.

Although this was the official organization on paper, it little resembled the reality of a platoon in the field in Vietnam. Rarely, if ever, were enough replacements available to fill the ranks depleted by battle casualties, illness, and completion of tours. Similar difficulties were experienced in securing men of the proper ranks for the various leadership positions. It was not unusual for a platoon to have less than half the authorized 43 infantrymen, with soldiers filling leadership roles one or two ranks above the stripes they wore on their sleeves.

It is a common perception by many people, especially those not familiar with the military, that the Army in Vietnam was a rigid organization. This is simply not correct. Constantly changing numbers of personnel required great flexibility. Platoons with four squads might have to reorganize into half that number after a significant fire fight, then add a squad a week later as replacements arrived. At the same time, vacancies created by casualties might elevate a fire team leader to squad leader and a squad leader to platoon sergeant or even platoon leader.

Men who live together in an environment of hardship and danger form a bond of brotherhood far beyond that of any other group. Casualties from fire fights were not merely numbers but close friends and companions. Despite the obvious emotional impact experienced with the loss of fellow infantrymen, the reorganization of the platoon occurred quickly—often while the explosions and the hail of bullets continued.

Rapid and effective reorganizations worked because the platoon and the Army as a whole were designed on an effective, proven system with a well-defined chain of command.

The US Army of the Vietnam period, as well as before and after the war, was organized so that all units and individuals were controlled in groups of two to five elements. As has already been illustrated, a platoon was composed of two to four squads, each divided into two fire teams of four or five men.

This system was mirrored throughout the Army. Three or four platoons made up a company, and four or five companies were in each battalion. A similar number of battalions were assigned to a brigade, brigades to a division, and divisions to a field force. Two field forces, which were equivalent to a corps in the pre- and post-Vietnam Army, made up the United State Army Vietnam (USARV) which was subordinate to the Department of the Army in Washington, D.C. An exception to this sequence, including the author's unit, were several separate brigades which were not subordinate to a division but reported directly to the field force headquarters.

At the head of each organization was a commander, who, while responsible for all those soldiers assigned to his unit, still directed his orders to those two to five subordinate commanders directly under him. This system, or chain of command as it is known, ran from the President of the United States to his appointed civilian Secretary of the Department of

Defense to the Secretary of the Department of the Army. From the Department of the Army the chain reached to USARV commanded by a general (four stars) to a field force commanded by a lieutenant general (three stars) to a division commanded by a major general (two stars) to a brigade commanded by a colonel to a battalion commanded by a lieutenant colonel to a company commanded by a captain to a platoon led by a lieutenant to a squad led by a staff sergeant to a fire team led by a sergeant, and, finally, to the individual rifleman. The exception, again, being in the separate brigades, where a brigadier general (one star) commanded rather than a colonel.

Platoons in Vietnam differed in unit designation, area of operation and, of course, individual characteristics. Yet we were more similar than different. The following pages tell the story of only one of well over 1,000 US infantry platoons that fought in Vietnam.

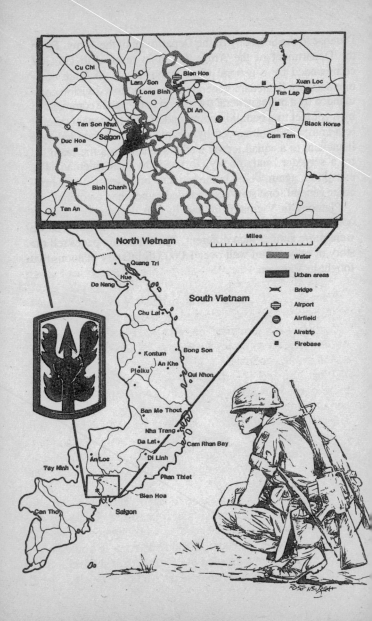

North Vietnam

South Vietnam

Miles

Water

Urban areas

Bridge

Airport

Airfield

Airstrip

Firebase

Cu Chi

Lam Son

Bien Hoa

Xuan Loc

Long Binh

Ten Lap

Ten Son Nhut

Di An

Black Horse

Duc Hoa

Saigon

Cam Tam

Binh Chanh

Tan An

Quang Tri

Hue

Da Nang

Chu Lai

Kontum

Bong Son

An Khe

Pleiku

Qui Nhon

Ban Me Thuot

Nha Trang

Da Lat

Cam Rhan Bay

An Loc

Di Linh

Tay Ninh

Phan Thiet

Bien Hoa

Can Tho

Saigon

INTRODUCTION

A war is a major event in a man's life. It was popular among many who fought to say that Vietnam "wasn't much of a war, but it was the only one we had." I can only add that it was enough of a war for me, for I am neither old nor young enough to want to experience another one.

I am proud to have served in Vietnam. I feel no guilt, have no regrets, harbor no memories I cannot cope with, and—except for a few terrifying moments and the many young men resting for eternity under neat rows of military headstones—I would change nothing.

What I do feel is satisfaction and pride in doing what had to be done, in standing up when called upon by my country and in being prepared to die if necessary.

I may have been naive in my love for and feeling of obligation to my country. My attitude was that the USA had been good to me; now it was time to pay a little back. The elected officials said the war was right and I had a duty to fight. That was enough for me.

However, I went to Vietnam not only because of the obligation I felt to do my duty but also because I did not want to miss the chance to experience the major significant event of my generation. I, of course, wondered what it would be like to go to war, and I dreaded the prospects of hardship, discipline, family separation and the possibility of death or debilitating injuries. Yet, I knew I did not want to let pass the opportunity to challenge myself and to experience the adventure. I felt it would be an irreversible mistake to avoid the war, for I knew if I did, I would never know myself to the fullest.

Because I knew this would be a critical period in my life, I kept a journal of my time in Nam. I made my first entry a few days before my departure from Texas, and it simply reads, "This starts what I hope to be a full book." It concludes a year later with "I AM HOME!" The pages in between hold my story; however, it is much more than only my story, for my experiences were much the same as those of thousands of others who went off to fight a war that many people felt was fought by the unwilling, led by the unqualified, to do the unnecessary for the ungrateful.

In my year in Vietnam, I walked the booby-trapped rice paddies of the Delta, searching for the elusive Viet Cong, and later macheted my way through the triple-canopy jungle, fighting the North Vietnamese Regulars. I served as an Infantry platoon leader, reconnaissance platoon leader and a company commander. I sweated, thirsted, hunted, killed. Somewhere in all my experiences, I overlapped the situations of nearly every Infantryman and many others who served.

After returning from the war, I allowed only my wife and my father to read my journals. I then packed them away in a cardboard box with all the letters I had written Linda. It was not until 1984, after a visit to the Vietnam Veterans' Memorial, that I decided to dig out the old journals and read them. I found my words of fifteen years earlier to be regretfully sophomoric. I readily admit the journal entries are not well-written and are fraught with idealism and, yes, occasionally, with cynicism. My daily entries are a combination of military jargon, abbreviations, and notes that had no meanings except to me. The quotes in the entries have no direct application to the date I wrote them. They are just words that meant something at the time.

Yet the entries painted the person I was then and, as I have slowly come to realize, shaped the person I am now. The writings appear here as I wrote them on the pages—pages often mud-splattered and occasionally blood-stained. I follow each day's entry with clarifications and honest efforts to explain the day as realistically and as understandably as possible. Letters home to my wife, brother, and parents, tucked away all these years, greatly assisted me in re-creating this day-to-day account.

I wrote this book with the intention of assisting the non-veteran, and perhaps even the veteran, to understand a small part of the Vietnam experience. By the time I finished, I realized that I had written it for myself, and possibly for my daughters and wife so they could better understand me.

PRE-JOURNAL

I am not sure that anyone is ever really ready to go to war. While the spirit and curiosity come easily, the knowledge and skills of warfare do not. Unfortunately, most battlefield expertise can only be gained the hard way—in combat itself.

Still, I felt comfortable with my training before reaching Southeast Asia. Four years at Texas A & M University had prepared me for active duty as well as any ROTC institution was capable. The Army's Basic Officer Course had provided more fundamentals, and the Airborne School had presented physical conditioning and served as a confidence builder. Ranger School had honed leadership, map-reading, and survival skills to a fine edge.

A brief tour with the 82d Airborne Division at Fort Bragg, North Carolina, had helped educate me about the Army. There most members of my rifle platoon were recent returnees from Vietnam, awaiting discharge or orders to go back for another tour. Their advice, usually combined with exaggerated war stories, was often more beneficial than the Army's formal training. At Fort Bragg I also learned how the Army really worked—and did not work.

Yet time passed all too quickly. My part in the Vietnam war rushed to meet me—but not always in the way I expected.

Soldiers departing for Vietnam were usually granted a 30-day leave in route. My wife and I spent the month traveling

4

cross country from North Carolina to Texas and California. Linda and I had been married for a little over a year and because of my frequent temporary-duty assignments to military schools already had spent less than six months together. It would be our third anniversary before we had been together for the equivalent of a year.

On our way to our parents' homes in Texas, we stopped at the Shiloh Battlefield Park in Mississippi, and I encountered for the first time what it meant to be a Vietnam soldier. As I stared across the field where American had fought American, an older man casually remarked to me, ''My great-grandfather charged across this field with the Northern Army.'' I replied that probably my kin had been waiting for his great-grandfather about where we were now standing. We talked for some time about the Civil War and the patriotism displayed by both sides. In the course of the conversation, I mentioned that I was on my way to Vietnam. He hesitated, gave me a strange look, hurried to his nearby car, and departed. I was left feeling that I had somehow been wrong even to mention my destination. Perhaps he had been more interested in discussing old wars than in the present one.

Visits to family members and old friends were equally disturbing. Those who truly cared troubled me with their concern and worry about my safety. Even more bothersome were those, especially of my own age, who were not in uniform and made no mention of the war nor my impending departure for it. Maybe they were just embarrassed at their noncommitment. However, in reality, it seemed more likely they felt superior for having avoided an unpleasant experience. Maybe they were right, but they do not know nor will they ever realize just what they missed.

Songs and poems are written about departures. Moviemakers love the soldier-departing-home scenes. I do not remember any dramatics nor music in the air when I left Texas. What remains in my mind is Linda's grandfather's last words to me. The retired farmer, over seventy years old, standing proud in bib overalls simply said, ''It doesn't seem right you going off to war and risking your life. Why don't they send old men like me and let the young ones like you stay home?'' Good question, Granddad. I had no answer then and even less of one today.

Perhaps the first realization of just what I was getting myself into came about a mile from my parents' house. After a fairly unemotional good-bye, I thought that the parting had not been too bad. That all changed when I glanced in the rear-view mirror and caught what might be my last glimpse of my parents' modest farm home.

Our next stop was Fort Bliss, near El Paso, Texas, to visit my brother Jim and his wife Judy. Jim had returned from Vietnam a little over a year before—just prior to Linda's and my wedding. He had displayed tremendous bravery in combat as an Infantry company commander. Among other awards, he wore the Silver Star, our country's third highest medal for valor.

Jim had married Judy during a brief leave home after a year in Vietnam. He had volunteered for a six-month extension to remain with his company. After only three days of marriage, he cut short his honeymoon by a week when he learned his unit was countering a large enemy offensive. He felt he was needed at what in other wars had been called the front.

Jim's job at Fort Bliss was as a basic training company commander. He showed me his troops and lamented that many were recent draftees under the McNamara 100,000 Project, which allowed into the Army young men whose mental capabilities were far below those of the previous standards. Jim and I shared the concern over these individuals—his for training them, and mine for leading and depending on them in combat.

Our brief visit at Fort Bliss was somewhat stressed. I did not realize it at the time, but Jim's mind must have been full of his own memories of the war and the awareness of what I was going into. He gave me no advice, for he, too, was confident of my training. His only guidance was that I should keep a diary of my experiences. I flippantly replied that a diary was what teenage girls wrote in. He answered, "Then call it a journal. You will be glad you did." As usual, he was right.

The next day I purchased a journal.

El Paso, Tex
    This starts what I hope to be a full book—covering what I hope to be an interesting and fruitful year—
    This afternoon I visited Jim's working place and around his Bde area—
    Jim's boss Col Burr said—VN will go on forever—I hope to do my part in proving him wrong—

In Flight American Flt 313 1900
    Linda Ann and I on our way to San Francisco—Had a wonderful time in El Paso—Mexico, Races, Ruidoso, etc—
    20 min layover Tucson, Ariz.

San Francisco Arrived approx 2200
    Good flight—
    Staying at Marine Memorial Hotel—SF looks like fun

Linda and I decided to fly to San Francisco to have as much time as possible to enjoy the city and ourselves before departure. My initial journal entry echoed brief philosophies learned more in the movie theater than in real life, but not likely much different from those of soldiers going off to war at any other period in time.

My detailing of flight numbers and times did not reflect a sense of precision and detail. I was simply interested in the process as this was only my second venture on a commercial airline. My introduction to flight had not been as pleasant.

Reporting to jump school a few weeks after college graduation and commissioning, I had shared the anticipation of the first parachute jump with my fellow students. What I did not reveal to them was that my first jump would also include my first airplane ride. I made a total of six take-offs and exits at

1250 feet before I was to find out what it was like to land in an airplane.

Our selection of the Marine Memorial Hotel was based on the recommendations of a friend. Also, it was one of few accommodations in the city that offered a military discount. It seemed strange then, and all that much stranger in later years, to be going to a war with so little support of the people we supposedly represented.

✈ **15 APRIL 1969**
Tuesday

San Francisco, Calif.
    Marine Memorial Room #615
    Today Linda Ann and I took a Graylines Tour of SF—beautiful day—impressive city—
    Saw a lot of "Hippies"—young—Look like they don't even know Vietnam is going on—Saw a Hippie girl changing baby's diaper in a busy park downtown
    Tour today covered—Golden Gate Bridge and Park, Japanese Tea Garden, Cliff House, Seal Rock, Alcatraz, Presidio, Twin Peaks, etc.
    Night—Went to movie "Love Bug"—funny—Later to topless bar

The Army had always promised fun, travel, and adventure, and San Francisco certainly provided the first two.

It is strange how some overused words become dated and are rarely heard except to describe their era of origin. Hippie seemed quite an appropriate description of the paisley and tie-dyed clothed children of the 60s. Their unwashed, tattered, and long-haired appearance ultimately became a uniform—

something that they had so desperately sought to avoid in their quest for individualism.

In some ways I envied their freedom and lack of discipline and regimentation. During my college years I had often dreamed of, and at times even planned, taking a year off to be a vagabond of the highways. Following my thumb I would see and experience America. But as with many things, the war changed all that. It forced us all to choose an identity. My route was the flag rather than the flower.

A Disney movie and a topless bar may seem an odd combination. Yet, perhaps both represented a way of life we were fighting for. In the dark confines of the theater, it felt good to laugh and escape the thoughts of my impending departure. Later, at the North Beach skin palace, the irony of the sagging breasts and stretch marks of the go-go girls at a club that promised excitement was quite apparent.

✯ 16 APRIL 1969
Wednesday

San Francisco, Calif.
   Slept late—Rode cable car to Fisherman's Wharf—Saw Ripley's Believe it or Not Museum, etc.
   Took day pretty easy—Bet I miss days like this
   Time gets shorter—

My bet was absolutely correct. However, it was not a wager one could want to win. The luxury of sleeping late, doing as I pleased, and having no responsibilities was soon to be so remote that these days would seem more a dream than real memory. Everything was so relaxed, yet intense and hurried at the same time. From food to sex to sightseeing to sex, it seemed we had to do it all while we still could.

It was fun, romantic, exciting, and frustrating. Time is always so difficult to use when there is little of it. Linda and I found it impossible to really enjoy the present with such an unpredictable future ahead.

---

17 APRIL 1969
Thursday

San Francisco, Calif
    Stayed in room most of day—
    Night—2LT Ron Pieper came in—He, Liz Livingston, Linda Ann and I took Night Club Tour—Ate at Hilton, saw female impersonations at Finocchios, then to Purple Onion (Walt Brown and girl singer), then to 365 Club with Woody Herman orchestra—Not too good of a tour—
    Took short walk through Chinatown
    Then on glassed-in elevator in Fairmont Hotel (HAVE GUN WILL TRAVEL filmed there) To bar—good

Ron Pieper and I had been in the same company at Fort Bragg and in the same platoon in Ranger School. We had spent much time talking about the war and our preparations for it. He and Liz had been seeing each other for some time and seemed quite close. Ron was reluctant, however, to make a commitment. Before our year in Nam was over, Liz was to meet and marry someone else. All I ever heard about her husband was that he was not a soldier. A year is a long time to wait, I guess.

I was tiring of San Francisco. Like the athlete who trains long and hard for the big game, I was ready to begin.

⍓ 18 APRIL
Friday

San Francisco, Calif.
   Goodbye to my wonderful wife
   Took bus to Travis AFB—No trouble till . . .
   Arrived about 1700—2030 they put us on buses—we thought to plane—
   Ended up plane had troubles—So am now at Brigadoon Lodge, Vacaville, Calif.—At Army expense—Staying with Marine E-7—6 months to go to retirement—Still back to Vietnam
   So first night—still in USA

I remember a World War II film that showed a unit departing for Europe with bands playing and the train station bedecked with flags and red, white, and blue bunting. As the train slowly pulled out of the station, the young heroine walked, then ran along the rail cars, saying a tearful good-bye to her warrior as he leaned out the window. His last words were that he loved her. Hers were that she would wait.

There were no bands or colorful streamers at the bus station for Linda and me. A few passers-by glanced at my khaki uniform but seemed disinterested. I tried to be glib, telling Linda, "If anything happens to me, I'll be the most surprised one there." I told her not to worry. She did not have to say she would wait.

We both held our emotions reasonably well in check. I left feeling I had failed to let her know just how much she meant to me and that the war was not more important than she. She later told me that she believed she would never see me again. There was no glory or patriotic hype in our departure, only sadness.

I do not recall many of my thoughts on the two-hour bus ride to Travis Air Force Base. I tried to think of the future rather than the past with little success.

Today Travis is a quiet base. During the Vietnam years, it was the bustling gateway to the war. By 1969 whole units were no longer sent to the conflict. Rather, replacements were sent, one by one, for those wounded or who had finished their one-year tour. Most of the replacements went through Travis, and the large waiting rooms were always full because planes departed around the clock. Often over a thousand soldiers, airmen, and Marines would be seated or stretched out on the floor napping with duffel bags as pillows.

I was so damn excited when we boarded the buses for the plane and then so disappointed to learn the adventure was not to begin yet. The Army's policy was that once you were manifested on a flight, you stayed with it. If mechanical or other troubles occurred, you waited. We waited. Only later did I learn that the 365-day tour clock began when manifested. So my first tour day in Vietnam was spent in a nice California motel. Murphy's Law states that "if something can go wrong, it will." Murphy must have been a soldier.

The Marine sergeant sharing my room was a quiet-spoken black from Alabama who had already completed two tours and had only six months until retirement. It did not really seem fair for him to be giving so much when others were giving so little or nothing.

🚁 19 APRIL 1969
Saturday

Vacaville, Calif
   Spent time resting, watching TV
   Once again getting ready for great adventure

Travis AFB, Calif
   1800 Ready to go—

> Was picked as a classified documents courier—Little trouble

> Honolulu, Hawaii
>   Hawaii for first time—30 minutes to refuel
>   Night—Misty rain—
>   Already looking forward to 6 months from now and R&R—
> Bet Hawaii will look good then—
>   Time for a beer—then on to Okinawa

Much of Army life is "hurry up and wait." At other times it is simply wait.

I did not know the classified documents' contents, which is probably the reason they were little bother. As a captain on the plane said, "What if something goes wrong? What are they going to do, send you to Vietnam?"

Hawaii, Okinawa, Guam, and Midway were all used at one time or another as refueling stops for the replacement flights to Vietnam. The fathers of many on my plane had fought in a more popular war over the islands a generation ago. We were aware that the battles to which we were going would never receive the praise and adoration of the World War II campaigns.

🕊 20 APRIL 1969
Sunday

> In Flight to RVN
>   TWA T2B3
>   Guess today was lost at International Date Line—
>   Saw Okinawa—45 minute layover—
>   Caught up with flight that 2Lt Pieper and 2Lt Biner were on—
>   On to RVN

Flight time from Travis AFB to Bien Hoa, Vietnam, with refueling stops, was nineteen and a half hours. With the exception of two young troops who chugged as much beer as they could hold in Honolulu, the flight was quiet and somber. Because no alcohol was served on the military charters, their beer buzz quickly wore off and they soon napped or read like the rest of us.

Appropriately enough the in-flight movie featured John Wayne. Even though this flick, Hellfighters, was about oil field fires rather than war, it was a typical hell-for-leather, flag-waving film by the Duke. For some reason it did not seem strange to be hours away from a war zone and still enjoying movies and hot meals served by airline stewardesses. They were friendly, courteous and helpful, like those on planes everywhere. Yet, they were different, too. The most noticeable difference was that they were older than the usual stews. The reason was simple. The Vietnam route paid more and those with seniority got the flights.

Our attendants—wearing rank insignia, unit pins, and combat decorations presented by previous passengers—were a little sad. I was not surprised to see tears in their eyes as we finally landed and walked down the ramp into Vietnam. After many trips between the US and Southeast Asia, they knew better than we that for many young GIs, their smiling faces, with tear-stained cheeks, would be the last American women they would ever see.

I was surprised to find Ron Pieper and Al Biner at Okinawa. Afraid the war would be over before we could get there, the three of us had all volunteered and frequently argued at Fort Bragg about who would be the first veteran. Since their flight departed a few minutes after mine arrived, I guess they won. For Al, the victory was short-lived, though, because a few months later his legs were shattered, as was his career as a soldier.

✈ 21 APRIL 1969
Monday

> Bien Hoa-Long Binh RVN
>   Arrived approx 0600
>   Short time bussed to Long Binh—My first look at VN—Saw my first RVN flag over a school—Motor bikes everywhere
>   80 degrees before sun came up—100's in afternoon—
>   Took my first big orange malaria pill—
>   Talked to Lt in club—Has some easy job in Saigon—Proud he is "getting over"—SOB
>   Hope I get an Inf job—After all that is why I am here
>   While awaiting assignment I am in 381st Replacement Company of 90th Replacement Battalion
>   Today is Aggie Muster—No chance to go to one—Did talk to LTC Baker, Veterinarian Corp, Class of '51, this morning

My first view of Vietnam was from the airplane as we made a rapid descent into Bien Hoa airfield. The sun was just rising, and in the early morning light along the horizon, I could see the Mekong River and Delta. The landscape was pocked with bomb craters, and bright flashes of outgoing shells from an artillery battery blinked in the dim light.

As we descended the portable stairway of the plane the two hundred men who were going home on the same plane cheered and shouted, "There's my turtle" (meaning "What took you so long?") and "You'll be sorry!" Their words seemed a bit more honest than the large sign that stated, "The U. S. Air Force Welcomes You To The Republic Of Vietnam."

Along with the greetings came a blast of heat that had me sweating before I reached the terminal. Massive amounts of war machines and materials were parked and stacked everywhere. The air was full of aircraft, including fighter jets and helicopter gunships. Ammunition, food, and medical supplies in abundance were waiting transport. Near each building were sandbagged bunkers with signs guiding new arrivals to their entrances.

Our stop at the terminal was brief. We were separated by services, and the Army incoming boarded large green buses for transport to the Replacement Center. Bus windows were covered in wire mesh to prevent grenades or bombs from being thrown in.

The short drive to Long Binh gave me my first look at the people and country I was to defend. It reminded me of the Mexican border towns that I had visited from my native Texas in that everything appeared extremely poor and dirty.

But there were distinct differences. Rolls of concertina wire, intertwined and stacked up to six levels high, surrounded military compounds. Guard towers dotted the landscape like tombstones in a cemetery. Because this was the dry season, everything was coated by fine dust stirred up by the many military vehicles and civilian buses and mopeds.

Greater than the visual impressions was the overwhelming smell of the place. While not totally unpleasant, it was unique, a combination of the orders of human waste, decaying vegetables, smoke from charcoal cooking fires, and gasoline fumes. Of all the things that remind me today of Vietnam, an occasional whiff of a similar smell puts me back quicker than any other stimulus.

The first stop at the Replacement Center was to exchange our greenbacks and coins for Military Payment Certificates (MPC). This brightly colored currency pictured rice paddy scenes and young women in native Vietnamese dress. The conversion into what was called "funny money" was to prevent the black market trade in dollars. It was difficult to get used to the many denominations and the lack of coins. The nickel and dime certificates were a bit smaller but were paper, nevertheless.

The best part of the Replacement Center was that its bar was always open. With Happy Hour prices of a dime a shot and regular prices of a quarter, who could afford not to drink? The prices, combined with the boredom and anticipation of assignment, kept the club full most of the time.

Many, perhaps even most, soldiers arriving in the war zone did not share my enthusiasm for getting in on the action. Secure, relatively safe jobs in Saigon and other built-up areas were highly sought. It bothered me to hear the rear-echelon types bragging about how easy they had it. I should not have worried about getting an Infantry assignment. They were the easiest to find and vacancies opened with every fire fight.

Graduates of Texas A & M have met on San Jacinto Day for decades wherever any could get together. I really did not mind missing a muster. I was rapidly forming more important ties.

Two last stops completed the Replacement Center in-processing. First, under supervision of a senior noncommissioned officer, we were told to brush our teeth with a special decay-preventing substance.

Our last stop was at clothing supply where we were issued five sets of jungle fatigues, two sets of boots, and socks and underwear. Everything, from shorts to handkerchiefs, was OD (olive drab) green.

---

22 APRIL 1969
Tuesday

Long Binh RVN Hqs 199th LIB ⅔
  Camp Frenzell-Jones RVN
    Today I got my assignment—199th Light Infantry Brigade—Initially I was very disappointed—Later I realize that it is probably as good as any other Infantry assignment—
    Came in with CPT Jeffrey Swiss—Armor branch from New Jersey
    Hard to realize this base camp is in a combat zone—Then again I hear Arty in the distance
    Saw 2 Aggies today—One assigned here, the other a Marine visiting
    I am assigned to 2nd Battalion 3rd Infantry—Part of the Old Guard

    Have been wondering what a "Light" Inf Bde is—No one
seems to know either
    Took care of in-processing today
    Night—Drank a little beer while I've got the chance
    Hot and dry here—Monsoons supposed to start in approx
3 weeks

At the Replacement Center the main criterion used in assignments was need: send the in-coming soldiers where they were
needed most. This usually depended on which unit had recently
suffered the most casualties. My hopes of joining an airborne unit
or the 1st Air Cavalry were ended by the large numbers of killed
and wounded suffered by the 199th LIB in the past weeks. I had
not even heard of the brigade until my assignment. However, the
disappointment did not last long. It was the Infantry and I soon
learned that mud, heat and bullets treated all grunts the same,
regardless of what unit patch they wore.

A jeep picked up CPT (captain) Swiss and me and transported us to our new unit. The driver had lots of combat stories
to relate but finally admitted that they were all hearsay. His
entire war had been as a clerk and driver, and he had never
been to the field.

The Headquarters of the 199th was at Camp Frenzell-Jones
at the eastern edge of Long Binh. Although located nearly
twenty-five miles from Saigon, it was within the large built-
up and well-protected area of the Saigon–Bien Hoa–Long Binh
complex from which the war was run. Frenzell-Jones had been
named for the first two members of the brigade killed in action.
Their early demise had earned them a brief immortality by
way of tin-roofed buildings, sandbagged bunkers, and miles
of the everpresent concertina wire. Their namesake was short
lived; the camp was turned over to the Vietnamese when the
brigade went home in 1972.

The camp, known in GI language as BMB, for brigade main
base, was composed of a multitude of wooden buildings approximately 20 by 80 feet. The floors were concrete and the
top two feet between the walls and the tin roofs were covered

only with screens. With fans, they were reasonably bearable. Sandbags stacked about half way up the walls protected peace of mind if not the body. Fully sandbagged bunkers were near each building.

The camp also contained a PX (post exchange), a laundry, a souvenir shop, clubs for the different ranks, and all the usual administrative and support agencies required for a six thousand-man brigade.

The first stop was at the brigade adjutant's office. He briefed us on the unit history, recent fights and the current areas of operation (AOs). Although all four of the brigade's battalions were short of officers, the only problem he emphasized was that of the 2nd Battalion 3rd Infantry—the Two-thirds—which was working in extremely wet and muddy terrain. The officer seemed embarrassed less than an hour later when he informed us of our assignment to the Two-thirds.

It was a long way from the 2nd Battalion 3rd Infantry at Frenzell-Jones to the regiment's 1st Battalion in Washington, D. C. The spit and polish ceremonial unit in our nation's capital would never have recognized, nor have accepted onto its parade field ranks, the combat soldiers of the Old Guard in Vietnam. We shared only the name and a unit crest that is shaped like a Revolutionary soldier's hat. Beyond the 1st Battalion's ceremonial duties of lowering the 2nd Battalion's dead into the cold ground of Arlington National Cemetery, they did not acknowledge our existence.

Processing into the brigade involved turning in and updating finance and personnel records. Filling out notification forms, whom to contact in case of injury or death, was a priority as was confirming the beneficiary of GI insurance. Also, I made arrangements for allotments to Linda and to the 10% savings program that was one of the benefits of the combat zone. The clerk informed me that while in Vietnam I would pay no income tax, but social security and rations money would be deducted from my paycheck. A grand sum of $30 a month for family separation and $65 a month for combat pay would be added. Later I learned that these tax benefits and combat pay were also awarded to anyone who happened to visit Vietnam, no matter how briefly. A one-day junket by a senior Pentagon officer or a brief resupply air mission by plane crews gave each a full month's benefits and pay.

On the clerk's recommendation, I took only $50 a month payment to myself. It did not seem like enough at the time; however, I would find little need for money. The debts one incurs in the rice paddies and jungles are not paid for in dollars and cents.

If war were as it is in the movies, first letters home from a combat zone would be filled with romantic verse and poetic descriptions of the land and people. My first letters to Linda covered pay, allotments, and copies of documents she would need. I included such romantic instructions as, "Just keep these papers—they are right so don't worry about them."

---

23 APRIL 1969
Wednesday

Camp Frenzell-Jones RVN

Started incoming training today—Pretty weak—

Met Battalion Executive Officer Major Profett—Got assigned to Company C—Charlie Co has lost many officers—WIA-KIA. Also platoon sergeants getting hit—What I hear Company is always stirring up something—Has been losing a lot of men to booby traps

C Co has few experienced NCOs—Most are Non-Commissioned Officer Candidate School grads

Looks as if I am in for a tough assignment—Then again I have had the best possible training.

One of the first "combat stories" I heard—Commanding General comes out to the Bn—Dead VC on road just outside—Says bury him—That night some GI digs up VC's hands—

Hands all that show above ground—Beer can in one—The
other shooting the finger

Most of the units in Vietnam conducted a week-long orientation for new troops before sending them to the field. The
199th conducted its in a small cleared field that was in the
shadows of a guard tower.

The training repeated much from stateside classes on first
aid, medical evacuation, field sanitation, and enemy methods
of operations. Particular emphasis was placed on booby traps
and mines, and we were run through a simulated course. Many
of us failed to find all of the trip wires and pressure releases
of the traps. The harmless smoke grenades that we tripped
were good reminders that no such mistake would be allowed
when we faced the real thing. At the close of the class a young
sergeant showed us the twisted, bent barrel of an M-16 rifle,
telling us it was virtually all that was left after a soldier's
failure to detect a large booby-trapped artillery shell.

The classes were not all that well presented, adding to my
impatience to get to the field—the boonies, in Army jargon.
The orientation did allow us to become more acclimatized to
the searing heat and heavy humidity.

We also had time to get various patches sewed on our new
uniforms. I felt somewhat self-conscious at the obvious short
time in country indicated by my bright new green fatigues.

The cadre of the orientation school, as well as most of the
soldiers who worked at the company and battalion rear headquarters, were all old-timers who were near the end of their tours.
Most had spent eight to ten months in the boonies and had been
rewarded with the more secure rear jobs for surviving. Some had
earned the positions by serving in such dangerous jobs as point
man and machine gunner. They were generally friendly, helpful,
and eager to tell war stories of varying degrees of believability.
Their reference to us was as FNGs, meaning "fucking new guy,"
or more politely, "funny new guy."

Frenzell-Jones was a relatively secure area. With the exception
of Tet of 1968, it had never received any type of ground attack.

An occasional rocket was fired into the compound with little damage. I quickly learned that the infantrymen generally ignored the few rockets while the clerks, cooks, and other permanent residents of the camp took the incoming shells seriously.

The grunts loved to repeat the story of the quartermaster officer who tried to get a Purple Heart for a twisted ankle received running from his bed to his bunker.

---

24 APRIL 1969
Thursday

Camp Frenzell-Jones RVN
I continue to get ready for the field
Moved over to Charlie Co—
Met Company Executive Officer 1 LT Walter Hawkins—from the Bahamas—Also several NCOs—Of course receiving much advice on going to field
Have already heard several GI methods to quickly end the war—
1.–Poison all the fish markets
2.–Cause a snow and 20 degree weather—then police up VC bodies
Wrote several letters—Staying at Charlie Co Hqs now

One of the many things I have never understood about the Army is its unique ability to shorten long titles to unintelligible acronyms and to make simple letters into longer words. We change Mobile Army Surgical Hospital into MASH. Then we take something simple like C Company and always call it Charlie Company.

Nevertheless, I reported to Charlie Company where I received a genuine welcome. Although I was an FNG, I immediately felt a part of the unit. Charlie Company, like all rifle companies, was basically an extended family of about 120 men. Its platoons and squads were closer kin but the basic allegiance was to the company. New members were welcomed because they would make everyone's job easier and a little more secure. To become a family member in good standing, you only had to do your job and survive. The longer you lived, the more status in the family was yours. There is a strong bond between those who have taken lives and faced death together.

Every soldier in a company is always convinced that his is the best in the battalion, if not the entire Army. He is also always convinced that his company consistently gets the toughest missions and the least amount of time off. Charlie was the typical company.

My first introduction to the Company was in the form of Hawk Hawkins, the Executive Officer. The position was highly coveted because XO duty was mostly in the rear.

Hawk had been lucky. After only three months of combat, he had been the only officer in the Company eligible to replace the old XO when he rotated home. All the other candidates for the job had become casualties.

Hawk was good—especially in getting whatever the field soldiers needed. Most of this procurement was by scrounge or trade—or outright theft, if required. After I received my issue rucksack, canteens, and carrying equipment, Hawk handed me a nice Air Force K-Bar survival knife. His only comment was that I was not to ask where he had gotten it.

---

25 APRIL 1969
Friday

Camp Frenzell-Jones RVN
   Continued Redcatcher training—Went to club—Had a band

from Philippines—Very good—Played some Country-Western music—

Today I was issued my M-16 rifle—I realize that I am here to keep my men alive and to kill and lead my men to kill—Or possibly be killed myself—This is what I have been trained for—This is what I believe is my duty—I feel privileged to be able to do so for myself and my country and my wonderful wife and family.

The 199th LIB had been formed at Fort Benning, Georgia, in April, 1966. After a brief training period at Camp Shelby, Mississippi, the Brigade deployed by ship and arrived in Vietnam on December 10, 1966. The source of the Brigade's nickname, Redcatcher, was never mentioned, and I often wondered if our obvious anticommunist moniker might have to be changed at some future time when we faced an enemy of a different ideology.

Life at BMB was fairly slow. The days usually revolved around meal times and the opening of the club in the evening. The mess hall served adequate chow, which later, after months of C-rations, would seem a banquet. While the troops went through a cafeteria line, the officers ate in a small screened-off section that had tables and a small wash area. Vietnamese women—less than attractive but friendly middle-aged women who spoke passable English—brought the meals on trays and saw that we had ample iced water and drinks. The continuing joke was that they were all Viet Cong spies and never came to work on days of rocket attacks. It seemed funny to us FNGs. However, I noticed the old guys did not join in the laughter.

I ate my evening meal at the officers' club where I could enjoy a steak or hamburger in one of the few air-conditioned buildings in the camp. Popular US beers, fine wines, and the best of brand name spirits flowed freely. The walls were lined with slot machines and several card games of various stakes were ongoing. A band played several nights a week. Movies, usually less than a year old, were shown when no live entertainment was available.

Here waitresses were young, attractive Vietnamese who definitely knew how to wear the fashionable miniskirt. They were attentive and friendly yet hesitant at the same time. I doubt if there was a story or line they had not heard.

The Vietnamese civilians with their ID cards and passes pretty well had the run of the compound during the day. When they finished their jobs at the end of each day, they were loaded on trucks escorted by MPs and returned to their villages outside the gate. Shortly after sunup they were picked up and brought back into the camp. It would be interesting to know just how many were working for the VC as well.

This night I joined one of the card games and quickly had a large stack of the funny money in front of me, though several hours later it had dwindled to nothing. Most of the dollars in my pocket soon followed. It made little difference to me as I thought it was a hell of a lot better to expend my bad luck at cards than in the booby-trapped rice paddies I would soon be inhabiting.

My sentiments upon receiving my rifle now seem more appropriate to a 4th of July speech or a B-grade movie. Growing up on a ranch, I had owned guns and hunted game for the table as well as sport since I was ten. As a result, I had easily qualified as expert or sharpshooter on the many rifle ranges. Although guns had always been a part of me, none had ever become such an extension of my body and mind as that black gun in Vietnam. For the next year, it would rarely be farther away than an arm reach.

26 APRIL 1969
Saturday

Camp Frenzell-Jones
  Zeroed weapon
  Finished getting ready for field

The sights on military rifles are adjustable for elevation and windage. By firing well-aimed shot groups of three rounds each, you can adjust the strike of the bullet to exactly where you aim. It is a fairly easy process and the experienced rifleman can usually accomplish his zero in nine shots or less.

The rifle range, located just outside the camp, was run by NCOs with the usual Army precision and strict safety measures. Wherever the US military goes, you can always predict that marksmanship ranges and flight lines are the same. If you have seen one, you have seen them all.

The only departure from standard procedures was an abundance of ammunition. We were allowed to "pop all the caps" that we desired. We were also given the opportunity to familiarize ourselves with the M-79 grenade launcher. The short, shotgunlike weapon could fire a 40-millimeter grenade up to 400 meters. The ones I had seen in the States always had a six-inch adjustable flip-up sight just in front of the breach. These sights had been removed in Vietnam, as all they were good for was to catch on vines and branches. With a little practice, almost anyone could fire it quite accurately and faster by feel than by using the fragile sights.

We were also allowed to fire one M-72 LAW each. This disposable launcher rocket was originally designed as a light antitank weapon, from which its name LAW was derived. Because the weapons were also good bunker busters, each infantry squad carried several. On occasion, especially if wet, they would misfire. All of ours on that training range worked well except one. Because it was dangerous to transport after its misfire, we had to destroy it in place so it would not fall into the hands of the VC and be used against us as a booby trap.

We had no demolitions, so, to explode the flawed launcher, we used a little GI ingenuity. With me as the senior person present, the NCO in charge placed the LAW approximately one hundred meters down range. We then placed ourselves behind a berm and shot at it with the M-79. The grenade traveled slowly enough so that we had time to duck before it reached the rocket. The NCO barely missed the first shot and made a direct hit on the second. We tried to be extremely careful, as he had less than a month until rotation. I kept my head down. Getting blown away during my first week on a training range did not seem an heroic beginning.

At the range I had my first contact with the saleschildren of Vietnam. Unless you were inside a US compound or in the deepest of the rice paddies or jungles, as soon as you stopped you were surrounded by eight- to twelve-year-olds selling or begging. These youths, regardless of age or sex, were referred to as "baby san." Their wares included soft drinks, beer, cigarettes, lighters, and often their sisters or mothers if you were interested. The soft drinks were hot, but for an extra nickel the baby san would roll them on a block of ice until reasonably cool.

Back at Charlie Company my last preparation was to pack up a rucksack and a basic load of twenty-one magazines of ammunition. Two more days of new-arrival training remained, but with the shortage of officers in the field, I was sent forward early. I was pleased with the decision; anticipation was building with every day at the brigade base.

27 APRIL 1969
Sunday

Elvira
    Got to Co—Was assigned 1st platoon—Has about 22 men—Plt leader is Sp-4—
    E-6 came in with me
    One of my squads made contact tonight—got 2

My first trip to the field was in the Company Executive Officer (XO) jeep as part of a small resupply convoy which carried food, ammunition, spare parts, and replacements like myself to the battalion forward headquarters. The battalion area of operations (AO) was the rice paddies and pineapple plantations about forty miles south of Saigon. During the drive, LT Hawkins pointed out the Saigon River and areas of the city itself, including the racetrack which had been the site of some of the heaviest fighting during Tet 1968. The 199th had been the unit that finally secured it after great loss of life. I was amazed to see that only a little over a year later, the horses were running again with the grandstands jammed.

As we left Saigon, I began to notice the Vietnam version of the corner gasoline station. The traditional gas station no longer existed, as large storage containers of highly flammable petroleum made ideal targets for VC attacks. The old stations' places had been taken by small roadside stands that displayed about a half dozen one-gallon containers of fuel. Once again the principal attendants were children.

The countryside was beautiful and the drive would have been pleasant if it had been done just for fun.

Our first stop was at Binh Chanh where the battalion headquarters and a supporting artillery battery of six howitzers were located. The base contained a few stucco buildings, originally built by the Vietnamese as homes and shops, and many heavily sandbagged bunkers. In one of the larger bunkers, I met the battalion commander, LTC (Lieutenant Colonel) John A. Mess. His welcome was friendly although businesslike. He showed me the battalion AO on a large map, explaining that everything had been quiet for the past few days except for encounters with booby traps.

Hawk showed me around the compound and introduced me to many of the battalion staff and officers of the company who were securing the area. They talked about how long it was until R&R or to rotation. They made humorous—but nonmalicious—remarks about my newness.

They had many questions about what was going on back in

' the world,'' as the States were called. Still, the core of conversation was about fire fights and operations. Although I was made welcome, it was obvious that full acceptance would be dependent on time in-country and action under fire.

Hawk bid his farewell after dropping me off at the helopad. After a short wait, the resupply UH-1 helicopter picked up me and four other replacements. I was finally off to join my company and platoon.

The short flight gave me a good view of the many rivers, streams and water-logged rice paddies. Located at the junction of two rivers, our destination, Fire Base Elvira, was bounded by water on one side and the ever-present dirt berm and concertina wire on the others. Oval-shaped and no more than 150 meters across at any point, Elivra contained the company's four 81mm mortars. Near the center was a wooden watch tower about twenty feet high. Other areas were filled with bunkers made of the top halves of large metal culverts covered in sandbags. Three feet tall in the center and about four feet wide by eight feet long, they served both as fighting and sleeping positions.

Elvira looked no more hospitable on the ground than it had from the air.

I saw little activity when I arrived except for a small detail that unloaded the Huey's cargo of C-rations and various supplies. Most of the men were sleeping in the shade of the small bunkers while only the two in the tower seemed alert. I soon learned that little occurred in the day time. The VC hid by day and moved by night. Charlie Company had learned to live and fight the same way.

A young soldier wearing only fatigue trousers and shower shoes introduced himself as the company commander's radio telephone operator or RTO. He led me to the main communications bunker and introduced me to CPT George Grammis, the company commander. Grammis had on his full uniform but also was wearing shower shoes. He explained that they were the general footwear inside the base. Everything was so wet outside that feet needed as much sun and air as possible to avoid rot and infection. Nearing the end of six months as

Charlie Company CO, Grammis seemed near burnout and was looking forward to his replacement's arrival.

Grammis made introductions to the artillery forward observer 1LT Don Jong and to his headquarters personnel. He talked briefly about the company AO and warned repeatedly of booby traps. His remarks were brief, as he was also deciding where to locate the company's squad-sized ambush for the night. He said I would be the 1st Platoon's leader and that Staff Sergeant Marple and the PFC who had flown in with me would both be joining my platoon.

We walked the few meters to the 1st Platoon sector and CPT Grammis introduced me to SP4 Roy Collier, who was the acting platoon leader. On his departure Grammis instructed me to join him in the communications bunker that evening.

Collier introduced me to the twenty-two men who were now my responsibility, explaining that the platoon was experienced, most of the men having been in the boonies from four to six months. He said that the platoon had difficulty keeping officers and sergeants and that three had been evacuated with wounds in the past few weeks. He was happy to be resuming his normal duties as squad leader. He added that he really had not been the platoon leader, as he and the other squad leader had been taking turns being in charge. This was not the Army I had been taught at Fort Benning, yet it seemed to be operating fairly well.

I spoke to the entire platoon briefly and told them a little about myself. I was careful not to come across too strongly or gung-ho. They were glad to have me, but their respect would have to be earned. My assurances that I knew I had much to learn from them was a good start.

A rifle platoon is supposed to be made up of forty-three men divided into four squads. The 1st Platoon, as well as others in Charlie Company, was operating with only two squads, as rarely were over twenty-five men assigned. My first reorganization was to establish Staff Sergeant Marple as the platoon sergeant. A soldier with his rank usually led a squad, but everyone seemed to be doing a job calling for a grade one or two higher.

SP4 Collier departed for his night ambush and the other squad prepared for perimeter guard. Where security had been minimal during the day, half the men were on guard at night.

I spent most of the night listening to the squads in ambush positions report the activity in their areas by radio. About 2300 hours we heard firing about a kilometer outside the perimeter. Collier's squad had caught a VC group of five or six moving across the paddies and killed two. It was frustrating not to be with them when the action I had craved was so close, but there would soon be days when enemy contact would not seem so alluring.

🛦 28 APRIL 1969
Monday

Elvira
    Left on 2 day mission
    Went on my first ambush patrol—No contact
    Paddies are really muddy—
    Flak jackets heavy—Water everywhere and monsoons aren't even here yet

The contact with the VC the night before had indicated that the enemy was increasing activity in our area. The company moved out early to recon the surrounding paddies and treelines and prepared to saturate the area with night ambushes. The company commander gave each platoon a route of march and points on the map where he wanted night positions. He showed us the locations of the other platoons so we would not fire on each other by mistake. The maps, divided into square-kilo-meter boxes, had intersecting gridlines and numbers which allowed us to plot each objective with a six-digit coordinate to ensure accuracy up to one-hundred meters.

Mapreading is one of a soldier's most important assets and was much-emphasized in training. The easiest way to lose the confidence of men was not to know the unit's location at all times. The reason was simple: knowing the six-digit coordinates was critical in placing artillery and air support on the enemy rather than on ourselves.

The 1st Platoon's area was about six kilometers, or "klicks," from Elvira. This march of only three and a half miles looked easy on the map. On the ground, it was hell.

The mud varied from ankle deep to well over the knees. With the temperature around one-hundred degrees, movement was slow and exhausting. Along with our weapons, ammunition, food, water, and other gear, we wore flak jackets, weighing about ten pounds, which were supposed to stop shrapnel from booby traps. Our burden totaled forty to fifty pounds. The RTOs and machine gunners carried an additional fifteen to twenty pounds.

New arrivals carried no extra gear. My RTO explained that before the day was over the oldtimers would likely be carrying the FNGs' gear because it usually took a week before new arrivals were accustomed enough to the heat and mud to carry their complete load. The veterans made comments but were quick to remind each other that they had gone through the same acclimatization process.

The rice paddies, squares and rectangles from 100 to 250 meters across, were bordered by small dikes about two feet high and eighteen inches wide. They made perfect pathways, and that was the reason we avoided them. The VC figured we would look for the easiest walkways and that is where they placed booby traps. Crossing the mud and water was much more difficult, but it lent to longer life.

At intervals of two to four klicks, there were canals or streams surrounded by thick nipa palm trees about ten to fifteen feet high. Looking like movie-set desert palms—except shorter and with much more foliage—the trees provided excellent hiding places for the VC, and we approached with utmost care.

We spread out across the paddies moving in two columns about twenty-five meters apart. The point man for each file was in the lead by twenty meters and each trailing soldier kept an interval of at least ten meters. All were close enough to support by fire but far enough apart so that a booby trap would only inflict one casualty. Each man tried to walk in the footsteps of the man in front of him.

Talk centered on the coming monsoon season. The "old" soldiers kept telling us horror stories about the constant rains. With more cloudy nights and decreased visibility, the VC would be on the move.

My first night ambush was uneventful—yet exciting and scary. Your mind races with anticipation when you sit in the dark waiting for your fellow human being to appear so you can kill or be killed. I was filled with a dread that the enemy might not appear, and an even more powerful dread that he would.

Our ambush positions were typically squad size, ten or eleven men. Just before dark the point man would approach the position designated by the platoon leader and check it carefully for booby traps. After he reported all clear, the rest of the squad moved in.

We usually located ambushes next to a paddy dike for protection and quickly set out Claymore mines with wires running back to the firing devices. With one quick downward thrust on the handle, we could detonate the rectangular mine and propel hundreds of buckshot-sized balls that would cut down anything to the Claymores' front.

We normally set the Claymores in a circle around the squad, concentrating them in the area of most likely approach. The RTO and I were in the center of the sector while the squad's machine gun was positioned to best cover the entire area.

Soldiers were close together in two- and three-man positions and scheduled watch in two hour shifts. We slept within arm's reach of each other so we could change guard with the minimum noise and movement. The heavy flak jackets served as passable pillows. Ammo magazines and hand grenades were stacked by each man.

There was no talking, eating, or smoking. When we had to urinate, we crawled a few feet from our position and did it on our knees. This way we limited our exposure to the skyline and also prevented noisy splashing. Those who snored were awakened. If a man repeated the noise, he had to sleep while wearing a gas mask.

Most of us smoked and it was difficult to go all night without a cigarette. We tried chewing tobacco, but few stuck with it. Our excuse was that it increased thirst. Maybe we were not as tough as we thought.

---

29 APRIL 1969
Tuesday

Elvira
Con't mission—Slow day
Another night ambush
Saw a gunship etc. hitting about 1200 meters from us
Everybody ran out of water—Hot

Spending an entire day moving and looking for the enemy was impossible. Without frequent stops and long breaks, the heat and mud would inflict more casualties than the VC. It was also necessary to try to sleep in the daytime so we could be alert during the night ambushes. Often the only shade was a makeshift awning made with ponchos.

Other than the constant threat of booby traps, the most dangerous areas while moving across the paddies were the nipa palm-lined water ways. My platoon was wary of these areas for good reason. The lieutenant who preceded me in the platoon had been seriously wounded by an ambush waiting in small holes dug at the base of the nipa palm trees. We frequently fired grenades from the M-79s into such areas before crossing the thick foliage. This reconnaissance by fire from several hundred meters' distance was designed to get the VC to commit themselves while we were still reasonably protected by the terrain.

The first two days in the field had been a good experience. I had learned much about my men and the particular ways of working in the rice paddies. My abilities to navigate and read a map had gained the respect of the platoon. They were also aware that I had carried my own load in the heat and mud.

The strange sounds and sights were already becoming familiar. The static on the radio was constant, broken only by hourly situation reports or calls about enemy activity.

This night was the first time I had seen a Cobra gunship firing in darkness. From an altitude of about a thousand feet, its red tracer bullets, fired at a rate of over 6,000 per minute, appeared as a solid red streak snaking to the ground. The term "hosing down" an area became much more understandable.

My greatest lesson of these first two days in the paddies was that water was our most precious provision. Since we were near the coast and the paddies were only slightly above sea level, high tides pushed salt water up the canals, causing much of it to escape into the paddies through dikes that had been damaged by bombs and artillery. As a result, there was no drinkable water other than what we carried on our backs. The gallon or so we each carried in multiple canteens was simply not enough for two days in the hot sun.

A soldier will share his ammunition, his food, and even letters from home. The only commodity you never asked from anyone else was water. It made little difference on this occasion. We were all out of the liquid by nightfall that second day in the field. It made for a long night. I would be without water on other days, but that first night of thirst is as vivid a memory as later victory or disaster.

🛩 30 APRIL 1969
Wednesday

> Elvira
>> Back to Co base—Good to get a drink of water
>> In my plt now have 1 E-6, 1 E-5
>> Plt is very young but seem to be pretty good
>> Today is pay day—

"Good to get a drink of water," is one of the greatest understatements of my journal. It was late morning before we completed the march back to the base. Most of us had been without water for over eighteen hours.

At the base water was stored in a two hundred gallon rubber container that was delivered in a sling below a helicopter. Our movement forward remained orderly, and each man filled a canteen as he passed. There was no pushing or arguing over who was next. The soldiers may have been young, but they were disciplined and understood teamwork. After everyone had filled his canteen, the squad leaders and I finally had our water. It tasted so wonderful that tears almost came to my eyes.

The rest of the day was spent cleaning our weapons and equipment. One of the squads would be going back out into the paddies for a night ambush.

We rarely knew anything about the rest of the battalion's operations. The brigade and other US and Vietnamese units were something we only read about in the *Stars and Stripes* newspaper. Our interest in the war beyond the company was minimal. I had known far more about the big picture back in the States than I did while in the war zone. Personal survival and taking care of my men overshadowed any curiosity about the general situation.

Payday was still a part of our small world. LT Hawkins flew in with pay vouchers and an ammo can full of funny money. Much of the MPC was returned with him for storage in the company safe back at BMB. All we could do with it at Elvira was get it wet.

✈ I MAY 1969
Thursday

Elvira

My journal entries for the next few days would only note my location. There was much to write about, but no desire, partly because of the busy routine, fatigue from having so much to learn, and the lack of sleep from accompanying the nightly ambush patrols. Mostly, however, it was from the let-down after the initial excitement. After less than two weeks in-country, much, if not all, of the glamour had faded. It was simply hard, tiring, dangerous, and usually boring work.

There was also a feeling of isolation and intense loneliness. No mail had yet caught up from anyone back home. It already seemed as if my previous life no longer existed.

Most of my re-creation of these days is based on letters written to Linda. She kept each one and they greatly assisted me in filling in the blank pages of my journal.

I was getting used to life at Elvira. One hot meal was brought in daily by helicopters or boat. An ample supply of soft drinks and beer was provided by the Company fund. An honor payment system was established by placing an ammo can next to the cooler. Although not closely supervised, the can always seemed to have sufficient funds to replace the empties.

During the day we worked to improve the defenses of Elvira: stringing more barbed wire, checking the Claymore mines, and filling and stacking sandbags. We also cleared our fields of fire by cutting vegetation and moved firing positions so that the enemy could not pinpoint them before an attack.

The 1st Platoon's housekeeping on May Day was to further cut back the nipa palms on the far side of the adjacent river. This was not a popular mission as the platoon had had a man blown apart by a booby-trapped 105mm artillery round in the same area a month before.

We proceeded carefully, each step and machete cut carefully thought through before execution. After we had cleared about ten meters deeper into the thick vegetation, a man called me over. On the ground lay a shriveled human hand, cut off cleanly just above the wrist. Evidently, not all the parts of the platoon's fallen comrade had been found. We dug a shallow hole and buried the hand.

✎ 2 MAY 1969
Friday

Elvira

A good day. The first mail from home finally caught up. A letter from Linda and one from her grandmother made the mail call a happy one for a change.

My letter to Linda on this day pretty well summed up operations around Elvira. It stated, "We have been very busy—mostly just looking without finding." I had not yet learned that it was much better to look than to find.

A good break in the routine was provided by a USO visit. Greg Morrison of the then-popular television series *Mission Impossible* flew into Elvira by helicopter. He was very friendly

and shook everyone's hands while saying that he was proud
of us. His visit seems more significant today as I look back
and realize that I never saw another movie or TV personality
at a field location the rest of my tour.

✈ **3 MAY 1969**
Saturday

Move to Binh Chanh

Fire bases were named for wives or girlfriends. My only
thought when we received word that we would be leaving
Elvira was to hope that the woman, whoever she was, was
more attractive and hospitable than her namesake. Even with
short notice we were packed and ready to depart within an
hour.

Our transportation part way to Binh Chanh was by medium-
sized Navy boats that could each carry a platoon. The boats
flew large US flags, and I felt proud to see the stars and stripes
steaming in the breeze. But we soon were reminded that boats
and the Navy only go where there is water. The last couple of
miles into our new base were covered, as usual, on foot.

We quickly moved out on a battalion operation. Three
companies maneuvered from different directions to surround
a village. When all were in place, a fourth company moved
through the area and searched it. These operations, called
cordons, were frequently successful, as the enemy was not
able to run away without encountering our blocking positions and ambushes.

Charlie Company's part of the cordon was to establish a
blocking position about two kilometers in length. We did this

by forming a series of squad ambushes, each about two-hundred meters apart. They were like night ambushes except we stayed in the same position until the operation was completed.

The company commander, who usually controlled the units from his command post in a fire base, was on the ground with us. I was glad that he set up with one of the other platoons because I did not want his supervision nor his cluster of radios and antennae, which always made attractive targets for the VC.

We spread out a bit more at daylight but held the same general blocking position. We knew the VC would likely wait until darkness to try to break out of the cordon. Guards were still rotated to keep watch, however.

While not on guard, we were able to relax, talk, write letters, or try to sleep in the heat. We kept the fog of mosquitoes at bay by generous use of repellent from four-ounce OD plastic bottles of "bug juice" we kept on our helmets.

Paperback books were carried in nearly every rucksack and were passed along after each reading. Westerns and Harold Robbins were popular. If not literature, at least they helped pass the time.

4 MAY 1969
Sunday

Binh Chanh

The cordon ended after the maneuvering company had completely searched the area sealed off by the rest of the battalion. By monitoring the battalion frequency on the radio, we learned that several VC suspects and some ammunition and food had been found. There were no casualties on either side. We would remain in the area conducting ambushes for one more night to try to catch VC moving back into the area.

In the afternoon we received a needed resupply of water. Several replacements were aboard the helicopter. Within hours, they were on their first ambush patrol.

Also aboard was the platoon's Kit Carson scout who had been in Saigon for a couple of weeks' leave. Kit Carson scouts were former VC or NVA who had rallied to the government of South Vietnam. Some had changed sides because of the loss of belief in the communists. Many more had changed sides because of hunger or fear of impending capture or death on the battlefield. Everyone was suspicious of them and placed little trust in their abilities or new-found loyalties. We had no great fear of their turning on us the weapons we had given them, however. If the enemy had ever recaptured them, death would have been the least harsh of their treatment.

The 1st Platoon Kit Carson was Tom. I never knew his Vietnamese name or much about his background. He spoke enough English to say he had surrendered during Tet of 1968 after several years as an NVA sergeant. He would occasionally, after a few beers, brag that he had killed many Americans before turning on his brother VC and NVA. Tom was truly a man without a country, and, regardless of the war's victor, he would be a loser.

Most of Tom's usefulness was in detecting booby traps and occasionally as a less than adequate interpreter. He had a sense of humor and laughed frequently. Tom was more a platoon mascot than an effective fighting man.

The resupply bird had also delivered sandbags full of mail. A large stack of letters from Linda, my parents, brother, and an old college friend let me know that the US Postal Service was finally fully aware that 2LT Lanning was in Vietnam. It was absolutely wonderful to catch up on the news of home, even if all the news was not good.

My brother Jim wrote that Judy had contracted German

measles. As she was in her first few months of pregnancy, they were greatly concerned about damage to the baby and asked me to include their unborn in my prayers while assuring me that I was in theirs. I felt bad to be adding to their worries when they had so much on their minds.

🕊 **5 MAY 1969**
Monday

Binh Chanh
    Orange pill day
    Busy week—Ran a lot of ambushes, RIFs and a cordon—Little contact—Now have 28 in my plt—
    Plt medic—PFC Bass—is conscientious objector—Good
    Change of COs last week—Old one was CPT George Grammis
    My plt is young but seems to be good
    Most of my men are over at whore house—Will be going back out tonight
    Still dry here—Except in the paddies
    In last year this Co has had 120 WIA, 20 KIA—My plt lost many a few months ago
    Brigade Commander Brigadier General Davidson
    So far I have little respect for the people of VN—either side
    We sleep in sandbag bunkers—when we are here—which is seldom.

Days in the field began with a one-hundred-percent alert for a half hour before dawn and after day break. This one-hour "stand to" was conducted because this period was the most common time of enemy attack.

After the "stand to" we started our day by taking the daily small white malaria pill. On Mondays a larger orange pill was issued, one best taken after eating a hearty amount of food.

Otherwise, it acted as a strong laxative. Except for my journal entries, the orange pill was often the only reminder of just what day it was.

The pills were handed out by the platoon medic, PFC Dorsey Bass. Doc Bass was a member of a religious family from West Virginia whose denomination was so obscure I had never heard of it and cannot recall it today. Doc said it was an offshoot of the snake handlers and poison drinkers, smiling as he told us they no longer did "those things." Whatever his convictions, they were strong, and he had been able to convince a tough draft board that his beliefs did not allow him to bear arms. He had not contested the draft itself and, as long as he did not have to carry a weapon and kill, he was willing to do his part.

Bass was a somewhat overweight black man. His dark framed, Army-issue glasses and thinning hair made him appear older than his twenty years. He was soft-spoken and somewhat a loner, preferring to read his Bible than to join in the talk. The troops respected Doc and seldom commented on his C. O. status because he never hesitated to expose himself to fire to treat their wounds. Instead of pulling guard, he monitored the radio. He was a good listener and was more a mother figure than a comrade-in-arms.

We spent most of the day walking back to Binh Chanh, a larger base with its own mess hall. The small village just outside the base provided what the troops had been without for a long time in the paddies—women.

I had no problems with the men's visits to the local bordellos. After all, if the men were there to fight for the country, they should be able to enjoy part of it. My only instructions were that they should go in groups for their safety and see Doc Bass for issue of prophylactics, which were considered a medical item. The men faced dangers enough without adding the risk of venereal disease.

One of my soldiers soon was convinced he was in love with one of the ladies. He felt his ardor was returned until he ran out of money and learned differently.

Our new company commander was CPT Jeffrey Swiss, who had come in-country with me. I was surprised to find him as my new boss since an armor officer's assuming command of an Infantry unit was unusual. Even though I had not been in the field long, I could tell he had much to learn.

The casualty figures for the company of only 120 men were provided by the battalion adjutant. The figures for the wounded were somewhat inflated; many soldiers had been wounded more than once, and after brief hospital stays or field care, they returned to the war. The killed-in-action statistics were accurate. You only die once.

The figures made it quite evident why a soldier with more than six months in the company was considered an old-timer. Few completed a full tour without joining one of the casualty lists.

Brigadier General Davidson was a tall, powerful-looking man and the highest ranking black commander in the war zone at the time. He had earned the position by serving as a Deputy Brigade Commander for over a year and extending his tour to get the command. He was well thought-of by all.

My opinion of the people of Vietnam was not high. It would become even lower with more experience.

6 MAY 1969
Tuesday

Binh Chanh

Life at Binh Chanh was somewhat easier than at Elvira. The three hot meals each day provided by the mess hall were a welcome break from C-rations.

The scraps and garbage were carried to an open dump area a few hundred meters from the base. Children and old women dug in the refuse throughout the day for food or anything usable for clothing or shelter. Americans gave little assistance. It was difficult—if not impossible—to tell just who was the enemy. Our job was to destroy, not to feed and care for, though the irony of our spending a fortune to kill Vietnamese while they were going hungry all around us did not escape me.

The surrounding paddies were not quite as muddy as those near Elvira, but the monsoons were due to begin soon. I had not kept such a close eye on the sky for rain clouds since boyhood on my father's drought-plagued farm.

Although I had only been with the platoon for a little over two weeks, I felt I already knew the soldiers pretty well. Living and working together twenty-four hours a day readily revealed personalities and capabilities. The average age of the men was slightly over nineteen. At twenty-two, I was the second oldest in the platoon. The men followed orders with little question. They complained about almost everything, but no more so than is traditional and expected of soldiers. As long as the duties and details were distributed fairly equally, they went about their jobs with reasonably good humor.

Only three of the men had been in the platoon for more than eight months. They frequently reminded me, and anyone who would listen, how many days remained until their rotation back to the States. Each asked for a job in the rear as soon as possible. I made no promises, as their experience was needed in the field. I did manage to see that they rarely walked point.

My letter home on this day asked Linda to order me another contact lens. I had lost one while I was attempting to remove it in a night ambush position. By the time the replacement lens arrived, however, I had decided no longer to wear them. The staggered sleep and guard schedules, combined with the dust, made continued wearing of the lenses impractical. Also, personal appearance had taken a distant second place to survival.

Linda was in Texas, staying with her parents until she could move to San Francisco to live with her friend Susan Hargrove when Susan's husband Tom left for Vietnam. They planned to sublet an apartment from Susan's parents, who were going to Lebanon for a year.

🛩 7 MAY 1969
Wednesday

Binh Chanh
   Today I found out Linda and I are going to have a baby—I'll be damned—This is certainly a happiness but also a great worry—I had no sooner started her letter when we got called to move out—Patrolled about 6k with an ARVN plt—Scary as hell moving at night—Finally got to finish letter about 3 hours after I started it—My prayers are with my wife and child
   Have been very happy with my navigation—Paralleled the ARVNs for 6k—Came out 50m from target

Reading a letter in a sandbagged bunker eleven-thousand miles from home is a hell of a way to find out you are going to be a father. I was ecstatic at the news.

Even before I got orders for the war, Linda and I had discussed having a child while I was in Vietnam, and she had stopped taking the Pill several months before my departure. Although it seemed that she had not conceived, we had certainly exposed her to the possibility. She wrote that the doctor said that she had the "Egyptian flu"—she was going to "be a mummie."

Her letter was lengthy, and I had read only the fact that she was pregnant when we received the rush order to move out with the South Vietnamese platoon. There was barely time for me to skim the rest of the letter before we departed on an extremely dangerous night mission, where we had no way to detect possible booby traps. I was never sure just why the patrol was ordered on such short notice. As usual, no explanation was made. For a few hours, the danger of night movement drove out of my mind any concerns of becoming a father.

When we finally returned to the base, I finished the letter by candlelight. Soon I had told just about everyone in the company, waking many to relate the good news. I was amazed that no one was particularly interested.

The pregnancy was never far out of my thoughts for the next seven months. Yet it really did not worry me. It was what we wanted and I had complete confidence in Linda. I had my war. At least now she would have her baby.

✈ 8 MAY 1969
Thursday

Binh Chanh
    Clearing nipa palm today—
    Found a Chicom grenade booby trap—
    When we blew it 2nd plt leader—LT Andy May from N. C.—was hit in chest—First blood I've seen—I was standing next to him—He will be out in a couple of days doc says—Not bad Thank God.
    Night—Went on cordon—Long night—Am getting run down

Our mission for the day was more busywork than anything of real tactical value because the line of nipa palm was nearly a mile from the fire base and did not interfere with observation or field of fire. Someone in Battalion Operations must have decided that physical labor was a cure for boredom.

The 1st and 2nd Platoons took turns cutting down the foliage and providing security. We proceeded with care. A week earlier the same mission had been given to another unit who had left before finishing the job. The palms made a prime area for booby traps because the VC knew sooner or later someone would be back to chop some more.

We had been working a couple of hours when one of the troops spotted a grenade booby trap augmented with blasting powder, nails, glass and pieces of old metal packed in a tin can. A trip wire ran from it to a nipa palm branch.

As a member of his platoon had found it, LT May took charge of destroying the grenade. Andy placed about a quarter pound of C-4 explosive next to the booby trap. He molded the puttylike substance around a blasting cap with a long fuse. After lighting the fuse, he walked to where the rest of us were waiting. I asked him if we were far enough away. He assured me he had done this many times and that we were safe.

When the C-4 detonated, it blew the booby trap as planned, but a small piece of jagged steel hit Andy in center chest, penetrating the skin and stopping against his sternum. After his surprise passed, he laughed at his mistake as the blood ran in a thin line down his chest. The wound was not serious enough to request a helicopter dust-off, so a jeep ambulance picked him up.

After a couple of stitches and a chewing-out from both the company and battalion commanders, he returned to duty. No Purple Heart was mentioned, as his injuries were considered to be his own fault. My feelings upon seeing this "first blood" were a mixture of relief that it was not worse and of embarrassment over our mistake.

After May had been evacuated, we returned to clearing the vegetation. My platoon command post—my RTO, Doc Bass and myself—was in a nearby hooch, a twelve by fifteen foot shack made of wood poles and thatched palm. In this tin-roofed, dirt-floored structure lived a woman and two small children.

The woman spent much time washing dishes and clothes in a muddy ditch just outside the hut. The older child, a girl of about five, held a small baby on her hip. There was no man at home. He was likely in the ARVN or possibly with the VC. Perhaps he had been the source of the booby trap.

On an old wooden table in the hooch, I wrote Linda about my joy in receiving word of her pregnancy. The girl with the baby on her hip watched over my shoulder. I had never paid much attention to children. In fact, I had never held a baby in my arms. After giving the girl some C-rations and chewing gum, I went back to work.

✎ 9 MAY 1969
Friday

Finished cordon—Long walk back in—Had all my men change ammo in magazines today.

Stayed back tonight—First time in about a week—I go out usually more than the other platoon leaders—Want to be with my men—They need leadership

Getting so I wake up at least 1 or 2 times an hour—Check guard etc.—It pays to be cautious—

Found a 105mm round booby trap today—Nobody hit it Thank God

Co CO offered a case of beer to anyone in ambushes getting a body count—One of my squad leaders said they could have gotten one last night but VC offered 2 cases if they would let him go so they did

The humor of a GI

The cordon was fruitless. The battalion had invested an entire day and night's effort with no results. There had been no direct contact with the enemy since Collier's squad killed two my first night in the field.

Constant exposure to the saltwater which filled the canals and paddies made keeping weapons clean a continuing task. We oiled our rifles and machine guns on nearly every break and, at least twice a day, disassembled, cleaned, and reassembled each weapon.

I was closely inspecting each man's weapon and equipment when my RTO, SP4 Jerry Woody, pointed out that much of the ammunition was becoming corroded in the magazines. This was simple to fix. We secured new ammo from the battalion ammo point and replaced all of the old rounds, which were returned to battalion for disposal. We did not want them to fall into the hands of the VC. The idea of facing our own bullets was not appealing.

Woody, a Georgia native who had been in the platoon for six months, had taken his turn on point and as a squad RTO before taking over the platoon radio since shortly before I joined the platoon. His Southern drawl was easily recognizable on the radio.

In Army language the radio was a PRC 77. GIs simply called it "the horn." To carry the platoon leader's radio was an honored position. It allowed Woody to keep up with what was going on in the entire company, a small benefit for carrying the extra twenty pounds and for identifying himself as a prime target by the antenna waving in the air. I never met an RTO who was not a very curious individual and a bit of a gossip at heart. So maybe it all evened out.

At nineteen, Woody had been around more than his fellow GI teenagers. He had dropped out of school in the ninth grade. On his own since that time, he had worked construction and driven trucks. He looked forward to returning to Atlanta and being a long-haul trucker.

Both of his arms were covered in poorly done tattoos—the type frequently applied by fellow prisoners in jail. Woody confirmed that was part of their origin, but he would only say that he had never done "anything bad enough to keep him out of the Army." The largest design was a crude heart with the word Mom, though he never mentioned his parents.

Woody was my constant companion. Never farther than arm's reach, he knew his safety as well as the entire platoon's depended on the communications he provided. He took care of me like a mother. At the briefest rest break, he could brew up a cup of coffee big enough for the two of us. His advice, assistance, and companionship were invaluable.

Finding and destroying the 105mm booby trap before it could do the same to us was satisfying. It was a small strike back at the bastard enemy that was the cause of our exhausting operations. The fact that the men were still alert despite the lack of activity was comforting.

10 MAY 1969
Saturday

Binh Chanh

The next few days would be the last of my regular journal entries for awhile. I was becoming exhausted both mentally and physically. Constant day patrols and night ambushes were wearing me down.

In the paddies we slept directly on the ground. Despite the heat of the day, the nights were cool. Lightweight ponchos and poncho liners at least kept the damp air from making it too miserable.

The poncho liners were in a green, brown, and black camouflage pattern. They dried quickly and provided much warmth for their light weight. Woody assured me that they would even stop bullets if you believed it hard enough.

My liner was one of the few things I later brought home. I still have it. Everybody loved his liner. Whether they were security blankets or represented the women we were sleeping without, I am not really sure.

The day's recon in force (RIF) displayed the superior marksmanship of the 2nd squad leader, SP4 Gallagher. Trained as a sharpshooter, Gallagher carried an M14 sniper rifle with scope. He swore that at a range of three-hundred meters he could fire the weapon and regain his sight picture in the scope to watch the round strike the target.

On our RIF, a man working in the paddies began walking quickly away. At a range of over five-hundred meters, Gallagher put a round at the man's feet as a warning for him to stop. The man scarcely moved a muscle until we arrived at his location. His ID card was in order, so we let him go.

✍ **11 MAY 1969**
Sunday

Binh Chanh

Much of my recollection of these days again comes from my letters home. In accordance with our talks before I left, Linda kept all my correspondence. It was not until my brother and parents learned I was writing about my Vietnam experience that they revealed that they, too, had kept each letter.

Why had they kept each letter for so long? We did not discuss the reason; we all knew why. Each letter they received might have been the last.

My letters home were based more on the opportunity to mail them than on the time to write. Usually correspondence revolved around resupply, when letters written by the platoon were placed in a sandbag and handed to the helicopter crew chief or pilot. They somehow always found their way to the proper postal channels.

Stamps were no problem. Everyone in the war zone was allowed to write "free" in the right top corner of the envelope. That, along with name, rank, serial number, and unit as a return address, guaranteed delivery.

Stationery, pens, etc., were provided for free also. Many of the sheets of paper had a small map of Southeast Asia in the lower corner. To better orient the reader, I frequently circled the general area we were in.

The longer I was in Vietnam, the fewer letters I received. Linda continued her daily correspondence, numbering each letter on the back of the envelope so I could read them in order. Jim and my mother wrote at least weekly. I received an occasional letter from someone at my parents' church or from old college friends. Other relatives also wrote periodically. One fairly regular letter writer was a great uncle whom I did not know very well. He was a veteran of both World Wars and understood the importance of mail to a soldier.

Some people promised to write and never did. Others wrote only the first month or so. Then, again, I, too, wrote fewer letters as time went by. The occasional letter from the tax collector for car-registration or property tax was received with humor and curses and ultimately forwarded to Linda for payment.

Incoming mail was the high point of any day we were fortunate enough to receive it. We did not keep our letters, however. After time for several readings, we burned them, ensuring they would not fall in the hands of the enemy to be used for propaganda purposes. It was often reported that units farther north heard letters to GIs read over Radio Hanoi.

One of the few letters I kept from Linda was the one informing me of our impending parenthood. It stayed with my journal, in a small waterproof bag in my rucksack, for the duration.

🐦 12 MAY 1969
Monday

Binh Chanh

More day-time patrols and night ambushes. Our movement through the paddies and villages surrounding Binh Chanh produced little except to show the locals we were in the area. This was supposed to discourage them from providing support to the VC. We likely did as much harm as good.

Their way of life was so different from ours, yet in other ways similar to our own. We went into the villagers' homes with no warning or request for permission to enter. In one thatched-roof, dirt-floored home, a large pendulum wall-clock chimed the hours. From what I observed, the villagers had neither regular jobs nor any type of scheduled activities. The presence of the clock was ironic in a land where time seemed to stand still.

The contrasts were always enormous. In one village we stopped while Doc Bass treated a small child for an animal bite. The boy's mother explained in a mixture of English and Vietnamese that the injury was from a mongoose, an ill-tempered pet kept to kill snakes and rats in the hooches. Doc's limited medical knowledge and supplies allowed him only to clean and bandage the wound. The woman and child both seemed grateful. We felt that we might even be doing a little to win the hearts and minds of the locals.

However, in the same village, Collier dragged a middle-aged man out of his hooch and accused him of being a VC. He punctuated his questions to the man with slaps and kicks until I stopped him. Collier's explanation for this was, "He's a fucking VC! Only gooks have moustaches."

The man's ID card was in order. With no weapon or military equipment found in the man's hooch, I had to conclude that Collier's convictions were the result of his own frustration over always finding booby traps but never the enemy who set them. He was not the only one who thought that if we had the people by the balls, their hearts and minds would follow.

The problem was knowing just who was the enemy. Hearts and minds aside, everyone referred to any Vietnamese as a gook, dink, or slope. No one really worried about "social" work. An infantryman's job is to kill and destroy.

13 MAY 1969
Tuesday

Binh Chanh

The intelligence officers at S-2 had decided that the enemy was becoming more active 10 klicks to our south. Most of the brigade was to develop a cordon around a large area of paddies and thick nipa palm. The Two-thirds was to have the most dangerous job of sweeping through the area.

A few soldiers were left behind to secure the fire base perimeter—mostly troops recovering from minor illnesses or injuries. Virtually everyone else loaded the helicopters for a quick insertion to seal off the suspected VC stronghold.

By moving quickly, we soon had surrounded an area of several square kilometers. Overhead the brigade commander controlled the entire operation. The battalion commanders, accompanied by their operations officers, alternated from ground CPs to their helicopter command and control airships. From these points of observation, they could ensure our circle was unbroken and direct fire on any enemy who made the mistake of revealing themselves.

We immediately found fresh VC trails. Small hand-lettered signs reading, "*Tu Dia*" and "*mins*" were on many paddy dikes. Others had no message other than a painted skull and cross bones. The signs allowed the VC to avoid their own deadly handiwork and warned the local noncombatants to stay out of the area. They made a strong psychological impact on us as well.

By nightfall we had destroyed several booby-trapped hand grenades found by the alert point man. Around some signs we found nothing. Whatever their purpose, we were all aware the enemy was near. Our apprehensions were heightened by the obvious fact that the VC knew we were coming.

As darkness covered the paddies, we stopped. Ambushes and blocking forces were carefully positioned to keep the cordon sealed. Artillery defensive concentrations were zeroed in near our positions. These "def cons" assured that the artillery had accurate data ready to put on the sights; with seconds' notice, we could have a wall of exploding steel around us.

The Charlie Company headquarters had brought one of our four 81mm mortar tubes. Its eighty-pound weight made it a bitch to hump across the mud even though the three main pieces were carried by a four-man crew. Its high explosive (HE) and illumination rounds added to our loads. However, we needed the firepower.

Because this was not a free-fire zone, artillery firing had to be cleared with local government officials to be sure rounds would not impact in friendly villages. The coordination process took several minutes while mortar rounds could be fired in seconds. Minutes compared to seconds often equated to lives lost and a body count not gained.

The first platoon had the added firepower of a 90mm recoilless rifle, a four-foot long cylinder similar to the bazookas of World War II. Designed for antitank use, it had been modified as an antipersonnel weapon through use of shells containing hundreds of one-inch arrow-shaped pieces of wire. Effective only at short ranges, it could break up any attack on a position.

The 90 was in the charge of SP4 Clayton, who also carried his usual M-16 as well as two shells for the gun. Clayton was a brickwall of a man. A black from Washington, D.C., he was the strongest man in the platoon. Still, with the extra weight, he had trouble keeping up. Clay did not complain. He loved the 90 and was glad to have it in the paddies; it usually remained on fire base perimeter-support because of the weight.

Whatever was out there, we were as ready as possible. I woke Woody at midnight for his turn on radio watch. He whispered, "This is bad shit, One-six. Tomorrow's going to be a long day."

One-six was my radio call sign as the 1st Platoon leader. The company commander was Six, the second platoon leader Two-six, and so on. In the field the entire platoon called me One-six or occasionally LT ("L-tee") for lieutenant; no "sirs" or salutes were rendered nor wanted—these would indicate me as an officer to a VC sniper.

As usual, Woody was right. We were facing a long day.

≥ 14 MAY 1969
Wednesday

On another Cordon
   Had 7 men hit today by an 81mm booby trap—
   My first real taste of death—Men hit next to me and behind me—

Last thing one man said before dust off was to see if his
flak jacket helped—It probably saved his life—
3 dusted off to heat—
A strange feeling for men hit to be calling for you

Light rain began to fall shortly after midnight. We pulled
our ponchos closer and cursed Mother Nature for adding to
our discomfort. The monsoon season had begun gently.

By daybreak the clouds had cleared and we continued our
sweep of the cordoned area. The temperature soon neared 100
degrees. Our paths followed the wettest, muddiest route to
avoid the many booby traps. Collier's squad, with my CP,
was on the right flank, SP4 Gallagher's squad on the left.

The air above was filled with helicopters of various command levels. The radio crackled with orders to push harder in
the sweep.

By noon the heat, mud, lack of sufficient water, extra equipment, and the fast pace had the entire platoon near exhaustion.
Three FNGs had to be evacuated as heat casualties, lessening
our numbers. We were soon to lose more.

In the early afternoon, CPT Swiss instructed me by radio to
move farther north into the nipa-palm line. I objected because
of the many booby-trap signs, but he explained that the order
was from battalion and though he agreed with my assessment,
we had to follow it.

On my instructions, Woody called Gallagher on the horn
and told him to move to my location. He would have to know
the changed compass heading as well as the new plan for clearing the area. Separating the squads was a small canal about
four feet across. A log crossed the span. At each end was a
small skull and cross bones sign. I yelled to Gallagher, telling
him not to use the log. He grinned and nodded his head that
he understood.

He took a wide berth around the log. As he forded the small
canal, a large black-clouded explosion ripped the air.

Gallagher was blown out of the canal to the near bank. The
radio handset I was talking on, connected by an expandable

cord to Woody's PRC 77, was jerked from my hand. Woody had been hit and blown backward six feet. Screams of "Medic!" "One-six!" and "Goddamn!" filled the air.

By the time I reached Woody, he had recovered the handset. As blood poured from his legs, he was calmly calling for a dust-off. Doc ran to Gallagher. Collier quickly established a security perimeter around the fallen.

In seconds we had counted the wounded as six. I reported to CPT Swiss that we would need at least two medivac helicopters. I applied mine and Woody's first aid dressings to his legs. Doc was working on Gallagher while other members of the platoon bandaged their buddies.

Gallagher had wounds from his feet to his head. One eye hung out of the socket. His sniper rifle, held across his chest, and his flak jacket had absorbed much of the shrapnel in that area. After a shot of morphine, he was able to talk. He looked up and said, "They beat us on that one, didn't they, One-six?"

I answered with a nod.

He continued, "I'm sorry. I should have seen it. At least now, I will be going home."

Gallagher never asked about his eye. His good shot of the previous week came to mind. He would shoot no more.

The next most seriously wounded was SP4 Clausen. A fellow Texan, from Breckenridge, Clausen was always bitching about having to wear his flak jacket. It probably saved his life. Still, part of the booby trap had penetrated the jacket and his chest. The bubbling blood indicated a hit in the lung. The sound of air escaping his body made it evident why they call them sucking chest wounds. With a compress bandage and lots of pressure, we finally stopped the air loss, but we had to get him out quickly, for the lung was collapsing.

The injured were spread over an area thirty-five to forty meters in diameter. Some of us near the blast had not gotten a scratch. Others, like Clayton, were hit at the far edge of the circle. Clay received minor but painful wounds in the ass. He had been leaning over to set the 90mm recoilless rifle on a piece of dry ground when the booby trap exploded. Both buttocks were bleeding profusely.

Two other men had minor wounds. PFC Manderson had several small punctures in his legs. PFC Hefferman had caught one fragment in his arm.

The first dust-off was already completed when PFC Molleda, maintaining a security position at the edge of the platoon, reported he thought he, too, was hit. Our wounded had risen to seven. Doc quickly cut away Molleda's fatigue trousers to reveal wounds in both legs. There was little blood but he was having trouble moving his limbs. We placed him on a stretcher and loaded him on the second dust off.

Molleda had arrived in the platoon on the same day as I. He was a quiet, hard worker who never complained. His English was so poor that frequently other Spanish-speaking soldiers in the platoon had to interpret. Molleda's tour would be a short one. We learned later the booby trap had broken both his legs.

Before the last dust-off lifted into the sky, a light observation helicopter (LOH) landed. Out of the LOH stepped a full colonel. By the name tag on his starched, pressed fatigues, I could see he was COL Smith, the deputy brigade commander. He wore a soft cap rather than a steel helmet and was armed with only a 45-caliber pistol.

Apparently he did not want to walk through the mud in his spit-shined boots. Calling me to his location and making no introduction, he angrily chewed me out for losing so many men from one booby trap. Pointing out the large area of the blast to him seemed to make no difference. He told me what I already knew; I did not need to hear from him that, as the leader, I was responsible.

Many of the platoon overheard the one-sided conversation. Several said later that we should have shot the son of a bitch. Their support was appreciated.

Along with the quickness of near-death, there was another lesson for me. Americans valued Americans' lives far above those of our Vietnamese allies. As the first medivac landed, the crew chief picked a badly wounded ARVN soldier off a stretcher on the chopper's floor, then threw the small man into the narrow area of the aircraft's engine to make way for Gallagher and the others.

After the last dust-off departed I was able to convince COL Smith to evacuate the weapons and gear of the wounded. A call to the company CP ensured they would notify the rear troops to meet the chopper and secure the equipment.

Several weeks later I heard that COL Smith was shot down and seriously wounded when he got too close to a fire fight he was trying to supervise. Rumors were that M-16, as well as AK-47, bullets were found in the wreck of the aircraft. It made a good story. It did not hurt our morale and sense of justice.

Inspection of the booby-trap blast area showed that the explosive was apparently a US 81mm mortar round. A hand grenade or two may have been added, which would account for the large amount of shrapnel. The trip wire was under the water of the canal. The log was the only safe way across the water. Later I sat on the log as I washed the blood of my soldiers from my hands.

We reorganized, with SSG (Staff Sergeant) Marple taking charge of Gallagher's squad. With only fifteen men left, we did not need a platoon sergeant.

The platoon moved another five hundred meters before nightfall. Each step was taken with fear of the present and images in mind of the past.

---

15 MAY 1969
Thursday

Cordon

Heard Nixon's speech today—Some of my men's comments—

"Damn, isn't that great—I can go home in 12 months"
"Peace—yeah, piece"
"Really"
"Another speech to please the politicans"
Also numerous unprintable comments

By noon we had completed the sweep of our sector of the cordon area. Except for finding and destroying several more booby traps, we inflicted no vengeance on the enemy.

My new RTO, PFC Roger DeForrest, had brought along a small transistor radio in his pack. It was against platoon policy to carry them outside the fire base because noise was not conducive to finding the enemy, but he assured me that he had not turned it on since we departed Binh Chanh. Though soldiers in the rear, or REMFS (for rear-echelon motherfuckers), could listen to Armed Forces Network Radio or watch Armed Forces Television at their leisure, the radio was a luxury we in the field could not afford.

DeForrest explained that he had carried the small radio in hopes we could listen to the highly touted speech by President Nixon. Mr. Nixon had previously announced he would discuss the plans for the first American unit pullout of the war. We all hoped it would be a "home by Christmas" message. But we knew better.

AFN radio played popular rock and roll, soul, and country music. Recordings of shows such as *The Shadow* and *The Lone Ranger* were also frequently broadcast. Perhaps the most famous voice on AFN was the Chicken Man. His early-morning show, which began with "Good morning, Vietnam," received more than a few laughs—and curses as well.

The President's speech was not well-received. His reference to us as noble American fighting men meant little to the tired, wet, scared infantrymen.

Following the President's message, we heard a newscast of the mounting casualties taken by the 101st Airborne Division to our north at a place aptly called Hamburger Hill. DeForrest turned off the transistor radio and returned it to his pack. We could see not even a flicker of light at the end of the tunnel.

Just before dark the platoon moved into a single-ambush position. We had good observation and could cover our sector from one position rather than two. The decision was appreciated by the fifteen men remaining in the platoon.

An hour after dark, Charlie Company's third platoon engaged two VC seven hundred meters from our position. The VCs' AK tracers were green while ours were red, so it was easy to distinguish between the friendly and enemy fire. We kept our heads down. Bullets and tracers, red or green, have no conscience about whom they hit.

We were delighted to hear on the horn that one of the enemy was killed and his weapon captured. The only thing that would have made it better would have been if they had killed both. We all hoped that the dead gook was the one who had set the "log-crossing" booby trap.

---

16 MAY 1969
Friday

Move to Binh Dien Bridge

Sketchy reports on the radio revealed that the operation had been an overall success. In addition to the body count and weapon capture by the third platoon, several other contacts had produced similar results. As usual, we never received a report of the total successes and losses of the operation. The first platoon was glad to be leaving the area. Regardless of the Brigade's happiness with the adventure, the 1st Platoon would mark it as a bloody, horrible memory.

The news that we would be extracted by helicopters was most welcomed. Maybe our luck was taking a new direction.

In the open paddies, a landing zone (LZ) for the birds was easy to select. While checking the area to be sure the choppers would not land on any booby traps, the second squad found a 155 millimeter artillery round with no obvious trip wire or pressure device. Still, the rusty six-inch-diameter shell had to be destroyed; however, the platoon's best demolition man, SP4 Clausen, was in a Saigon hospital.

I had received some demo training in Ranger School, so the explosives duty became mine. After placing a half-pound of C-4 next to the round, I lit the long fuse and ran to the platoon's position over three-hundred meters away. Following the loud explosion, we raised our heads over the paddy dike to take a look, but we hit the dirt when we saw and heard a large chunk of the missile heading our way. It arced through the air like a softball heading to the outfield and landed with a splash in the mud less than ten meters in front of us.

We walked out and took a look at the piece of metal that had traveled six times farther than the 155's normal bursting radius. It was about three inches wide and eight inches long; it was supposed to break up into small pieces on detonation. Apparently, due to its age and time in the hot sun, this one jagged piece had been able to hold together to seek its destroyer. The incident only added to our good feelings about leaving the area.

A short time later, we heard helicopters approaching from the distance. In seconds we were airborne. Minutes later we landed on the asphalt surface of Highway 4 at the edge of the Binh Dien Bridge.

The bridge spanned about 125 meters across the Kinh Doi River, which flowed into the Saigon River about twelve klicks to the east. Highway 4 was the main roadway from Saigon to the Delta region. It was an important civilian transportation artery as well as the main ground supply route for the military in the southern third of the country.

The necessity of guarding the bridge was made evident by

twisted wreckage of the two previous spans that had been
blown by VC sappers.

The Charlie Company CP was in a large house at the south
end of the bridge. CPT Swiss assigned the third platoon the
bridge itself. The second platoon was to guard the north approach and the first platoon was to secure the south end and
the CP.

We moved into our sector after the departing platoon gave
us a quick tour. They left their Claymore mines and wires in
place. At each bunker was a diagram of the mines' locations.
We quickly settled into our new home.

✄ 17 MAY 1969
Saturday

Binh Dien Bridge
   Got to go into Saigon to see my men—They had already
been moved from 3rd Field—Most to Japan
   Went to PX—Some of the Betty Crocker assignments
over here are easier than stateside Inf jobs—
   Everybody calls the USA "the world"

LT Hawkins visited the company with paperwork for CPT
Swiss to sign. He also brought a jeep trailer full of beer, mail,
and a hot meal. Even Army chow tasted good after days of C-
rations.

I borrowed Hawkins' jeep to visit my wounded men in Saigon's 3rd Field Hospital. DeForrest went along to ride shot-
gun. The XO's driver knew the way to the hospital; he had
made the trip many times before.

The streets of Saigon narrowed near the hospital. We passed
a large cemetery which, the driver explained, contained many
graves from the French involvement in the fifties.

The hospital was much bigger than I expected. A large white stucco structure of several stories, it resembled the hospitals back home.

DeForrest and I left the jeep in charge of the driver. Without him there to secure it, the radio, as well as the jeep itself, was likely to disappear.

Several of the white-uniformed staff of the hospital stared disapprovingly at our dirty uniforms and boots as we entered the building, still carrying M-16 rifles and bandoleers of ammo. Hand grenades hung from our web gear.

A disheveled Army captain, wearing nurse insignia, was at the main desk. She looked as if she had not slept in days. I handed her a list of my men, which she delivered to a specialist in charge of the files. While he searched, the nurse led me through large open wards full of patients. Beds were so close together the attendants could hardly walk between them.

The nurse explained that the hospital was grossly over-crowded because casualties from Hamburger Hill were still flowing in. The less seriously wounded were being returned to their units; the more critical were being transferred to Japan.

When we returned to the desk, the clerk confided that the files were a mess but thought that two of my men had been released back to BMB that morning. A couple had been sent to Japan. As for the others, he was not really sure.

Medivac helicopters and ground ambulances continued to arrive. I felt out of place. There was nothing we could do to help except get out of the staff's way. As we returned to the jeep, I noticed that even the smell of Vietnam was welcome after the antiseptic odor of 3rd Field Hospital.

Our next stop was at a nearby PX. DeForrest had a long list from the platoon asking for *Playboy* magazines and for food not in green cans.

The American MP at the PX door explained to us—not any too politely—that we would have to leave our weapons outside. His attitude was that we dirty grunts were not really welcome. Entering the building, we understood why. Its air-conditioned shelves were filled to overflowing with name-brand everything. The store could have easily have been at Fort Bragg or on Main Street back in the world.

We gathered the items on the lists as quickly as possible. Again we felt out of place. Most of the patrons looked at us as they would at whores in church. Just smelling our fatigues was about as close as many of them ever would get to the real war. The grunt term "Betty Crocker" seemed most appropriate for the Saigon warriors. They would have looked more at home in aprons baking cakes than in the paddies.

❧ 18 MAY 1969
Sunday

Binh Dien Bridge
Same, same

In learning foreign languages the first words memorized are usually "please," "thank you," and "Where is the bathroom?" I never learned what these phrases are in Vietnamese. Every grunt did know how to say "Stop!" "Come back here," and "Get the hell out of the way." Other communications, such as "Fuck you," "beer," and "boom-boom" seemed to be the same in any language. Some words were merely repeated loudly as if volume and persistence would transfer their meanings. "Same, same" meant no change, boring as usual.

The 1st Platoon sector for security of the bridge was composed of five heavily sandbagged bunkers, identical to those at Elvira, Binh Chanh, and probably every other American defensive position in Vietnam. One squad was sent out on ambush each night, leaving only two men at each bunker. We never slept for more than two hours at a time. A complete night's sleep was becoming a vague memory.

Within the wire-surrounded bunker line were a half-dozen Vietnamese hooches inhabited, as usual, by old men, women, and children; anything not carried or guarded disappeared in short order. One of the huts had a small battery-operated television. The inhabitants were well-aware of their positions, however. Each hut had a bunker in its center. The top served as a dining table by day and a sleeping platform at night.

❧ 19 MAY 1969
Monday

Little easier duty here—
Am down to 18 men—Need replacements—
M-16 nearly blew up in my face today—Another man's weapon.
Many of the kids here speak English—All the cuss words—Most can't remember when GIs weren't here
Today is Ho Chi Minh's birthday

Hefferman and Clayton returned to the platoon from their stay at 3rd Field Hospital and BMB. Their stories of beds with sheets, good food and beer made their wounds almost seem worthwhile. They made little comment on the removal of the shrapnel from their flesh, though they proudly displayed their newly awarded Purple Hearts.

Other routine personnel matters continued. A replacement arrived; one man departed for R&R; another soldier returned to the States on a thirty-day emergency leave to attend his father's funeral.

SSG Nat Flores returned to the platoon from body escort back to the world, having been requested to accompany the casket by the dead man's family.

Escort duty was a good break from Vietnam. No one really wanted the honor, however. None of us wanted to lose a friend to get a temporary ticket home. The death of others only reminded us of our own vulnerabilities. As the popular Country Joe and the Fish song about Vietnam said, "You, too, could be the first one on your block to come home in a box."

Flores, a Texan from Taylor, was popular with the men and an excellent leader. Even though he only had a few months left in his tour, he returned to the "first herd" as platoon sergeant. SSG Marple was now the 2nd squad leader while Acting Sergeant Collier still had the first.

I was becoming more acquainted with the forty or so villagers within our compound. We saw no young men around. Yet nearly three-quarters of the inhabitants were children under twelve years of age. Whenever the men had been present, they had obviously made the best of their time.

A waifish girl of about ten was always around the bunker DeForrest and I shared. She spoke fairly good English, especially obscenitites that I had not learned until I joined the Army. We could not pronounce her Vietnamese name, so at her request, we called her Gina. Gina ran errands, passed along village gossip, and even helped fill sandbags. She also assured us that she would guard our equipment from theft by the other children. Whatever her motivation, it worked. We gave her enough C-rations every day to feed her entire family. I did not really feel sorry for her. Yet, I hoped my own child would grow up in a better world.

In response to my question about how long Americans had been at the bridge, Gina replied, "GIs always been here."

The children of the village never seemed to play like the kids back home. No toys were evident. Older children took care of the younger ones. Others fished or gathered plants for the table. Everyone moved at a slow pace. Sitting in the shade was a major pastime. They rarely laughed or seemed very animated except for one day when I saw them in a circle laughing with glee. I glanced over their shoulders to see a large rat that had been soaked in kerosene and set afire. The rodent tried to crawl out of the circle but was knocked back by his stick-wielding tormentors. Death finally brought an end to their game. A boy picked up the rat by the tail and walked away. Whether he was going to dispose of it or eat it, I did not know.

My journal entry about the M-16 incident is puzzling. I should remember such an occurrence. Other lines on the pages bring back complete conversations, the surrounding terrain, people's faces and even smells. This entry brings back nothing. It did not make its way into my letters home either. Strange that something that could have killed me was not important enough to remember.

In the late afternoon, we received word that the 3rd Platoon had taken casualties from another booby trap.

Shortly before sundown they returned to the bridge. I sat in as CPT Swiss debriefed the platoon leader, 2LT Norm Sassner. Norm explained that the platoon had spent much of the day on a Navy boat patroling the canals. Several times the boat had pulled up to the bank and dropped its front ramp so the platoon could go ashore on short recon-patrols.

On the final patrol of the day the point man had triggered a trip-wired hand grenade. The soldier had received serious leg wounds and the platoon sergeant had taken shrapnel in the legs and penis. A wound to the genitals was the most feared injury in this war, as in any other conflict. A man's first question to the medics was not "Am I going to make it?" but rather "Do I still have my balls?" (Everyone felt much better when the sergeant returned from the hospital a month later. He assured us his penis was fully operational. It goes without saying that this gave us all confidence in modern medicine.)

A bloody bandage on Sassner's leg showed that he, too, had been hit. After dusting off his two soldiers, Norm had removed a small steel fragment from his thigh with the medic's tweezers. Norm requested no Purple Heart for his wound. Like most of us, he believed the battlefield superstition that a "cheap" Purple Heart would lead to really deserving the next one.

More bad news came a short time later. The 1st Platoon would be going to the same area the next day.

Ho Chi Minh's birthday passed without further incident. We observed it with special vigilance to catch anyone who might try to make the destruction of our bridge a gift to Uncle Ho.

Later that night I wrote my brother by flashlight. His recent letters had said that Judy's baby was developing fine despite the measles. Time would tell.

═══════════════════════════════════════

✍ 20 MAY 1969
Tuesday

Bien Luc
   OPCONed to Co B ⁵/₁₂ today—Bad area—They hit two Chicom booby traps—Felt fortunate we all walked out—
   Found one woman in labor—Men wanted to leave her alone—I made her walk to LCM to be evacuated with the rest

Trucks arrived at the bridge early in the morning to carry us to the 5th Battalion, 12th Infantry AO. In the small village of Bien Luc, I found the Bravo Company commander. We had first met during Redcatcher training at BMB, so we briefly exchanged stories about our experiences during the past few weeks. He then explained the day's mission.

The 1st Platoon was to sweep through a paddy area to some isolated hooches and a small village of farmers and fishermen. All civilians were to be moved to a nearby canal where they would be transported by Navy landing craft marine (LCMs) to Bien Luc. There they would be met by Vietnamese interrogators. After questioning and reissue of the national identification cards, they would be returned to their homes.

The Bravo CO showed me on the map where we were to

link up about noon. He also pointed out a location where we should meet the battalion's Alpha Company on the left flank. This coordination would ensure the entire area had been swept. After exchanging radio frequency and call signs with the Bravo RTOs, we moved out.

Before leaving the bridge CPT Swiss had given me a new experimental protective suit. The "gook suit" was similar to the flak vest except it hung apronlike from shoulders to below the knees. The first point man, PFC Tex Turnage, wore it for only a few hundred meters before stopping. Tex took off the heavy apron as he walked back to my position.

"One-six, this damn thing will kill me before the gooks do," he said.

I walked back to the point with Tex and put the suit on myself. After about one hundred meters, I told Tex he was right. No one could wear the heavy suit in the heat and stay conscious long enough to need its protection. Another well-intentioned project by the research and development folks went down the drain.

A short time later Turnage found a booby trap as he crossed over a paddy dike. It was a home-made grenade of black powder and metal fragments stuffed into a small red-labeled, mackerel-in-tomato-sauce can. We destroyed it in place.

It was not long before DeForrest received a call from the adjacent unit. They could see us across the paddies and requested we pop smoke to identify ourselves. A few seconds after I pulled the pin on a purple smoke canister, they identified "goofy grape."

We carried several colors of smoke. By requiring the other unit to identify the color, we could both be reasonably sure that the VC were not monitoring our radio frequencies and popping their own smoke to confuse the issue. This was a particularly good technique when working with gunships and air support to ensure the fire power was placed on the dinks rather than on ourselves.

The platoon leader of the adjacent unit was a young sergeant. His CP was in a thatched hut by a small canal that divided our two areas of responsibility. The sergeant proudly showed me two of the mackerel-can grenade booby traps lying on a table. Instead of destroying them in place, he had held the pin and handle in place by hand. Then he had taken the trip wire and wrapped it around the charging handle to hold it down. That was one of the dumbest things I had yet seen. When I told the sergeant my opinion, he shrugged his shoulders and said he thought they would make good souvenirs.

DeForrest and I were glad to leave the hooch and return to our side of the canal. An hour later hand-painted mine and danger signs began to appear on the dikes. As we took a short break, we heard a loud explosion in the area to our right, where Bravo Company was searching. On the radio we could hear their request for a dust-off for their wounded.

Halfway through our sector we came upon a woman and two children herding three water buffalo. I pointed in the direction of the village where we were to meet the Bravo commander. After much shouting and gesturing, I convinced her to lead the way. With the three buffalo and the locals walking in front of us, we felt a little safer from booby traps.

Using civilians in this manner is, of course, against the Geneva Convention agreements. I really did not care. What were they going to do? Send me to Vietnam?

We reached the rendezvous village shortly after noon. The men helped put the water buffalo in a small pole pen. Then they searched the woman's hut and several others for weapons and military supplies. Each hut had large crockery jars holding about twenty-five gallons of water. Except for their water, we took nothing belonging to the villagers. We herded the twenty or so inhabitants into an open area in the center of the compound. The platoon from Bravo brought in about eighty more women and children. An LCM was called to pick them up.

Through the Bravo Kit Carson scout, we instructed the old-man village leader to tell the people what was going on. They showed little interest and, surprisingly, no fear. Even our assurance that they would be returned to their homes the next day brought only blank stares.

I thought about my pregnant wife as I forced, at rifle point, the woman in labor to the LCM landing area. She could not be left in the village. Anyone remaining in the area would be considered VC. I justified my lack of feeling for the woman by thinking that perhaps a doctor would be at Bien Luc, the LCM's destination. In reality, that was unlikely.

Two small hooches were still to be searched. They were separated by about 100 meters from the rest of the village. A small trail next to the canal led to their dark doorways. Near the first hooch, in the middle of the trail, we saw a red mackerel can grenade in open sight. A trip wire from a nipa palm to freshly dug dirt glistened in the sunlight a bit closer to our location.

The villagers showed their first signs of nervousness as we pointed to the huts. Finally, a platoon from Bravo moved parallel to the trail toward the hooches. Their Kit Carson scout led the way. He pushed the old man of the village in front of him. After going only a few meters, the man began to chatter loudly in Vietnamese. With sobs, he collapsed on the ground. Even with kicks from the Kit Carson, he refused to proceed.

I watched from the edge of the village as the Kit Carson cautiously continued. Suddenly, with a loud explosion, he disappeared into a black cloud of smoke. An object that looked like a football sailed in slow motion through the air and landed near me. It was the scout's foot blown off just above the ankle. The jungle boot was still neatly tied on the appendage.

The Kit Carson was dead. The old man, unhurt by the explosion, soon would have been if the Kit Carson's American friends had not been stopped by the Bravo CO. They still managed to literally kick the shit out of him before they listened to orders instead of their hearts.

The company commander told another platoon to check out the huts. After a loud argument with the platoon leader, he walked over to me and said it was my platoon's turn to give it a try. I told him not to ask us to do what his own people refused to do. He seemed near to losing control of his company as well as himself.

Finally, I told him we would clear the huts, but my way instead of his. Taking two M-79 gunners, an M-60 crew and a couple of riflemen, I moved to the edge of the canal where there was a group of sampans. We loaded into three of them and cautiously rowed near the back of the hooches. On my orders, the M-60 raked both structures with several hundred rounds. The M-79s followed with ten or so grenades into each. One hut blew up with a secondary explosion.

We rowed back to the village center. I told the company commander that I felt he could report the area clear. As for the secondary explosion, he could report it as booby traps destroyed, or whatever he wanted.

Our part of the mission was complete. The LCM arrived and we boarded with the villagers for the ride to Bien Luc. The moans of the woman in labor were the only sounds except for the boat's engine and the lapping of water. We were back to the bridge just before traffic was stopped for the night.

21 MAY 1969
Wednesday

Binh Dien Bridge
More of easier days at Binh Dien Bridge

LT Hawkins again displayed his talents in taking care of the company, arriving at mid-morning with a large barbeque grill and two huge boxes of fast-thawing frozen steaks. In insulated food containers called mermites were baked potatoes and fresh salad. At noon the entire company had their fill of our best meal in over a month.

Time passed quickly on the bridge. During daylight, military vehicles and civilian buses and cars crossed the river in a steady stream. Traffic noise was almost like that back in the world except for the frequent punctuation of rifle fire from the bridge guards. Soldiers on the span were instructed to fire at anything floating down the river to detonate mines that the VC might send down the water way. The shots also discouraged enemy frogmen as well as providing good target-practice for the troops.

Small boats using the river displayed prominently the yel-low-with-red-stripes RVN flag. They stopped several hundred meters short of the bridge where a twenty-foot Vietnamese Navy patrol boat armed with 50-caliber machine guns checked them before allowing them to pass. These RVN craft were called rag boats, a term easy to understand after seeing them.

In the center of Bien Dien village was an oval pond ten meters in diameter, teeming with large carp that the villagers raised to supplement their rice diet. I spent many hours on its banks feeding the fish C-ration crackers. Many of my journal entries were written as I sat smoking and thinking of days when I had fished in my father's farm ponds.

Walking back from the pond to my bunker-home took me past the rear of several of the huts. One day I passed a young woman naked to the waist standing under a thatch awning. Using a small basin of water and a cloth, she was bathing. When she noticed me, she immediately turned her eyes, covered herself as much as possible with the cloth, and ran into the hut.

I was much surprised at her embarrassment. The entire company bathed or swam in the river completely nude with no regard for the villagers. Piss tubes, made of artillery shell containers dug into the ground, were out in the open near each bunker. I never saw any modesty among the GIs. We went about as if we were around animals rather than human women and children. In our minds, it was they who were the barbarians, not we.

The somewhat easier days at the bridge also offered the opportunity to get to know the other members of the Charlie

Company better. The Artillery Forward Observer (FO) LT
Don Jong was an avid hearts player. Many an hour was spent
with Jong, Sassner, and the RTOs trying to avoid the Queen
of Spades.

🛩 22 MAY 1969
Thursday

Binh Dien Bridge
  Time goes on—
  Elvira caught hell last night
  Was in charge of Bridge today—Rest of Co. gone on cor-
don—
  Felt good to be in charge
  Red Cross Dollies by for a few minutes today—Was not
impressed

  "For those who fight for it, life has a special flavor the
protected never know."

    Found penciled on C-ration box after Battle at Khe
    Sanh last year—Printed in OVERSEAS WEEKLY

Alpha Company had occupied Elvira since our departure.
Under the cover of the now nightly rains, a squad of VC had
sneaked to within a hundred meters of the fire base and fired
several rocket-propelled grenades (RPGs) into the compound.
Several Alpha soldiers were killed and many more wounded.
No apparent losses were taken by the VC.
  That was the first contact in the vicinity of Elvira since
Collier's squad killed two my first night in the unit. It was an
excellent example of how inactivity led to carelessness which
led back to bloodshed.

While CPT Swiss and the rest of the company were gone on the daytime cordon, I was responsible for the bridge. It felt good to have the additional responsibility. The seed of hope for getting my own company was planted. I was still over a year from making captain, and most company commanders were senior captains with four or more years service. In the peacetime Army, it would be impossible for anyone of my rank to get command. An awareness that Vietnam was the impossible had already dawned on me. To get a company, all I would have to do would be to produce—and stay alive. Staying alive would be the hard part.

As I was checking the guards on the bridge that afternoon, a small convoy of trucks stopped. 2LT Ed Mullins, whom I knew from Fort Bragg, was in the lead jeep and called me over. He was now assigned to the 9th Infantry Division to our south. Traffic began to back up so our exchange of war stories and "Have you heard from . . . ?" were cut short. It did not seem at all unusual to run into a friend eleven thousand miles from home.

As for the Donut Dollies, I had not yet been gone from the world long enough to appreciate the sight and smell of round-eyed women; their appearance would improve the longer I was away from home.

✌ 23 MAY 1969
Friday

> Platoon size day RIF—Only contact was a water buffalo—
> Charged my point
> Results: 1 water buffalo WIA

The mission for the day was a six-kilometer recon in force (RIF). These patrols and the nightly ambushes were a part of the bridge security plans. It was hoped that any enemy build-up would be detected before a consolidated attack on the bridge could be mounted.

The point man for the day was PFC Harrison Hines. A black from the inner city of Detroit, he was a cool, experienced infantryman who knew the mean temperament of water buffalo. Vietnamese children could lead the curved-horn beasts and even ride on their backs, but the buffalo disliked Americans. Some said it was because we smelled different. Other swore all water buffalo were VC in disguise.

Hines tried to make a wide circle around the animal, which was grazing in the middle of a paddy. Suddenly the buffalo snorted, pawed the ground and, with a bellow, charged. Hines stood his ground. When the angry buffalo was about ten meters from him, Hines raised his M-16 and calmly fired twice. The buffalo dropped to its knees, then slowly regained its feet, shook its head a few times, and staggered away. The platoon cheered Hines's coolness and marksmanship, and some broke into laughter.

The rifle fire had attracted the attention of a small boy in a nearby hooch. He ran across the paddies and caught up with the buffalo. With a small stick, he tried to herd it home. Hines's only remark was that he thought he deserved a body count for the damn VC buffalo.

24 MAY 1969
Saturday

Moved to FB Claudette

My letter to Linda on this day said that I thought we would be staying at the bridge for several more days. My thoughts and the Army's were, as usual, not the same. About noon we received word to prepare to move in two hours to Fire Base Claudette.

I was not glad to be leaving the bridge. It had been almost pleasant compared to Elvira and Binh Chanh. Time had passed quickly, although I later thought that we had stayed at the bridge much longer than a week. It was a time of maturation and confidence-building for me. I no longer felt like an FNG.

We arrived at Claudette after an uneventful ride to the northeast of the bridge. The fire base was located at the edge of the village of Xom Huong at the juncture of the Kinh Cau and Kinh Xang canals. We never used the village's real name—to us it was Claudette only. The canals, dug by the French before World War II, were referred to as Blue North and Blue South. After all, if you do not learn the local language for "thank you," why learn how to pronounce the geographical names?

Claudette was very similar to Binh Chanh. The forward battalion headquarters, our direct support artillery battery, and other support elements had been recently relocated to the fire base.

Charlie Campany's sector included the usual bunkers—and ruins of a French fort. Within the wire was also a small Catholic church, complete with steeple and cross. The church brought curses rather than reverence from the men: Catholic villages did not allow whorehouses. The lack of pleasure spots at Claudette would not be immediately important, however. CPT Swiss relayed from the battalion commander that we should keep our rucksacks packed. We would be moving out early the next morning on an extended operation to the west.

✎ 25 MAY 1969
Sunday

FB Claudette—Pineapples
  Moved in last night—Set ambush—This morning within 15 meters found 8 punji pits & one frag grenade booby trap—
  I stepped in one punji pit but luckily didn't get a scratch. Pits we found were 3 x 4 x 3 feet with 15 to 20 sharpened sticks in each.

Surrounding Claudette were hundreds of acres of pineapple plantations that had not been tended in many years because of the war. Pineapples still grew on the spiny, low bushes. They were delicious the first few days, but after a week became as monotonous as C-rations. Today I still do not care for the fruit.

The pineapple fields varied in size from a couple of hundred meters to a kilometer square. Small canals and thick vegetation of nipa palm, cane, and tall grass grew in-between.

Punji pits with their sharpened sticks were a well-known weapon of the VC. Every report about the war seems to emphasize their wide use. But by 1969, punji pits were a rarity. The VC, supported by the NVA, Chinese, and other Communist countries, now had an abundance of far more lethal weapons. Explosive booby traps, mines, and Claymores were far more effective than the primitive stakes.

The pits could still inflict debilitating injuries, however. The human waste smeared on the stakes caused severe infections with the smallest scratch. I was fortunate in that my boot slid down the side of the pit, pushing the stakes away from my leg. SP4 Homer Aultman, from Mississippi, who occasionally alternated with DeForrest in carrying my radio, pulled me from the hole. As if warning me about cracks in a sidewalk, he calmly said, "Watch your step, One-six."

This date marked the first anniversary of my service in the US Army. Much had happened in that year, and as I write these words after nearly two decades in uniform, it seems much like a very unusual play: A long-running performance where the climax occurred in the first act.

====

🚁 26 MAY 1969
Monday

> Airmobiled to this location—Choppers got one coming in—My 2nd sqd found the body—This was reported on radio—RTO SP4 Garcia—San Antonio, Tx: "We found the M   F   —His head is nearly shot off, leg blown to hell—Holes & blood everywhere—Man! He's beautiful."
> No more contact today—
> Freedom bird (plane back to States) flies over—Some one yells, "Pop smoke!"

Vietnam was a helicopter war. One of the disadvantages of a Light Brigade like the 199th was that we had limited airmobile support. With the exception of a few command and control ships (C&C), all our helicopters had to be borrowed from outside Brigade assets. As a result, we rode less and walked more.

The advantages of the helicopters were mobility and firepower. We were treated to a fine example of the latter as we neared the landing zone (LZ) which had already been prepped by artillery. Cobra gunships came in firing 2.75-inch rockets, 40mm grenades and minigun 7.62mm ball and tracer ammo. As we neared the LZ, I could see the ordnance impacting. It looked as if nothing could survive such an onslaught. I was wrong. As the choppers flared before setting down, a lone VC jumped from a ditch and raced across a paddy dike.

The eight ships of our lift all fired on the lone enemy. The left gunner on our ship was cussing because he was on the wrong side and not able to join in the kill. The VC toppled from the dike like a tin target in a shooting gallery.

We were on the skids of the chopper, jumping to the ground before the bird fully landed. The pilot barely touched earth before he was back in the air gaining altitude.

The choppers got credit for the kill. As infantrymen, we still had a major advantage over the aviators—we got to go through the dink's pockets. The few papers on the body were sent to S-2 for any intelligence value. Personal effects, such as the star-pattern belt buckle, cigarette lighter, and a small amount of money were kept by the platoon. The body we left in the paddy to rot. We did not bury enemy dead unless we were staying in the area. All dead men smell the same, regardless of their cause.

Garcia was right—he was beautiful. This gook would set no more booby traps.

Our new area of operations was in the flight path of Bien Hoa. The planes climbed quickly as they departed, but on clear days we could still recognize the freedom birds as they headed for home. Popping smoke might get us helicopters, but freedom birds were available to us only after 365 days.

In 1969, writing in my private journal, I could not write "mother fucker." Times do change. Perhaps some of my lost innocence is not all for the good.

🖎 **27 MAY 1969**
Tuesday

Continued operation—
Lost one man—Heat casualty

The monsoon season was well upon us with twice daily downpours. At about ten each morning and again at four in the afternoon, sheets of rain fell for about an hour. After dark, the rains were lighter and less predictable.

Between the rains, the sun shone with tropic intensity and in combination with the constant high humidity was almost as dangerous as the enemy. About the only first aid we could render a soldier with heat exhaustion was to put him in the shade and share our meager water supply.

Our daytime sweeps varied in length from three to six kilometers. We carried lightweight ropes with small grappling hooks tied on the end. The point man, when reaching a particularly suspicious area, would throw the hook forward, then drag it back, hopefully springing any trip wires present. We also fired the M79 grenade launcher into suspicious areas to detonate anything explosive in the vicinity.

At night we continued to break into two separate ambush positions. The rain made it easier to stay awake but much more difficult to sleep.

Our ambush efficiency was greatly enhanced by the use of starlight scopes, similar in appearance to a regular telescopic rifle-sight but about four times larger. Looking through a rubber-insulated eyepiece turned even the blackest night up to five hundred meters away into a green-tinged field of vision. Distance and movement were slightly distorted. A little practice with the scopes, however, gave us clear observation.

The scopes' only flaw was that they rapidly consumed their batteries. The many spare batteries they required along with the scopes themselves, added to our burden.

28 MAY 1969
Wednesday

Continued mission
Some of my men's civilian occupations:

> SP4 Autlman—Off shore oil roughneck
> PFC Hefferman—Printer's helper
> PFC Russell—"on the street"
> PFC Toolate—Wants to be pro baseball player
> PFC Grey—High school band director
> PFC Purcell—Heavy equipment operator

Few of the platoon's men had been regularly employed before working for Uncle Sam. Most, like Russell, had been "on the street" before being drafted. A couple of the men were volunteers, but not many. If one joined the military by choice, signing up to be an infantryman was not a popular option.

The Navy and Air Force, manned entirely by volunteers, had little problem filling their ranks. Those who chose the Army usually ended up as grunts based on their failure to qualify for a support role in the Military Occupational Specialty (MOS) testing upon entry into the service.

The Infantry MOS was 11B, officially pronounced "11 Bravo." Soldiers referred to it as 11 Bush because that is where the grunt was found.

There was, of course, no one in my platoon with a white-collar background or even an inclination in that direction. Few were from that heritage by birth either. I never met an officer or soldier who even knew anyone with an Ivy League education.

A high-school diploma was generally the highest degree attained. Our generation was to become the most educated in our country's history, but this did not apply to the Vietnam veteran. PFC Grey was the exception. A graduate of a small college, he had been drafted while teaching at Alvin High School, Alvin, Texas. A couple of years older than I, he was the oldest in the platoon.

All a man had to do to avoid the draft was to stay in school with a deferment until he was twenty-six years old. At that magic age, he was no longer considered for conscription. Many of today's lawyers and Ph.D.s strived for their academic degrees solely to miss another type of struggle—the one to survive in Vietnam.

My letters home included, along with more personal matters, brief descriptions of the soldiers. The correspondence to Linda on this day dealt with her recent concern about smoking during pregnancy. I told her she had enough worries without trying to quit.

29 MAY 1969
Thursday

In daytime position after humping 3 kilometers—Personnel sighted at 1000 meters—My plt gave chase—2 long hours later we have our prisoners—four 10-year old kids

Defining an area as a free-fire zone meant that anyone in it was enemy. The paddies were rarely free-fire zones because many civilians lived and worked in our AOs. During the day we had to be very careful not to shoot a farmer carrying a hoe who looked much like a VC carrying a rifle. After the curfew, however, all of Vietnam was a free-fire zone. If it moved, it was enemy.

The four people we saw about a klick away did not appear to be armed. Still, they should not have been so far away from the nearest village. They ran and our chase was long in time but not in distance. With the preponderance of booby traps, no one moved quickly in the paddies.

When we caught the kids, all they were carrying were small canvas sacks containing crablike creatures they had caught in the paddy waters. Our Kit Carson, Tom, explained after questioning the children that they ran because they were afraid we would shoot them. Their fears seemed logical to me. We let them go.

---

30 May 1969
Friday

> 2nd plt got 1 body count—VC had an AK47—I got to fire it later—Accurate
>
> My plt's actions in 6 days:
>> Found and searched 1 body from chopper kill
>> Destroyed 5 bunkers—small
>> Destroyed 9 small punji pits—1 large
>> Blew two 105 dud rounds—one booby trapped
>> Blew one 40mm duster round
>> Found and destroyed 1 grenade booby trap
>
> Losses:
>> 1 man heat casualty
>
> Today I was checking out 105mm white phosphorus round dud to see if it was booby trapped—On my hands and knees— My pen light falls out of my pocket and lights—(it is still fairly dark) I shook for five minutes—laughed for ten

The dead VC's weapon was a Chinese copy of the standard Russian assault rifle. It was accurate when fired in single shots but was difficult to control on automatic. The M-16 was just as accurate on single and much more manageable firing on full automatic, or "rock and roll."

There were lots of debates about which rifle was better. Personally I preferred the M16, largely because the ammunition was lighter and we could carry many more rounds. Regardless of the arguments, we liked this particular AK47. It was now in our hands rather than the enemy's.

The AK47's slender twelve-inch spike-type folding bayonet was removed and kept by the second platoon members as a trophy. The weapon itself was turned in to S-2 because fully automatic weapons were not allowed to be taken home as souvenirs.

Although I approached the artillery shell with great caution, I was becoming confident of my ability to detect and destroy booby traps. The penlight was a good reminder that regardless of my skill, no mistake could be allowed. My shaking was much more sincere than my following nervous laughter.

🛦 31 MAY 1969
Saturday

Back to Claudette
   Weapons and equipment maintenance
   Conversations heard on operation:
      SP4 Blaylock—Tenn: Hucke, you ever seen a live
                                chicken?
      PFC Hucke—Brooklyn, N. Y. : No
      PFC Russell—Harlem, N. Y. : Hey, man, ain't you
                                ever been to the zoo?
      PFC Russell used to be a member of the Mighty Midgets—
   a Harlem street gang

Orders to return to the firebase were most welcomed, even if they meant another long walk.

First order of business at Claudette was to clean our weapons and equipment. When that was completed, we worked on the bunker-line defense, adding Claymores and making sure the automatic-weapon fields of fire intersected.

Once all of this was done, we could clean ourselves.

We timed our quick baths in the adjacent canals so that we came out of the salt water during the afternoon rain—our way of rinsing the brine from our bodies. I never heard anyone complain of the smell of fellow soldiers. We all smelled the same after a few days of mud, sweat, and fear.

Clean uniforms replaced those we had worn for the last week.

While we were in the field, we wore the same uniforms, and only those badly torn or rotted were replaced, delivered with our resupply by helicopter. We wore no underwear because if we did, the constant hot dampness caused chaffing and open sores. Some of the men were able to wear their jungle boots without socks. I never could. We removed our footwear whenever possible during the day to dry our feet. At night, in the field, we never took our boots off.

We returned to Claudette for payday. My month's pay was less than it had been back at Fort Bragg. Combat pay was added but, because Linda was living with her parents, we lost the $110 housing allowance and $30 family separation allowance. This would change when she moved to San Francisco.

Linda's address would have been easy to falsify to get the additional allowance. We were honest, though. Tempting fate with a lie did not strike us as an appropriate option in my present circumstance.

✈ I JUNE 1969
Sunday

Claudette
    Memorial services for PFC Plante—WIA just before I took
over plt. Died in Japan last week
    Impressive and saddening—Helmet on rifle—Empty boots—
A good tribute to a soldier

Medical evacuation of wounded was tremendously rapid.
Often a casualty was picked up by the dust-off helicopter and
delivered to a hospital within twenty minutes of being hit.
Medical care was top-notch as a result of superior training
and—unfortunately—experience.

Only half of the current strength of the first platoon had been
in Vietnam when Plante was hit less than two months before.
Remembered as a good soldier, he was thought to have received the million dollar home-returning wound. No one had
expected he would arrive there in a gray casket.

The memorial ceremony was impressive. It allowed the men
to bid a traditional farewell to a fallen comrade. Yet, it seemed
to me to make the men dwell unnecessarily on the ever-present
threat to their own lives. I vowed that if I ever gained a company command, we would skip such reminders.

✈ 2 JUNE 1969
Monday

Back to the pineapple
    Tonight while moving to position, artillery of 82d hit my

second squad—Mistake was made by CPT Swiss and artillery—3 hurt
    SP4 Gancanz—Hit in back
    PFC Bass (medic)—Hit in hand and knee
    PFC Turnage—Hit in hand
    SSGT Marple was the squad leader
    The screams of the RTO trying to stop arty was something
I care to never hear again—
    All we could do to help was pray—
    I did get on radio to ensure they got security, etc. out

We departed Claudette early in the morning for a long recon
back into the pineapple. We rarely received written orders or
even a verbal rendition of the Fort Benning Infantry School
five paragraph operation order we had been taught. Generally
we were given a six-digit coordinate to which we were to
move. This would later be supplemented by additional en-
coded coordinates via the radio for night ambushes.

Our platoon AO bordered on an area being worked by the
3rd Brigade of the 82d Airborne Division. CPT Swiss had not
plotted this boundary correctly on his map. As a result, he
ordered one of my squad ambushes into the 82d's AO. As
Marple's squad moved into their night position, they were
spotted by an artillery FO in the 82d.

Marple's squad was fortunate that they were in an extremely
muddy area. The artillery rounds buried in the goo before exploding, greatly reducing their bursting radius.

I could hear the artillery impacting about five hundred meters from my platoon CP. Marple's RTO, SP4 Garcia, shouted
his initial transmissions in Spanish. I did not need an interpreter to understand the crisis. A call to LT Jong quickly got
the artillery stopped.

Marple reported that none of the men was hit too badly.
Doc Bass, himself wounded, came on the horn confirming
Marple's evaluation. Soon the dust-off arrived and the three
were evacuated.

None of the wounded men received a Purple Heart, as the

wounds were classified as "injuries due to friendly fire." It did not seem so friendly to the men in the impact zone.

A week-long investigation at the various higher headquarters would reveal that CPT Swiss had inverted a couple of the grid coordinates and the 82d's artillery had not properly coordinated their target. An honest but costly mistake. Our confidence in the company commander was shaken, yet we all knew that any of us might have made the same mistake.

---

3 JUNE 1969
Tuesday

Continue operation
  Rains like hell
  Set up position in 3 to 4 inches of water

  From READER'S DIGEST June 69 "Seen in dept store selling U. S. flags—'These colors will not run' "

Three replacements joined the platoon from the resupply bird, keeping the platoon's strength at twenty. We were now without a medic, but word from the rear said Doc and the other two men would rejoin us after a couple of weeks in the hospital.

Even in the rainy season we were usually able to find fairly dry spots for our night ambushes. On this night we were not so fortunate. We alternated with half the men on top of a dike while the others crouched in the shallow water. Our war often seemed as much against the elements as against the VC.

My letters home over these few days were far more cheerful than my diary entries. Letters often were a refuge from the real condition that surrounded us. I noted to Linda that I had slept on a cot the night back at Claudette. This was only the second time in over a month that the bare earth had not been my resting place.

Also, I acknowledged a package of food she had sent that contained M&Ms, Lifesavers, and other hard candies. I tried diplomatically to explain that these items were already issued to us in a Special Purpose (SP) packet on each resupply.

Linda had also sent an aluminum pan of popcorn which I tried to pop over heat tablets. These foil-wrapped compressed-fuel tabs that looked like small bars of blue soap burned easily at the touch of a match. The only problem with them was that if they were not ventilated properly they gave off awful-smelling, lung-racking fumes. For coffee water, heat tabs worked wonders; for popping corn, they left something to be desired. Nevertheless, I reported to Linda that it was "slightly burnt but delicious."

My letter ended with the short question, "Are you going barefoot?" This was, of course, in reference to the old adage, "Keep them barefoot and pregnant."

✈ 4 JUNE 1969
Wednesday

Pineapple
   More rain—
   Most of my letters from the world lately have been full
   of people complaining—I appreciate the letters but wonder
if they know how good they have it

In the field we were hot during the day, cold at night and wet and filthy most of the time. We were either bored or absolutely terrified. Still, there were few real complaints. Everyone pulled together. Americans of virtually every ethnic and regional background were represented in the platoon. We shared our meager possessions with generosity. Certain individuals had more responsibility than others, yet every task was performed by each. We resembled an extended family—a family of leaders and followers, but also a unit that worked for the common good and survival of all. The longer we were together, the tighter the bond became.

The caring of families and friends back home was critical. At the same time, we felt far from those support groups. The longer we stayed in Vietnam, the more distant seemed the reality of day-to-day life back home.

Our happiness often depended on such small things as something to eat other than C-rations or simply a night without rain. A cold beer or soda became more important than an entire "night on the town" in our previous lives.

I do not think any of us fully realized our part in history or that we were experiencing perhaps the greatest events of our lives at so early an age. We did feel good about ourselves and each other. We were damn good soldiers, in the finest army in the world. As infantrymen, we had a cockiness that is common to those who consider themselves elite. We felt that the rest of the Army, as well as the Air Force and Navy, existed only to lend us support.

Sure we complained. But we strongly resented any comment or innuendo that we were not doing an important job—a job that few wanted or were capable of performing. Our day-to-day life was not characterized by hardship: It was beyond hardship. When we received letters or read articles about problems back home because of weather, money, or living conditions, we smiled and shook our heads. Correspondence about car accidents, lost jobs, or broken love affairs seemed ludicrous. If anyone wanted to find out about a hard life, let them join us.

We were experiencing enough pain, fear and discomfort in a single year to last a lifetime—that is, if we were lucky enough to survive so long.

☞ 5 JUNE 1969
Thursday

Continue mission
   More rain—
   Officers in Charlie Co as of this date:
      CPT J. A. Swiss—Armor—New Jersey
      1LT Bill Little—Inf—New Jersey—USMA 2nd plt
      1LT Don Jong—Artillery—California—OCS
      2LT Norm Sassner—Inf—Florida—OCS—3rd plt
   Today LTC Mess came out to pin silver bar on me—Only
thing it really means is more money

Daytime patrols, night ambushes. One day was much the
same as the next. Without my journal and letters, most of these
days would have blended into an indiscernible blur of mud,
sweat, and boredom.

Andy May had got a job in the rear. Bill Little, one of the
few West Point graduates in the battalion, joined the company.
A likeable guy though a bit too serious, he, like all the rest of
the officers in the company except myself, was a bachelor.
Over the coming months we would become close friends.

LTC (Lieutenant Colonel) Mess flew in to the company CP
about three klicks from my platoon position. The long walk
across the potentially booby trapped area to get to him took
some of the joy out of no longer being a second lieutenant.
My duties would not change with the silver bar. The extra
hundred dollars a month for the same work was nice.

As the brunt of jokes, second lieutenants are often portrayed
as naive bumblers and called "butter bars" because of the gold
color of their rank insignia. By 1969 in Vietnam, they received
more respect since there were few old NCOs in the units.
Often the second lieutenant was the most knowledgeable soldier in the platoon. His abilities to call in artillery, air, and
dust-offs were qualities not to be joked about. There was still

much good-natured ribbing about "second looies" being "wet behind the ears," but little of it was serious.

🛬 **6 JUNE 1969**
Friday

Pineapple
   Today we found a bunker line—While destroying them I checked out a bomb crater for a cache—In it I stumbled over something—Ended up being a 500 lb bomb—
   Report from hospital—All my men doing fine

Our artillery frequently fired what were called harassment and interdiction (H&I) missions. When no specific enemy target was identified, areas such as trail junctions and nipa palm lines were randomly hit in hopes the enemy might be present. H&I missions also kept the enemy from moving freely.

The result of our firepower was that the enemy had to dig in everywhere he went; we found his bunkers regularly. It was difficult to destroy a hole in the ground, but we did our best by tearing off the overhead cover of logs and caving in the sides of the structures.

When we found bunkers, we used rifle cleaning-rods to probe the soil, searching the area for supplies and weapons. We paid particular attention to stream beds and areas under bodies of water.

Bomb craters pocked virtually the entire landscape. Typical craters were fifteen to twenty feet in diameter and six to eight feet deep. Depending on the season, they were at least half full of water.

I do not know how the unexploded bomb came to rest in the water-filled crater. The VC may have found and hid it for later disassembly and remaking into booby traps. Regardless of how, it was scary as hell to realize I was standing on five-hundred pounds of ordnance. If it had detonated, there would have been nothing left but a memory.

My confidence in my demolition work was strong, but destroying so large a bomb was too big a job for me. A radio request secured the assistance of an explosive ordnance demolition detachment (EOD).

There was a second motive for requesting the EOD team. The entire platoon was out of cigarettes and no resupply was due until the next day. Since the helicopter crews and EOD personnel were flying back to the rear after their mission, they gladly surrendered their smokes.

✄ 7 JUNE 1969
Saturday

Back to Claudette
    Choppered back by chinook—
    I was Co CO for a few hours while CPT Swiss went in to sign statements ref. artillery incident—I could run this Co.— In fact, wish it was mine—
    Results of actions 2–7 June
    Found
        58 bunkers—approx 4x6x4—2 ft overhead cover—all destroyed
        1 500 lb bomb—EOD destroyed
        1 2.75 rocket marking round
        2 81mm mortar rounds
        1 electric bomb fuse
        1 US Claymore
    Losses
        3 men WIA—Arty
    I have best plt in company—and the company knows it

The list of actions over these five days shows that much of the damage we did to ourselves. In addition to the casualties inflicted by our own artillery, all the ordnance we found had been made in the good ole USA.

The seed of desire—wanting my own company—had sprouted and was growing rapidly. Ego, of course, was a factor. But I honestly felt that I could do the job. The things that were making the 1st Platoon the best would work at the company level as well.

The key ingredient to a good unit was the men's having confidence in their leaders at all levels. Platoon leaders were not supposed to walk point; I did on the occasions when I thought it was necessary for mission accomplishment and at times just to show the men I would. When planning operations or ambushes, I listened to each soldier's opinion. After decisions had been made, I demanded full compliance.

If a soldier had problems or complaints, he was heard out. Questions were answered. The good of the platoon was valued over individual desires. Respect for the sergeants was required, but a concern for subordinates was equally as important. At all times, everyone was aware that he was a soldier—but also a member of a team in which each played a critical role. Rules were followed—but no rule was set in concrete. Each could be bent; none would be broken.

The platoon's reputation was good because the platoon members thought they were good. The attitude was positive. We laughed at each other and with each other about our living conditions and personality quirks. We taught, and learned from, each other.

Within the platoon there were sometimes difficulties, of course, but most conflicts were kept within the unit. We solved or lived with our own problems.

After days in the field, the anticipation of returning to the fire base was enough to make everyone smile. The large, twin-rotor CH 47 Chinook, called "shit hooks" by the troops, easily carried us in minutes over the muddy terrain that had taken us days to traverse on the ground.

At Claudette we were greeted by Doc Bass, Turnage, and Gancanz. They seemed little-changed except for Turnage. Tex had been one of the real hell-raisers in the platoon. Beer and women had consumed his thoughts and actions. He now had a cross in the elastic band of his helmet.

In answer to my questions, Tex told me that when the artillery had first begun to land around him, he had fired his weapon in the air in useless anger. Suddenly he had stopped and begun to pray that he would not be killed. Religion had found the young soldier in the muddy paddies.

Tex occasionally reverted to his old self in future months, but not as often or as intensely as before. He attended every chaplain service, regardless of its denomination. Tex had gotten religion; he was just not sure which one.

The pleasure of returning to Claudette was somewhat diminished by my discovery that $40 was missing from the gear I had left behind at the fire base. A few of the other soldiers were also missing money, equipment, and personal items.

No one suspected the few members of the Company who had stayed behind. Their security measures may have been lax, but grunts do not steal from other grunts—at least not those in the same company. Either the village babysans or some of the support troops had done the pilfering. It really was not that important; we possessed little of any value and there was no place to spend the money anyway.

≈ **8 JUNE 1969**
Sunday

Claudette
    Services this afternoon—
    Got in 2 replacements—They said they had been told in
rear to get in 1st plt if possible—
    Officers meeting in bunker—All swatting flies and keeping
body count—Yes sometimes we get a little bored

Catholic and Protestant chaplains held the first formal religious ceremonies we had been provided in well over a month.
It was coincidental that the day was a Sunday.

There were only two kinds of chaplains in Vietnam: Those
who were good and those who were not. The good ones sought
out grunts in the field regardless of denomination. They were
good for morale and were great at leaving a sense of calm and
well-being behind. Other chaplains were rarely, if ever, seen
in the field. Never leaving their BMB chapels, they adminis-
tered to their assistants and to those in the rear. Whether they
feared for their own personal safety or felt that we grunts were
godless individuals, I do not know.

In the field there was a complete tolerance of individual
beliefs. Each man could attend services or not. Most did, although often they did so because they had nothing better to
do.

Claudette offered the opportunity to catch up on the news
back home by way of the daily *Stars and Stripes* newspaper.
We argued about sports news and jeered disasters such as
storms and floods. Unless the events occurred in someone in
the Company's "back home," we were not too concerned.

One *Stripes* article that caught my attention was about a high
school superintendent in New England who had fired one of
his teachers. The teacher had required her class, including a
student whose brother had been killed in Vietnam, to write

essays on the inhumanity of the war and how we should not be involved. I wrote the school official to state my support for his actions. A few weeks later the superintendent answered, saying that he had received far more censure than support.

≈ **9 JUNE 1969**
Monday

Claudette
    Many rumors about the north going around—I have a bad feeling about going up there—
    Have some of my men in positions in an old French fort—Most of it torn or blown down—One tower and flag pole on parade field still standing—Could almost vision French troops there 15–20 years ago—Bet their thoughts about the same as ours

Rumors run rampant in a combat zone. Everyone hears from someone that everything imaginable will or has happened. Frequently the rumor mill is a much faster source of information than official channels. At times it is about as accurate.

We had been hearing for the past few weeks that the 199th would soon be moving to an area of operations north of Saigon near War Zone D. The enemy would no longer be VC. Our new AO was reportedly controlled by at least five regiments of North Vietnamese Army Regulars (NVA).

I spent the night in the old guard tower of the French fort where three of my soldiers manned a 50-caliber machine gun. The fort had probably garrisoned a company of troops. Whether its demise was from enemy assault or just years of neglect, we did not know.

With the exception of what I had picked up in books by

Bernard Fall, I knew little about Vietnam's history. The Army provided no information about the country's past. Knowing what we were fighting to preserve might have made a difference.

🚁 **10 JUNE 1969**
Tuesday

Claudette
   A thought today—Since in Vietnam I have written little about my wife & expected child, parents, brother & sister-in-law. Even though they fill my thoughts often—Guess it's because love is something hard to write about—Also loneliness—
   Today one of my men attempted suicide—Actually he's just trying to get out of field

   "Cut off one's right to risk his life, and progress would end and society would atrophy and die."

                                           "The Risk Taker"
                                           R. Daley
                                           PLAYBOY June 1969

Inactivity usually caused more problems with the soldiers than being busy. A PFC who had been in the platoon only a few months took from the medic bag a bottle of pills that were for treatment of insect bites. The soldier's squad leader found him before he swallowed all of the pills and quickly took him to the battalion aid station where vomiting was induced.

My initial reaction was to try to get the soldier court-martialed. After a long talk, I agreed to give him a second chance. After all, maybe it was not really crazy to try to get out of the

war. Also, if convicted and jailed, he would have gained his
objective of leaving the field.

The soldier responded fairly well. His squad leader put him
on dirty details, filling sandbags and stringing concertina wire.
He also pulled more than his share at point for the next weeks.
Soon he was accepted back into the fold and was never again
a major problem.

I liked the *Playboy* quote. I still have little use for those who
do not take risks or accept challenges. The *Playboy* pictures
were not bad either.

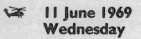

☞ 11 June 1969
Wednesday

Claudette
 More fire base type work

Studies have concluded that many migratory peoples move
as much to get away from their own shit as they do to find
new food and sustenance. In a fire base containing well over
one-hundred men, human waste disposal was a constant problem. The solution was small wooden latrines, platforms built
over 55-gallon drums cut in half. When the containers were
nearly full, diesel fuel was added and set aflame. The smell of
burning shit dominated the air of the fire base. Shit-burning
detail was a great threat to even the most malingering soldier.

Adjacent to our bunkers was an old French mine field several times larger than a football field. Markers warning of danger were posted in several languages, as neither side knew the
exact location of the mines. It was a no man's land where only
vegetation could survive.

In the midst of the pineapple fields a few klicks to the northwest, rising to the height of a five story building, was a statue of a squatting Buddha. The fat effigy stood mute, gazing across the landscape where guns now ruled rather than religion. Its limestone-and-cement features were pocked by rifle and rocket fire. Whether the damage had occurred by accident or by bored vandals testing their marksmanship, we knew not—nor did we care.

There were mysteries about the statue. Why was it several kilometers from the nearest village? Why a monument to Buddha in a predominantly Catholic sector? Who built it and why? We never knew. Its only apparent use was as a prominent navigational point.

---

12 JUNE 1969
Thursday

> Moved out to a big operation west of Elvira
> Airmobiled into area
> Bad area to move in—looking for caches, etc.

Before we lifted off, CPT Swiss informed us that this would be our last operation in the present AO. We would be returning to BMB for a couple of days of rest and reequipping before moving to the jungle fifty miles northeast of Long Binh.

The rumors had been correct. The idea of a standdown back at BMB caused an excitement not unlike that of visiting a city after months in the country. It also brought anticipation, for no one wanted the distinction of being the last Charlie Company casualty to the paddy booby traps.

It seemed appropriate but forbidding that my last mission in the AO would be back where I had started—near Elvira.

✈ 13 JUNE 1969
Friday

> Moved into blocking positions along a big stream.
> My CP in ruins of old Buddhist Temple
> This afternoon VC opens up on us from across blue with an AK47—one KIA, one WIA—from A ⅔ next to us—As we dove for cover DeForrest said, "A good place to die"—meaning the temple—Gunboats got the three VC
>
> Tonight on ambush Co CP group with four of my people saw 15–20 VC—We were on the other side of VC—400 meters—Fire about six inches above our heads for two hours—Then gunships etc.—CP group opened up too soon—Result all we found was dropped equipment and blood—No bodies—
>
> About as scared as I have ever been—My first real fire fight

The cordon had closed rapidly, causing the VC to try a suicidal daylight breakout. Their rifle fire had allowed them to reach the stream where the Navy gunboats quickly ended their escape attempt.

The A Co casualties were hit less than a hundred meters from my CP. The mud walls of the old temple stopped several rounds as we returned the enemies' fire, driving the VC into the gunboat sights. The fight lasted less than a minute. It did not take long for VC or Americans to die.

Shortly before nightfall, we moved into ambush positions. The company CP, with my four men as support, set up on the least likely avenue of approach.

The VC had slipped in between the company CP and the first platoon. By opening up too soon, CPT Swiss had not allowed the enemy to reach a position where we both could have put effective cross-fire on the VC. As a result, much of our fire pinned *us* down with our own bullets.

Gunships and artillery attempted to seal off avenues of escape, and illumination rounds turned the night into day. These artillery flares separated from canisters high in the air and slowly floated to the ground at the end of a small parachute. The empty canisters fell much quicker.

Sassner radioed that the illum canisters were falling near his platoon. When asked how close, Norm responded, "They are falling on both sides. They have me bracketed." Because the canisters could land no closer without hitting someone, the illumination was briefly halted and replotted.

This was my first real fire fight. I was frightened—actually, scared as hell is a better description. Still, I remained calm on the radio and delivered my instructions with confidence. Nobody panicked. Everyone did his job. As the fire fight lengthened and built in intensity, we stacked our grenades and ammo a little closer to us. When the illum briefly stopped, I took my K-bar knife out of its scabbard and stuck it in the ground beside me. I do not know how much good I thought it would do if guns and grenades could not do the job, but the action made me feel better anyway. DeForrest and I even managed a laugh over the third platoon's predicament with the canisters.

Sporadic firing continued for some time. In the confusion, the majority of the VC escaped, carrying away their casualties.

At sunup we searched the area finding blood trails, bloody bandages, and ammunition and pieces of equipment. We had obviously hit several VC. Our disappointment at finding no bodies was tempered with our relief at having taken no casualties ourselves.

After the relative calm of the previous week, two fights in one day certainly got everyone's attention. The difference in sounds of the AK and M-16 rounds cracking over our heads was distinct yet both firmly communicated their message. It was commonly said you never heard the shot that killed you, but we never received a report on the accuracy of this statement from either side's KIA.

It was not long before jokes about the third platoon's dodging illum cannisters and my platoon's men shooting at each

other were making the rounds. Since none of our blood had
been shed, it seemed pretty funny in retrospect.

🛩 14 JUNE 1969
Saturday

> Big RIF—Lost one man to heat—Then airmobile back to
> Claudette—Time to clean up then back out on ambush
> Set up plt size ambush at big statue of Buddha—Spooky
> place but good position—
> This morning while on RIF we found what looked like a
> fresh grave or cache site—We dug awhile—Then set off demo
> to blow a hole—My plt was about 10-20 meters away behind
> a bank—When we blew it we found it was a grave—Mud etc
> came down on us—whole plt stank like hell but thought it
> was funny

It was not the mud that stank—it was the etc.

We did not deliberately set out to desecrate a grave. The
site looked like a supply cache. Since no villages were nearby,
if it was a grave, then it would have to be VC. We hoped it
might even be a body from the contact the night before, though
the stench told us it was not.

Because it was impossible to dig foxholes in the muddy
paddies, we carried no entrenching tools. The demo charge
was a much easier method of digging than using our bare
hands.

We washed off as much of the stink as possible in a small
canal and reported to Battalion that we had found a VC grave.
I added that it was not fresh. DeForrest could not hold his
laughter as he held his nose while nodding in agreement.

Our airmobile back to Claudette was supposed to complete

our final mission among the pineapples. Just before dark, however, Battalion Operations decided a platoon ambush was required as part of the nightly firebase security. We moved out quickly in the direction of the Buddha. As we passed through the gap in the wire, Turnage tripped a wire. Fortunately, it was an early-warning trip flare that had been set by the squad guarding the gap in the wire. The guards thought it was funny that they had not told us about the harmless flare. Neither Turnage nor the rest of us saw it that way.

The shrine's base offered a good ambush site, as the fields of fire down the intersecting trails were excellent. Collier remarked that we had been spending a lot of time in church lately.

✈ 15 JUNE 1969
Sunday

    Claudette
       Clean up
       Back to BMB—Seems longer than 2 months since I was here—
       Steaks & drinks—

It took most of the day to clean our gear, police up trash and make final improvements to Claudette. Troops from the 82d Airborne were taking over the firebase. We wanted it in good shape for their arrival.

In a festive mood, everyone was looking forward to the standdown. A few complaints were uttered about the damn trucks being late. Still, it was a time of many jokes and much bragging about how much beer would be drunk that night.

On the three-hour ride to BMB, we crossed the Bien Dien

Bridge. A Vietnamese family was now living in a burnt-out personnel carrier alongside the road. I looked for Gina as we sped past. She was not in sight, but I felt sure she had found another GI platoon leader to take care of.

We arrived at BMB at dusk. Hawkins and the first sergeant took charge, briefing the troops on the schedule for the next few days, including classes on our new AO. Much more welcome was the news about times set aside for a company party and trips to the PX.

Also the troops were informed about regularly scheduled transportation available to the local "laundry." This brought cheers from the soldiers who had been around for awhile. The laundry was not for dirty clothes; it was a strip of bars and bordellos just outside the gate.

After the briefing, everyone turned in his weapons, ammo, hand grenades, Claymores, and all other lethal devices. By locking up the weapons, we would avoid injuring ourselves, each other, and the BMB warriors. If needed, the weaponry could quickly be reissued.

The rear troops gave us a wide berth. The next day, the entire Battalion would arrive at BMB and for a few days field troops would fill the clubs and PXs. None of the REMFs would be welcomed or, for that matter, easy to find.

By the time everyone had showered in the large bathhouses fed by water stored in old aircraft-wing fuel-tanks, jeep trailers full of iced beer arrived. Steaks were soon on outdoor grills. The party began.

✎ 16 JUNE 1969
Monday

Camp Frenzell-Jones
   Big party—Band—Stripper—Good time
   Myself & LT Jong took over EM Club and set up the Co—
We have some damn good men—
   Am getting bayonets for men before we go North
   Got a replacement in, PFC Michael Jones from Atlanta,
Ga. We worked together at Sweetwater, Tex AT&T proj-
ect—He got $3.25 an hour, I got $1.65

The party continued.

More steaks were grilled. Beer by the trailer load continued to arrive. A Filipino band played popular music on an outdoor stage. Songs about homecomings or any tune that mentioned a hometown or state were well received. The Vietnamese stripper took it all off to show us what we were fighting for. She seemed embarrassed at first. As more and more MPC funny money was thrown on the stage, she managed to shed her inhibitions. The loudest cheers went, however, to the occasional freedom bird taking off overhead from nearby Bien Hoa.

The outdoor activities ended at dusk, and the party moved to the enlisted men's club where Jong and I convinced the officer in charge that it was "Infantry only" night. The REMFs could go one night without their beer. We were doing them a favor anyway; their presence would only have gotten their nicely pressed uniforms and shined boots a little rearranged by the field soldiers.

I once read that Napoleon said you "could do anything with a bayonet except sit on it." I had rarely seen bayonets in Vietnam. The general consensus was that they were just extra weight. I did not agree. A bayonet could be used to open C-rations, cut brush, dig holes, or for about anything. After a few inquiries, I found several footlockers full of the eight-inch weapons in the company supply room. The clerk required that I sign for them so his records would be straight. He cautioned that I would get in trouble if any were lost. I replied, "What are they going to do? Send me to Vietnam?" He was not comforted.

The bayonets accomplished their purpose: they were good for the platoon's morale. The added single pound of weight was not important. We now had the weapon that most typified the Infantry. The bayonet was about as basic a killing tool as you could find.

 17 JUNE 1969
Tuesday

Camp Frenzell-Jones
    We get another day here—O. K.
    Went to O Club—LT Jong and I won $200 off 7th Support officers—Did our hearts good to take the BMB warriors—BMB rocketed tonight—Nothing close—No sweat

I awoke at about eight o'clock. Sweat drenched my body as mosquitoes buzzed in clouds around me. My trusty poncho liner lay where it had been kicked to the floor. My head hurt; my mouth tasted terrible; I had a world-class hangover.

Jong and Sassner returned from breakfast. With a grin, Don handed me a beer and said, "War is hell, One-six. Drink up."

Much of the day was spent assembling maps of the new AO. We also reported to the medics to receive shots. They did not tell us what they were for, nor did we ask. There was some mention of yellow fever, typhoid, etc. As I had had all those shots before leaving Fort Bragg, I figured the medics just enjoyed harrassing us.

The rockets were fired from several miles outside Frenzell-Jones. They were large 120mm projectiles that made a pretty good impact. As they were landing on the other side of the compound, we did not leave our hooch. We did watch the rear troops' death-defying runs to the bunkers. Later reports said the only damage inflicted was one latrine destroyed.

Linda had now arrived in San Francisco. Her letters related that the apartment she shared with Susan was ten minutes from Letterman General Hospital at the Presidio. Susan's husband Tom had just arrived in-country and was working as an advisor farther south in the Delta.

My letters from BMB to Linda were about missing her. I wrote even more about how good my soldiers were, and I enclosed the address of Don Jong's mother and encouraged Linda to look her up. I also noted that with a pay raise in July, we would be receiving $702 a month. That is not much now, nor was it then. Soldiers come cheap.

✎ 18 JUNE 1969
Wednesday

Camp Frenzell-Jones
    All day devoted to getting ready for move
    Troops are restless—Raising hell
    Issued first Article 15 since I've been here—PFC Russell—Failure to obey order from NCO—The man was given a chance

Classes became more intense. A demonstration on how to use a litter lowered by cable from a medivac chopper showed us the method of extracting casualties when no LZ was available.

Due to large AOs and thick jungles, we would no longer have mortars at company level. The Charlie Company mortar platoon now became the fourth rifle platoon. This was not a popular decision among the mortarmen. In the future they would be walking rather than staying in the fire base.

Again it was a case of inactivity causing problems. No one admitted it, but we were ready to see the jungles. Testing ourselves against the NVA was not a challenge we looked forward to, though it was one we readily accepted.

If a man refused an order from an NCO in the low intensity of BMB, he would likely do the same in the demanding environs of the field. Russell's instructions were simple: he was to tape map sheets together. Russell felt he was having to do more than his share.

The Article 15 is nonjudicial punishment. It fined him seven days' pay but did not go in his permanent records. After the proceedings were over, Russell again was ordered to tape the maps. He shrugged his shoulders, smiled, and went to work. By the time we left BMB, the incident was forgotten. Russell went back to being a good soldier.

After dark, Delta and Charlie Companies began hollering insults at each other across the small dirt road that separated the companies' billets. Most shouts centered on which was the best unit, but an occasional reference was heard to sexual relations with one's mother or doubts about paternity.

After one too many "mother fuckers" and "bastards," a small battle ensued. No one crossed the road. The weapons were the red star clusters and green hand flares carried for night signaling or target markings. The troops fired the flares at each other by striking the base sharply with their palms. With a loud, fire-trailing "*woosh*," the colored projectiles traveled several hundred meters.

By the time each company had fired six or eight of the devices, everyone was hiding behind the sandbagged walls and having a good time. Norm Sassner and I watched from a distance. After the flares stopped, we walked in and checked for damage. Except for a few minor burns, everyone was okay.

We carried the remaining flares back to the company supply room.

✎ **19 JUNE 1969**
Thursday

Black Horse
    Truck convoy to here—Dangerous road but no contact
    Troops staying outside—Scrounged all afternoon getting them tents—Raining like hell—Finally did get them
    Co CO has bad foot—If we move out before a few days I am in charge

The party was over.

We were up before daylight and just after sunup were on trucks heading northeast on Highway 1. The lowland rice paddies were soon behind us. The two-lane asphalt road, which had the vegetation cleared for a hundred meters on each side, took us into progressively thicker jungle. After about twenty-five miles, we began to pass rubber plantations, huge trees in neat, uniform rows.

A layer of sandbags lined the truck floor. Cobra gunships roared overhead serving both as observation platforms as well as fire support. Everyone was facing outward in the open trucks. At a large horseshoe-shaped bend midway to Xuan Luc, we saw many rusted and burnt vehicles that had been victims of previous ambushes.

At Xuan Luc we passed the new Brigade Forward Headquarters. We turned east, soon leaving Highway 1 and continuing down a gravel road to firebase Black Horse. Each village we passed had a small compound of ARVN or regional/provincial defense forces. The latter were better known as Ruff Puffs—they were much more puff than ruff.

About ten miles off the highway, we reached the fire base named after the black-horse shoulder patch of the 11th Armored Cavalry Regiment. The 11th ACR was one of the few armored units in Vietnam. The tankers lived well. They had their own PX and clubs and a work crew of locals.

Battalion headquarters set up operation of their CP in the northwest corner of the base. After only a brief stop, A, B, and D Companies deployed into the surrounding AO.

CPT Swiss had been having trouble for some time with an infection in his foot. Called trench foot in previous wars, it was known to us as immersion foot. Swiss and the Battalion Commander had thought he would get better while on standdown. When there was no improvement, LTC Mess decided to keep us at the base until a new company commander arrived. I had hoped to take over for at least a few days, but my time had not yet come.

The base was crowded. With most of the ACR units in for refitting before moving north, no buildings were available for the Infantry. I finally found a sympathetic first sergeant who provided us a small wooden hooch and enough tents to get the company out of the rain.

My letter to Linda noted that at the end of the month I would be returning to BMB for seven days as the acting XO: Hawkins had managed to wangle a second R&R out of country.

20 JUNE 1969
Friday

Black Horse
Got news today CPT Swiss going to Brigade

New CO CPT McGinnis from North Carolina
20 minutes later we moved out—into rubber plantations
First operation up here in the north

The change of command of Charlie Company was without ceremony. CPT Swiss called the officers together, introduced CPT Jim McGinnis, shook our hands, and departed with a friendly warning to "keep your heads down."

McGinnis spoke only briefly. He had been working in Brigade Operations and was on his second tour, having spent his first with a Special Forces team as an NCO before going to OCS. Although already a combat veteran, he admitted that this was his first experience with regular Infantry. His friendly, confident, easy-going manner made a good first impression.

McGinnis showed us grid coordinates of the area where we would be operating. Trucks were to arrive momentarily. He said that he would get to know us in the boonies and concluded with, "Saddle up."

The trucks took us back northwest to Highway 1, where our mission was a company-sized RIF through a rubber plantation that covered over twenty square kilometers. The mature trees were about eighteen inches in diameter and thirty feet tall. Laid out in precise rows, the plantation reminded me of the tombstones in a military cemetery. Some of the rubber trees showed recent work. The bark had been cut in a descending spiral from the six-foot level for a couple of feet. At the bases, pieces of flat tin diverted the raw latex into small crockery bowls.

All it took to get the sticky white sap oozing from a tree was to make a small cut with a sharp object. Several of the men tried milking the trees but soon stopped when they discovered how hard it was to get the gunk off their knives and uniforms.

McGinnis told us that no workers were then authorized to be in the area. Once off the highway, we were in a free fire zone.

The equipment we had carried across the paddies had been

greatly supplemented. Now we carried machetes, entrenching tools, and empty sandbags for reinforcing our defenses at night.

The rubber plantations were not quite as hot as the paddies. Shade covered the ground from trees that were only ten to fifteen feet apart.

Moving as a company was a new experience. My platoon had the point. We were not as spread out as we had been in the south because Brigade Intelligence reported that booby traps were a rarity. The threat was the well-armed NVA units who operated in groups of from twenty-five to over two-hundred. Every kilometer or so, the company halted. Platoons then circled out in a cloverleaf fashion to check the entire area.

At dusk the company broke into two perimeters about a klick apart. McGinnis' command post and the third and forth platoons were together. The first and second platoons' position was at the juncture where the rubber plantation met the jungle.

Bill Little and I shared a foxhole; our RTOs dug in next to us. We observed that our jungle fatigues were taking on the red tinge of the dirt we now lived in—another difference from the paddy mud that had been our previous home.

It rained all night. Dull popping noises kept us anxiously awake. When later operations in the rubber plantations produced the same sounds, we finally figured out that after the sun went down and the tree branches cooled, a nutlike growth cracked in the changing temperatures. Even knowing what caused the noise did not lessen our anxiety.

✈ **21 JUNE 1969**
Saturday

> Long hot RIF
> A tree fell 200 m away—One man opened up—Everyone nervous
> Setting up in Co positions
> New CO is No. 1—He said he had heard good things about me—He lets me run my plt as I see fit
> Delta Co got hit hard today—CPT Petrosilli—A used-to-be Lt in our Co was hit—2nd time to Japan

My opinion of the new CO's being Number 1 was not just based on his patronization of me. McGinnis was taking charge. His calmness and willingness to listen quickly gained our confidence. He was obviously having problems getting used to the heat, rain, and long marches, but he carried his own load. As with any commander, we called him the "old man." This seemed particularly appropriate as McGinnis was at least ten years older than the rest of us.

"Number 1" was a term that GIs and Vietnamese alike used for expression of praise. Number 10 was just the opposite. Everything was either 1 or 10—there were no degrees. Of course, there were far more Number 10s.

Pete Petrosilli had been a rifle platoon leader in Charlie Company before my arrival. A gunshot wound to the leg had sent him to Japan four months before. He had returned to lead the mortar platoon briefly while we were at Elvira. After promotion to captain, he had assumed command of Delta.

Delta Company engaged an equivalent-sized NVA unit. Although they had several killed and wounded, the Delta grunts inflicted far worse on the enemy. All was under control until the final dust-off.

Pete had taken some minor RPG shrapnel in the buttocks. He evacuated all his casualties and reluctantly got on the

last medivac himself. As it lifted off, a gook, ignoring the
Red Cross on the air ambulance, hit the bird with another
RPG. The resulting crash nearly killed Pete. His cheek and
jaw bones were crushed, and he sustained a broken leg and
internal injuries.

---

22 JUNE 1969
Sunday

> Linked up with some ARVNs—more searching
> Rains 3 to 4 times daily—Wet & muddy all the time
> Also leeches sucking blood
> We linked up with APCs today—Co took 2 plts in a
> sweep—He put me in charge of 2 plts to sweep around the
> other side of mountain—Tracks got lost—Had to straighten
> them out—Ended up CO also got lost—Lost commo with
> Battalion—I was taking all traffic—Ended up everybody had
> to follow my trail
> Felt funny when 3 sgts., 2 Cpts., and 1 Lt had to ask me
> where they were

This was our first operation with the armored personnel carriers of the Brigade's one company of tracks. Armed with a
50-caliber and two M-60 machine guns, their effectiveness
was limited by their lack of mobility in the jungle. I was lucky
that my column had stayed near a mountain, which aided my
navigation.

The jungle floor and its stagnant pools of water were full of
leeches about an inch or two in length with a diameter of a
pencil lead—until they had gorged themselves with our blood.
Leeches really did not hurt. When they clamped on to us, they
emitted a pain-killing secretion that also prevented blood from
clotting. We did not know we had picked up the dark-colored

dinner guests until we saw or felt their thumb-sized bodies affixed to our skin. They particularly liked to inch their way up our legs to our crotches. It was never pleasant to find one of the creatures. Finding one on the testicles was even more revolting.

Insect repellent caused a leech to release his suction and drop off. A bit of salt from a C-ration made the mucous body turn inside out in a bloody dance of death.

Bug juice around our fatigue trousers, which were tucked inside our boots, kept the leeches somewhat at bay. We also generously sprayed the repellent on the ground before we slept. Still, the suckers found our good ole red American blood. We never got used to them. They were just another irritant that became part of our lives.

23 JUNE 1969
Monday

> Set up on side of a mountain tonight
> SP4 Garcia and one of the ARVNs talked for an hour—I in Spanish, I in Vietnamese—Never could figure it out but they seemed to be communicating
> Am getting so I can work with the ARVNs

The ARVN seemed relaxed, appearing basically happy with their situation. There would be no end of the war for them after only a year. None of them seemed to be in a hurry, particularly to face the enemy. They liked our C-rations and filled their rucksacks.

We were now deep into the jungle. Brush and vines covered the ground and small trees reached to a height of about six feet. Another layer of trees grew to about twenty-five feet. Yet a final growth of large trees, reaching heights of about a hundred feet, towered above the lower two layers of vegetation. This triple canopy virtually blocked the sunlight.

No breeze penetrated the damp jungle. The dark floor was stifling hot, and the unrelenting smell of rotting vegetation filled the air.

At frequent intervals were thickets of bamboo. Varying from small clumps to patches thirty meters in diameter, their six-inch-thick stalks were impossible to cut through. The inevitable zigzagging around them made navigation difficult.

At least thirst was not the problem it had been in the Delta. Fresh streams of fairly clear water ran at frequent intervals. A purification tablet per canteen made it bitter but safe. Some of the soldiers added packets of Kool Aid to make the water more palatable.

🛩 24 JUNE 1969
Tuesday

Continue mission
Today we airmobiled to help out Alpha in contact—Had an NVA Regiment on a hill—By the time we got there NVA had left

We were in thick jungle when the radio crackled with Alpha Company's contact followed by Battalion's ordering us to the nearest pick up zone (PZ). Moving as quickly as possible, we still were nearly an hour covering the short kilometer to the PZ.

No sooner had we reached the clearing than the slicks came over the horizon. Their blade noise changed to a distinctive whoop-whoop as they turned toward us. Our loading was SOP as groups of six men sped down the open area with no group containing more than one M-60 or radio. Leaders were careful to get on different choppers. If a bird went down, we did not want to lose a group of critical weapons or leaders.

The flight of eight helicopters carried half the company at a time. Blood was up and running hot. As we jumped from the skids, the men were shouting so loudly that I could hear them over the rotors. Charlie Company wanted part of the action.

When we learned the NVA had broken contact, we were disappointed—and somewhat relieved. Alpha lost one killed, the dinks four. After hearing reports of the fire fight, it was evident that the first word, about a regiment-sized enemy, had been greatly exaggerated.

🐦 25 JUNE 1969
Wednesday

Continue mission

After it was determined that the NVA were no longer in the area, CPT McGinnis received orders for Charlie Company to conduct a reconnaissance in force (RIF) to the south.

Our movement halted about an hour before dusk. The lead platoon leader selected a site for the night defensive position (NDP) and the platoons occupied their sectors based on a clock system. The direction of movement was considered twelve o'clock. From twelve to three was the lead platoon sector, from nine to twelve the next platoon, then from three to six and from six to nine the remaining platoon. The company CP set up near the center of the circle.

Because of thick jungle, the perimeter often was more oval

than circular. Claymore mines, trip illumination flares and intersecting fields of machine gun fire were the first priorities. Half of the men remained on alert while the others worked. Trails or other likely avenues of approach were covered by sending out three-man observation/listening posts. Depending on the situation, they might stay in the positions all night or return to the perimeter just before dark.

LT Jong called in nightly artillery defensive concentrations. Marking rounds of aerial smoke bursts were always fired before shooting the high-explosive steel.

We dug holes deep enough to protect a prone man and stacked sandbags and logs for added protection. Then we stretched ponchos on sticks about eighteen inches above the ground with the ends either staked with more sticks or tied to trees or logs with extra boot laces.

The makeshift poncho tents were strictly for sleeping. Soldiers on alert sat outside the poncho hooch so they could hear without the distraction of the rain pelting on the fabric.

We slept directly on the ground. The men carried air mattresses but used them only at the fire bases. In the boonies, the soldiers' rolling over on the air-filled pads made too much noise.

After the NDP was completely established, platoon leaders checked their sectors. McGinnis usually made a brief tour, stopping to visit with the grunts as he made his round.

It was now time to eat. A few of the soldiers ate three full meals a day, but the combination of the heat and the monotony of C-rations made most of us rarely hungry.

I usually ate most of a complete C-ration in the evening. After stand-to the next morning, a cup of coffee brewed in an empty C-ration cracker can was breakfast. At noon a can of fruit, a pound cake or pecan nut roll was all I wanted in the heat.

26 JUNE 1969
Thursday

Jungle
   After moving all day we were ready to set up NDP—2nd plt on point heard gook voices—My plt set up a block in a creek and 2nd moved in—After a brief fire fight we withdrew—Called in arty and set up for night
   One man wounded—Shot through mouth—Had to use hook on chopper to raise him out of jungle

On the battlefield, skill and experience are critical, but at times luck is the deciding factor. If we had halted a few hundred meters earlier, we would not have heard the enemies' voices. If we had not been moving with stealth, they would have escaped or ambushed us, but not all the luck was on our side. Darkness was approaching and we had to make our attack quickly.

McGinnis assembled the platoon leaders, ordering the third platoon to remain on our small hill to secure our rucksacks so we could move in unencumbered. The fourth platoon was to establish a blocking position on a hill two hundred meters to our left. My platoon was to move down a small stream to our right while Little's second platoon proceeded directly toward the voices. Jong plotted artillery to seal off the far side.

About two hundred meters down the stream a trail led from the far side to the water. On the bank a pair of wet black pajama trousers was still dripping. Apparently, a gook doing his laundry had heard our approach.

Just as I called McGinnis to inform him we had been detected, the second platoon opened fire about 150 meters to our left. By the sound of the barrage, they were firing every weapon they had. We could not directly see the enemy through the thick foliage, but we directed our fire at the reports of the AK47s.

As the gooks' fire diminished we pushed up the trail. I had never seen Tom scared. He was shaking so hard that we could barely understand him as he said, "Beaucoup NVA! Beaucoup NVA!"

Artillery was now blasting the jungle. Jong brought it to within a hundred meters of us. Fire from the gooks diminished to sporadic shots by a weapon none of us could identify.

Though it was now completely dark, we all wanted to sweep through the gook camp. McGinnis' order to return to the secured hill was a good one; however, as in the darkness, we might have fought each other rather than the dinks.

Sassner guided each platoon into sector. Little's platoon was the last to return, his medic half-carrying a rifleman who had taken a round through the lower face. Apparently the soldier had his mouth open when the bullet entered. Its exit took out some teeth and part of the jaw and cheek. He was bleeding heavily.

McGinnis had already called in a dust off while Sassner had secured a bomb crater inside the perimeter that provided enough clearance for the chopper to drop a hook-sling for the casualty.

We began to dig in. DeForrest and I soon discovered that in the darkness we were sharing our position with a large bed of black ants. We withdrew without a fight. The huge ants left red welts from their bites.

Jong continued artillery off and on throughout the night to prevent the gooks' returning to remove bodies or equipment. Some of Little's men reported fighting their way to the edge of bunkers before withdrawing. My platoon had made it far enough for us to see what appeared to be low, thatched hooches.

During the long night I decided not to return to BMB as Hawkins' temporary replacement. I did not want to leave my platoon. McGinnis agreed while rejecting my recommendation that Sassner go instead. He needed us all in the field.

✈ 27 JUNE 1969
Friday

Moved into contact area—Search found:
    7 large bunkers
    9 hooches
    1 cook shack
    2 bodies—1 male 1 female—KIA
    100 lbs. of various clothing & boots
    55 lbs. of rice
    1 printing press
    1 typewriter
    3 large bags of documents—(Later found to have secret info—Also names and addresses of VC supporters in area)
    Much cooking equipment
    Sewing gear
    1 SKS with ammo
    1 US M-2 carbine ammo
    Misc ammo & misc equipment
    $160 in VC money—Found by me—Split among 1st plt
    Medicine—Much

At daylight we went back into the contact area following the same plan as the previous evening. Just beyond the point where we had halted the attack was a latrine and wash area. A few meters later we came to the bunkers. Some had tables built on top, covered with thatched roofs supported by bamboo poles.

Another hut protected a cooking area where a large pot of now burnt rice sat on dying embers. Next to the cook shack lay a dead gook wearing only shorts, sandals and a covering of flies. An SKS rifle was a few feet away.

The body had been hit many times. DeForrest and I noticed a small sack tied around the body's waist at about the same time. We cut the bloody canvas strap and found the roll of South Vietnamese piasters. The paper bills, called "Ps," would buy the platoon beer for awhile.

On the other side of the bunker complex, Little's platoon discovered the source of the odd sounding weapon we had heard the night before. The M-2 carbine lay next to a dead young woman. She was far too bloated for her enlargement to have been the result of the heat. We wondered why a pregnant woman had stayed, fought and died while others were escaping. We joked that the woman and unborn child should count as two bodies. No one expressed any regret about killing her. She had the opportunity to do the same to us. In fact, she had tried very hard to do so.

After the entire complex was secured, we began a more detailed search. Several blood trails led into the jungle between the fourth platoon's blocking position and the artillery barrage. More blood and bandages showed we had killed at least five or six more. We claimed only the two we had weapons in hand for. The others were reported as probable kills.

We ignored the dink bodies after we searched them. Tom, DeForrest and I had our CP within five meters of the male gook. We heated water for coffee and ate our lunch as we discussed how quickly the maggots had begun their work.

The other gooks had escaped with little but their lives. Eating utensils were still on the table. Packs, ammo and food were neatly stacked in nearly every bunker. Rice was in bags and long sack-like cylinders. Tom showed us how these containers could be easily carried around the neck like a loose scarf. We cut open the containers and poured the grain in the creek and the latrine. Equipment and clothing we burnt. Ammo, documents and the small printing press was carried to an LZ a couple of klicks away for transfer to the S-2.

The typewriter contained an unfinished report. Intelligence later sent us an interpretation that said the report was from the commander of the camp, saying new US units were operating in his area. He wrote we would not venture far enough into the jungle to find his headquarters. He had been wrong.

Other documents revealed that we had found a rest area for the 274th NVA Regiment which was composed of NVA and a consolidation of local VC. We presumed the woman was with the latter.

We burned the hooches. They had been camouflaged so well under the triple canopy that they were impossible to spot from the air. From the ground we had to be within ten meters to make out their barest outline.

The two weapons were awarded to the second platoon. They had made the initial contact and had been in the thickest of the fighting. There were sufficient souvenirs for all. McGinnis kept the Vietnamese typewriter because his wife taught high school typing classes back in North Carolina.

We also found several diaries. Neatly drawn pictures of people and animals along with poems adorned the pages. We wanted to keep them but sent them to the S-2 because they might contain some intel value.

In the late afternoon we moved to the LZ from which the documents had been extracted. We felt better setting up our NDP in a place the enemy did not know as well as their camp.

Spirits were high. We had done significant damage to the enemy while only taking one WIA. We had surprised and defeated the enemy on his own turf.

My letter to Linda briefly described the fight. I also asked her if she had any ideas for baby names. Although I had promised her I would give her full details about events in my life, I did not include anything about the rotting body of the pregnant woman we had left in the jungle camp.

🌺 **28 JUNE 1969**
Saturday

> Took a 6-man recon back to VC base camp—Found more bunkers etc.

> Returned to Co and led them in—Was in charge of blowing
> bunkers—Took 4 lbs.—Dug in from top—Tried first time
> from bottom—Didn't work—Also scary as hell with charge
> lit trying to climb out of bunker—
>
> Light contact with 1 VC today—No damage either side—
> Nervous perimeter tonight—
>
> This bunker complex is a once a tour chance for most of
> us—Few people have ever seen one with almost all the equip-
> ment inside

If the NVA had reoccupied the bunker complex, they would
be alert for our return. I figured that a small group could move
in much more quietly than the entire company. We could
quickly be reinforced if we detected more gooks. McGinnis
agreed.

As we left the perimeter, Little joined my patrol. I did not
ask if he had permission from the CO. Bill did not want to
miss a possible action and he was willing to join us as just
another rifle rather than as a lieutenant.

We approached the camp from the side that Jong had attempted to seal with artillery. More blood trails indicated the
redlegs (Artillery) had also gotten a few. Our cautious movement only covered a few meters a minute. We halted frequently and just listened. After an hour and a half, we reached
a bunker line we had not discovered the day before and confirmed that the enemy had not returned.

The patrol returned to the company to lead them back in by
the new route. We had barely moved when a grunt in the third
platoon at the tail of the company opened up on full automatic.
A returned burst of AK fire had us all diving for cover.

When everything calmed down, the soldier with his rifle
still smoking said a dink had come down the trail to his right.
Because he had broken his glasses the day before, he could
not see well and had thought the approaching soldier was an
observation patrol (OP) rejoining the platoon until the man
turned and ran.

As he seemed unaware of the recent fight, the dink was
probably on his way to the camp with a message or for a rest.

McGinnis reported the brief contact and requested the Battalion TOC have the rear medics get the soldier a new pair of glasses.

Bunkers in that part of the complex contained little, having been far enough from the initial contact to allow the dinks to take their supplies with them.

We had now located twenty bunkers in the camp. These were much larger than the ones we had found in the Delta. About five feet wide and eight feet long, they were dug out to a depth of three to four feet and covered with logs six inches or more in diameter. Dirt was piled on the logs, giving about two feet of overhead cover. Small entrance ways that served as gun ports were at each end. Shallow trenches just deep enough to cover a crawling man connected many of the fortifications.

Our problem now was how to destroy the bunkers. A chopper load of C-4 had been humped in from the LZ. On my first attempt to blow one, I molded four pounds of explosive around the center logs inside the bunkers. After lighting two fuses which ran to blasting caps to ensure that at least one would work, I then had to crawl out of the low ceiling hole. With the smell of the burning fuses in my nostrils, my six-foot-five-inch frame moved amazingly fast.

When the charge blew, the top of the bunker rose, shuddered and dropped back in place. I had only wounded the bunker. I was glad. The idea of crawling out of nineteen more of the holes had no appeal. My next try was to dig a small hole in the dirt on top of the logs and emplace four more pounds of C-4. When the tamped charge exploded, it blew the logs and dirt downward, filling the bunker. One down and nineteen to go. It took most of the rest of the day. I used the opportunity to train more of the platoon in demolitions.

✎ 29 JUNE 1969
Sunday

> Got ready to airmobile back to Black Horse—
> I chose NDP position as usual tonight—
> My plt spends most of the time on point

It rained hard all day. We stayed close to the LZ in case the weather broke enough for helicopters to pick us up and take us to Black Horse. It never did.

We kept close watch on the trails leading to the destroyed bunker complex, but there was no action. Apparently the enemy, too, was waiting out the rain.

By now our soaked bodies had dampened our high spirits. Jungle fatigues worn for nearly two weeks were literally rotting off of us. We looked forward to a break. We felt we deserved it.

✎ 30 JUNE 1969
Monday

> Ready to airmobile to Black Horse—Called off—Weather trouble
> Have heard no news of any kind in a long time
> A lot of the men are getting ringworm
> Search & destroy on way to new PZ—On a break my men cut down a 12-inch rubber tree with a machete—Just to be doing something I guess

> "Thou shall have a place also without the camp, wither thou shalt go forth abroad;

> And thou shalt have a paddle upon thy weapon; and it
> shall be, when thou wilt ease thyself abroad, thou shalt
> dig there with; and shalt turn back and cover that which
> cometh from thee."
>
> Deuteronomy 23:12–13

The rain continued. All we could do was wait.

We had had no resupply in several days and I had received no mail on the last chopper. A week of no letters was a long time.

The ringworm fungus was difficult to treat in the constant wetness. Some of the men had it on their chests and faces. Except for a small patch on the back of my hand, I had been able to avoid the itchy growth. Doc carried large, white, chalky pills that helped somewhat.

The Bible quote seemed a good one for a soldier whose latrine was a shovel and the earth itself.

🦋 **1 JULY 1969**
Tuesday

> Finally airmobiled to Black Horse
> On 11 day mission we got 3 hot meals
> Got in 2 more replacements—That makes about 27 field
> strength

It was absolutely wonderful to return to Black Horse. The Battalion now had taken over several of the sandbagged buildings from the 11th ACR. Clean bodies and sets of fatigues not only felt good but also made us feel lighter.

My platoon was at its largest since my arrival. With promotions and replacements, my platoon now had four NCOs.

None, however, had been in the Army for more than a year or were over twenty years old.

First Sergeant Melvin Ploeger was running the Company headquarters at Black Horse. Soldiers and officers alike called him Top. The other first sergeants occasionally referred to him as Red. I doubt if anyone except his mother ever called him Melvin. A bit overweight, red headed and constantly sun-burned because of his light complexion, Top did his best to be mean as hell. He was usually successful. No one had enough nerve to ask his age, but we figured he was over thirty-five, making him the oldest man in the company.

Top had nearly twenty years in the Army. As First Sergeant, he was responsible for the company's administration and logistics. Although no one would admit it, we all liked the bastard.

Top and I had a running battle about when I would get my Combat Infantryman's Badge. The regulations stated that a soldier had to be an Infantryman in the field for thirty days and/or have engaged the enemy.

My first question for Top upon arrival at Black Horse was about my CIB. He barked, "Leave me alone. You get the CIB when I think you have earned it." He added a "Sir" and a smile. A few hours later, he gave me a copy of the orders awarding me and several others our CIBs.

CIBs were awarded somewhat loosely in Vietnam. Many an Infantryman wearing the badge, especially senior officers, saw little combat. Personally, I felt on that day at Black Horse the same way I feel now: I have received no higher award or honor than the rifle and wreath of the CIB.

Almost as good as the news of the CIB was the large stack of mail. I placed the ones from Linda on top by postmark date. I read each closely, re-read them and then put them back for a last reading before I destroyed them.

My letters to Linda from the boonies were short. From a fire base or BMB, they were much longer. I tried to tell Linda as much of the details, good and bad, as possible. It was better for her to know than to imagine.

To my parents, I was much more brief and vague. By now they had had sons in Vietnam for nearly two years. I had seen them age quickly during Jim's tour and I did my best to reassure them. It did little good, of course.

Letters to Jim were general. He knew the specifics from first-hand experience. Years later he would tell me he thought it would be a miracle if both of us survived. He was troubled by the idea that his making it home lessened my chances. I yearned to talk to him and to share our fears and triumphs. (Oddly, we never have really discussed the war. I do not know why. Perhaps we understand without talking about it or maybe we just do not want to relive it.)

My letter to Linda from Black Horse included, "I love and miss you very much—Still I am as happy as I can be under these circumstances—We are doing a job that has to be done and we are doing a damn good job of it—Killing these people leaves no bad feelings at all."

✒ 2 JULY 1969
Wednesday

> Airmobiled back to jungle—
> My plt on point again—
> Have a scout dog with us—Don't really think he is too good but he's nice to have around for the troops to pet

The helicopters carried us to a small, marshy LZ some twenty klicks northwest of Black Horse. Delta Company followed once we had the area secured. After everyone was on the ground, Charlie Company headed southwest and Delta moved to the northwest.

My selection of the NDP for the company was poor. We

had good fields of fire on the hillside, but the rocky soil made digging in nearly impossible. We scraped out what we could and used rocks and logs for more cover.

The scout dog was trained to detect the enemy as well as booby traps. His keen senses supposedly would give us an early warning when he froze into a motionless position. As long as the handler was by his side, the dog was quite friendly; when left alone, he would let no one approach.

Scout dogs were only good the first day or two out because they tired quickly in the heat. Special food had to be carried for them as well. At least they were smart enough not to eat C-rations.

Not on a one-year tour, the dogs stayed in Vietnam until they could not or would not work any more, then were destroyed. The possibility of communicable diseases contracted in Nam being transferred to dogs back home meant that they were in the war for their own duration.

⌐ 3 JULY 1969
Thursday

We continue to move—

Got word at 1100 that Delta was in heavy contact 1 klick away—We moved in to help

When we got there Delta already had wounded—1st & 2nd plts moved in to help—Tried twice, pushed back both times—PFC Hefferman WIA—Shrapnel left cheek, face—Not bad—Made it to 30 m from bunkers

Delta had a man wounded—Screaming—His plt ldr was KIA trying to get him—This is not plt ldr's job

Finally all we could do was drop back—Call in arty and air

Final count 9 KIA-MIA, 16 to 20 WIA—US

Dust off had to hook them out

The next few days' journal entries were all written on 6 July. They are rather precise, calm and unemotional. In fact, those were days of absolute confusion, chaos, and death. It was one of the few battles in which I was involved that was reported by the television networks and worldwide press. For a few hours we were in the middle of the day's hottest fight in Vietnam. It was a day that would bring a Medal of Honor, a Distinguished Service Cross, and a mass of lesser valor awards and Purple Hearts to a group of very brave men. It was also a day that sent green Army cars to the homes of the next of kin back in the States.

Because the first platoon had been on point the day before, we were the trail platoon in the company movement. When we changed direction to move to assist Delta, we had no idea of the magnitude of the battle.

All was quiet when we reached the Delta position. A large group of wounded was being treated in an area behind a low hill. A lieutenant I had met briefly at Black Horse was sitting against a tree. A bloody bandage was wrapped around his wrist. His West Point ring prominently gleamed through the drying blood.

I tried to talk to him, but he did not answer. His glassy eyes stared into the distance. That officer was the only person I ever saw in a condition of mental shock. Though his wounds were minor, he had just quit. His was as close to an act of cowardice by an American soldier as I ever observed.

Another hundred meters along the trail, I came upon McGinnis and CPT Lewis, the Delta commander. Lewis, a tough-looking man about McGinnis' age, was drawing on the ground with the barrel of a .45 pistol. A bloody field dressing was clinched in his teeth. His RTO explained while Lewis drew pictures.

The teenage radio operator calmly told us their point man had been hit in the legs by machine gun fire. The platoon medic and then the platoon leader had been killed trying to get to the screaming soldier. The three were just across a large deadfall of logs and branches a hundred meters to our front.

Each time the platoon had reached the deadfall, the enemy had resumed the machine gun fire. A dust-off trying to drop a jungle penetrater for the wounded had been hit and had to withdraw.

The RTO continued. During the last attempt to reach the wounded man, the gooks had thrown hand grenades and fired RPG rounds. McGinnis, Lewis, and the RTO agreed on a plan. My platoon and Little's were to assault the enemy position from the left flank. Delta was to attack in the same direction as before.

Delta Company was losing its effectiveness as a unit. All its officers were dead or wounded. Lewis rallied together about twenty men to try to retrieve his dead and injured. The point man's cries for help still mingled with occasional bursts of random fire. The gooks were using him as bait.

I stayed on the far right of my platoon assault line. Twenty meters away, I could see Lewis getting ready. Blood ran down his chin, soaking his fatigue shirt. His eyes were calm, however. I noticed he wore the right shoulder patch of the 101st Airborne from a previous tour. This was not his first fight.

As soon as the second platoon was in position on my left, the entire front opened fire and began to crawl forward. Tracers from two enemy machine guns were intersecting at the deadfall. RPGs and grenades impacted the killing zone. We made about fifty meters into the thick jungle. A call on the radio ordered us to pull back.

We met again with Lewis. His RTO explained as Lewis drew more pictures that they had made it across the deadfall. More men had been hit and the rest had had to pull back. Lewis tried to talk. His top teeth and palate had been knocked loose by pieces of frag grenade. He could only grunt.

We waited for the other two Charlie Company platoons to get into position where they could support by fire. Sassner reported that the jungle was so thick that they could do little good.

Lewis held up one finger. He wanted to try one more time. We moved back to our positions as Jong dropped salvo after salvo of artillery into the gook position. He was working with the Delta FO who was bleeding from a leg wound. The arty halted only briefly when gunships rolled in with rockets and mini-guns.

We resumed the attack. It took a half an hour to make it to within thirty meters of the enemy position. Tree branches and leaves fell like hailstones as the enemy bullets cut the vegetation above our heads. Five meters to my left, Hefferman took grenade fragments in the face, but he continued to fire his red-hot M-60. In the relative open area to my right, I could see that the enemy's fire was now concentrating on Lewis. Grenades filled the air, going both ways. Many failed to explode. Frightened hands on both sides forgot to pull the pins in the heat of the battle.

We could move no farther forward. Again we were ordered to withdraw.

Tears were now in Lewis' eyes. His RTO was no longer with him. A weeping Delta soldier said the RTO had jumped on a grenade to save Lewis.

Lewis motioned he wanted to try again. McGinnis explained the situation to the Battalion and Brigade Commanders who were orbiting the area in their C&C birds. By now, the fight had been going on for nearly six hours. Darkness was closing around us. The Battalion Commander ordered us to withdraw and get the wounded evacuated. Sounds no longer came from the deadfall.

Lewis was growing weak from the loss of blood. Sassner was working a couple of hundred meters to our rear to clear an area for a dust-off. The night was black when we finally were able to get six of the wounded on the bird. I noticed that the lieutenant with the minor wound was the first to be wrenched up on the cable. Lewis, still protesting, was last.

We formed a joint perimeter with what was left of Delta. A young sergeant and their artillery FO took charge. Twenty or so wounded were inside the perimeter. They were quiet except for one soldier who kept getting up to show a large hole in his biceps. A shot of morphine had killed the pain and a tourniquet had stopped the bleeding.

After many checks of rosters and reports from the surviving leaders, we determined that nine men were missing. The count was eight for some time. Finally, someone asked where a replacement was who had reported in two days before. Not even in the company long enough to be on the roster, he was now with the dead.

Little took a small group outside the perimeter. Exposing a strobe light, he directed a resupply helicopter to a bomb crater where the crew could kick out more ammo. We reloaded magazines and distributed replacement grenades. It was midnight before we were refitted and dug in because we had to prepare holes for the wounded as well as for ourselves. The moon briefly broke through the clouds; we felt exposed in the dim light.

I had little time to think about anything until about one in the morning. At last, all was relatively calm. Suddenly I was ravenous. I had had nothing to eat or drink all day. I emptied a quart canteen without stopping. Rummaging around in my rucksack, I pulled out the first can I found. With all the events of the day, I still recall that can of beans and franks. It was delicious. Perhaps it was more the reminder to my senses that I was still alive than the flavor of the food itself.

As I look back, two other things seem locked in my mind. The first is the large swarm of yellow, purple, and black butterflies that had stayed around us all that day, oblivious to the fight. The second thing is that the gooks had been firing white tracers. Green and red we had all seen many times, but not white. Later we figured out that all tracers are white the first twenty to thirty meters out of a gun muzzle. We had been that close.

Little came to my position in the middle of the night. He wanted to try to go back and recover the MIAs under the cloak of darkness. By now the enemy area was being hit by F-4 jet bombs and napalm. His idea was more frustration than sensibility.

Lewis later received the DSC. He deserved it. His RTO, CPL Michael F. Folland, was posthumously awarded the Medal of Honor. His citation read in part:

CPL Michael F. Folland while serving with Co. D, 2d Bn, 3d Inf 199th Inf Bde distinguished himself on July 3, 1969 in Long Khanh Province as his patrol moved through a dense jungle area and was caught in a heavy crossfire. Folland ran to help his commander assault the enemy. The force moved forward until it was pinned down by machine gun fire. Folland stood up to draw enemy fire while his commander tried to destroy the positions with a grenade. While the officer prepared to throw the grenade an enemy grenade landed in their position. Folland warned his commander who hurled it from their position. A second grenade followed and again Folland shouted. After seeing that no one could reach the grenade, he threw himself on it absorbing the impact of the explosion and saving the lives of his fellow soldiers.

✒ 4 JULY 1969
Friday

C Co moved back up Butterfly Hill—This is the name the troops called it—My plt leading—Mission: Get the 9 MIA out—After several recons by fire we moved in and found them—9 men—All close together

9 men dead—Maggots already working on them—Not a pretty sight—Still we had to go in base camp—We moved in—I had to lead—Plt was scared and shook—My RTO and I hit the bunkers—Throwing grenades etc—Thank God NVA had already pulled back

We began searching

I checked many bunkers & small tunnels—You take a bayonet and dive in after a grenade—Not good for nerves

A hell of a 4th of July

We still had no idea of the enemy situation. The fact that they had stayed and fought so hard indicated they had something worth defending. From their firepower and the variety of their weapons, we estimated there were at least a hundred of them. The biggest question was whether they were still in place or had withdrawn.

Gunships and jets hit the area again at daybreak. The helicopter pilots reported they could see bunkers and bodies that appeared to be American.

Just before we moved out of the NDP, a resupply chopper kicked out additional C-4 for blowing an LZ. Sassner quickly had an area cleared which was large enough for dust-offs to land and evacuate the wounded.

Along with the C-4, the resupply bird delivered a large bundle of body bags. We never packed around these gray containers with their sewed-in carrying handles, partly because we did not want the extra weight but mostly because we did not want the reminders of our own vulnerabilities. We preferred to cover our dead with ponchos and have the bags delivered when necessary.

We began our return to the enemy's position with an artillery barrage. Jong kept calling it in a couple of hundred meters to our front, moving it forward at our pace. At the near side of the deadfall, we began our fire.

Crawling quickly over the downed trees, we reached the bodies of the Delta dead. The nine were in an area the size of a small room. They were so close that some lay on top of others. Off to one side was the RTO's blasted body. His radio was at his side.

We lay among the dead as we continued to pour fire into the bunkers we could now see just ahead. We paused long enough to confirm we had found all nine bodies and to set the safeties on the dead men's weapons so that our crawling over them would not accidently discharge a round. We avoided unexploded grenades and RPG rounds.

The sight and smell of the maggot-riddled bodies slowed

the platoon. If the enemy was still present, we were in the worst possible position. I motioned the men forward. De-Forrest and I, in the lead, quickly reached the bunkers. We dropped grenades in each and ran to the next ones. Thirty meters deep into the complex, we had already passed three lines of fortifications.

We threw more grenades. As soon as each exploded, we dove into the narrow opening of the bunker. We could see nothing in the dark, smoke-filled enclosures. Drawing bayonets, we patted and stabbed our way blindly until we confirmed that no living thing was present.

The enemy had vanished in the night. Our foothold in the complex expanded as the rest of the company moved in. After our perimeter was established, I returned to Little's platoon, which had the job of filling the body bags. Members of Delta Company were assisting with the identification of the dead. We thought at first that one of the bodies was an enemy soldier. Closer examination and questioning of the Delta sergeant revealed the man was a GI of Chinese ancestry. One man had fallen with his arm extended in the air. On his hand, now frozen in rigor mortis, was the gold glint of a wedding band.

Our search of the enemy area began in earnest. Bunkers extended in every direction, covering half a square kilometer. In the two bunkers nearest our dead were mounds of expended shell casings. The large drum-like magazines that fed RPD light machine guns covered the bunkers' floors.

Both bunkers contained pools of blood. An NVA pith helmet sported a bloody hole. Nearby, a stretcher made of tree limbs and a poncho was covered in more blood. Deep in the complex, a much larger bunker that had been used as an aid station produced bloody bandages and clothing with bloody bullet and shrapnel holes. Numerous blood trails led to the south. I do not know what body count we claimed. It was apparent that many of the enemy had died. But they had not left a single body.

It soon became obvious why the enemy had fought so hard.

Weapons, food, medicine and supplies of all types were being found and brought to the center of the perimeter.

A few hours later, I saw Little at the growing mound of captured equipment. As he inspected the booty, he told me he would much rather have assaulted the bunker-line than placed the dead in the body bags. He walked away, paused and, with a half grin and a shrug said, "Happy Fourth of July, One-six."

---

5 JULY 1969
Saturday

Continue search of NVA base camp—Findings:
  150 RPG5s
  50 RPG7s
  50 RPG Boosters
  2 82mm mortar tubes & base plates
  3 82mm sights
  12,000 AK47 rounds
  1 AK47
  1 AK47 modified (folding stock)
  200 lbs rice
  200 lbs noodles
  100 lbs misc food
  3 large medicine cases
  1 60 mm mortar tube
  10 82mm rounds
  100 blasting caps
  100 hand grenades—Russian, Chinese, US, East German, homemade
  30 large bags of documents
  500 lbs of demo
  10 20-lb Chicom Claymores
  2,000 rounds M-60 ammo

Many blood trails
Much more misc equipment

Based on the supplies and the number of bunkers, we raised our estimate of enemy to two hundred. The complex had apparently served as a training area as well as a supply center. A thatched-roof classroom with logs for seats had wire obstacles set up to teach breaching techniques. Political slogans and pictures of US weapons lined the walls.

Documents indicated that we had found a base camp of the 33d NVA Regiment. Held in reserve during Tet of '68, it had never been committed in the offensive. It was well-equipped, fully manned and, as we discovered, a good fighting unit.

The realization that everything we found had been carried all the way from North Vietnam was some consolation for our losses. The magnitude also indicated the retreating gooks must have had many dead and wounded to carry away to have left so much equipment behind.

Mail arrived on a resupply ship delivering demolitions. Four letters from Linda were most welcome. Sitting on one of the bunkers, I wrote her about the last few days and I acknowledged a list of baby names she had sent. Life went on.

---

6 JULY 1969
Sunday

"Butterfly Hill"
   Things on 5 July also found on 6 & 7 & 8 & 9 July
   We got mission to continue thoroughly searching area and destroying it
   I did part of demo work
   Sqd of Engineers brought in to help and to build LZ
   All of this is a good find—But not worth 9 lives

By the third day of searching the complex, we had found over fifty bunkers. Engineers were flown in to help destroy the camp and cut an LZ so we could begin extracting captured supplies.

Their first job was to blow down a mahogany tree. The beautiful tree was over three feet in diameter, towering above the triple canopy. With a loud blast, the engineers brought it down, but it fell the wrong direction, crossing the small LZ we had already prepared. Removing the downed tree added a day of hard work.

The initial search of the base camp had almost been a fun-filled treasure hunt. By now, the troops were tired of the digging, looking, and carrying.

Grenades, mortar rounds, RPG rockets, and the Claymores were stacked in a bunker and blown up with a C-4 charge. After some discussion on how to get rid of the twelve thousand AK47 cartridges, I told McGinnis I would take care of them.

My solution was to stack the ammo and the five hundred pounds of gook C-4-equivalent in a pile. Since the enemy demo, in hard, yellow two-pound bricks, burned similarly to C-4, I thought it was better to try to burn it. If we exploded the pile as we had the other ammo, most of it would likely be blown across the jungle. The gooks might later recover some of the rounds. This way, I would destroy ammo and explosives at the same time.

I formed a long, thin line of C-4 leading to the large mound. After testing a similar line, I decided I would have plenty of time to safely run across the two hundred meters to the company position before the fireworks started.

I lit the C-4 fuse and ran like hell. About thirty meters into my flight, a big *woosh*—accompanied by a flash of light—nearly knocked me down. I dove behind a large tree as the AK rounds began to explode like popcorn in a popper: A single pop, followed by several more, and then so many pops, they could not be distinguished individually. Green tracers filled the air.

In a few minutes all became quiet. After a wait of another ten minutes, I cautiously peeped around the tree. A large blackened mass of melted metal was all that was left.

Walking back to the company, I wondered if many GIs had ever been pinned down by twelve thousand bullets. McGinnis and the rest of the troops were still hunkered behind bunkers and logs. Before he asked, I told him it worked just like I had planned. His only response was "Bullshit."

🦋 7 JULY 1969
Monday

"Butterfly Hill"
  I could still be back at BMB as acting XO—Am glad I turned it down—I feel as though my NCOs and men need me
  My men say I talk in my sleep—Shout coordinates—Yell get down etc—Guess this is typical
  Snakes, rats, bugs, ants—Get bit by one or all daily
  Still being a combat Infantryman is the greatest feeling in the world

Butterfly Hill was a serene name for a violent place. The colorful creatures would disappear on occasion but always returned. I never saw another butterfly my whole tour.

The sleeptalking was fairly routine for those who had been in the field for awhile. Our nerves were on edge, but far from out of control. In some ways, I have never felt more alive than during those days in the company of fighting men.

At the same time, my own chances for survival continued to come to mind. On the back page of my journal I wrote a brief last will and testament. Although the Army lawyers would have done it for free, I had never gotten around to it. I did not have much to leave to anyone anyway, but my few sentences, witnessed by two NCOs from the platoon, would have to do.

One of the search groups found a large container with over twenty-five pounds of a white powder. In my attempt to identify the substance, I smelled it, and, not recognizing its scent, I wet my finger tip and brought a taste of it to my mouth. I quickly learned that it was persistent CS. This long-lasting tear gas equivalent was used to neutralize tunnels that could not be destroyed. Where the gooks had picked it up was a mystery. Crying and gagging, I lay under a tree for an hour while DeForrest poured water on my face in an attempt to wash the gunk away. My plight provided great entertainment for the weary GIs.

---

8 JULY 1969
Tuesday

"Butterfly Hill"
Raining all the time—
Have bamboo poisoning on my right leg and arm—Consists of running sores—Could get a profile but I will stay with men
The sight of the 9 dead GIs keeps coming to mind—I pray that we stay good and lucky
What I would give to see my wife and family—
Items I got in base camp:
  Anti-US literature
  I NVA E-6 Sgt rank
  I NVA canteen
  I operating mask—homemade VC
  I Chinese cleaning kit for rifle

We were rarely totally dry. When the sun broke out, I would hang an OD T-shirt on my rucksack till dry and then place it in a water-proof bag. When it got cool at night, I would put it on.

Bamboo poisoning was the result of pricks from the sharp thorns. Puss-filled sores the size of pencil erasers and about four inches apart covered one of my legs. Doc Bass washed them with hydrogen peroxide a couple of times a day. As they healed, they left small black holes.

There were many other souvenirs of the base camp I could have kept. I was not too interested because I knew I would have to carry anything I picked up.

Though the NVA and VC rarely wore rank, I found the set of sergeant's rank insignia wrapped in plastic stuck in the logs of a bunker and gave one to McGinnis, as he liked souvenirs. The operating mask found in the blood-soaked aid station was simply a handkerchief with a piece of clear plastic sewed in for vision.

We all got a kick out of the anti-US literature that told of mutinies and desertions in US units and encouraged blacks to turn on their white comrades. They served only to make us laugh; they were too small for toilet paper.

✎ 9 JULY 1969
Wednesday

"Butterfly Hill"

We got ready to be extracted to Black Horse. One bird of Engineers crashed—Didn't burn—CO later said he was going to put me in for a medal for pulling injured out, setting security, etc—Didn't really think I did that much—Only medal I want is the one for being in country 6 months

Black Horse
   One of first things I saw was Life mag. July 7, 69—Article
on Vietnam dead—Saddening—Mixed feelings on article
   Talked with CO—I could go in for permanent XO in Aug—
He said he needed me in field—I will stay in field—This is
where I am needed

The Engineers had completed preparing the LZ and helping
us blow the bunkers. Helicopters bringing in additional demolitions had back-hauled the captured weapons and supplies.
The 82mm Chinese mortars were taken back to BMB where
they sat in front of Charlie Company and the Battalion headquarters as reminders of victory—and defeat as well. I never
looked at them without seeing the nine bloated bodies with
butterflies flying above them.

Butterfly Hill had not yet taken its last GI life. The Engineer
squad overloaded their helicopter. I could tell by the sound of
the chopper on take-off that the pilots were pulling all available
power. The bird rose steadily but not fast enough. It flew
straight into the top of the trees at the end of the LZ, making
a half-left and falling to the ground on its side.

Several of us had begun running toward the chopper as soon
as we heard the rotor blades striking the trees. DeForrest and
I covered the two hundred meters to find both pilots okay.
They were feverishly shutting off all the electrical power in
hopes the escaping fuel would not catch fire.

The pilots' injuries were minor because they were strapped
in their seats. The Engineer squad and door gunners were not
so lucky. Several were unconscious. A jagged bone protruded
through the leg of another. One door gunner seemed all right
as I helped him pull his M-60 machine gun out of the wreckage.

By the time we had everyone out of the wreckage and established security, dust-offs were on the way. These birds of
mercy always responded rapidly, but never as fast as when
fellow aviators were down. Despite the efforts of the medic,
one of the Engineers died before the medivac arrived.

While we were loading the injured on the dust-off, another chopper from the downed bird's aviation company landed. The pilot must have been new in-country. When he saw the dead body and the bloody injured, he leaned out the chopper door and threw up. Despite the situation, several of the grunts could not restrain their grins at the heaving aviator.

Our return to Black Horse was delayed so we could secure the crash site. It was late afternoon when a major arrived on still another chopper. He explained that he was the crash investigation officer and that the determination about whether the crashed bird was recoverable was his decision.

The major was explaining to McGinnis that we would have to secure the bird overnight so it could be lifted out by a CH47 Chinook the next day when I noticed his Texas A & M class ring. After introducing myself, we talked briefly about the chances of the Aggies in the coming football season.

After talking about our Texas hometowns, I explained to the major what we had been through and that we all wanted to return to Black Horse.

The major made no reply as he walked back to the crash site. In a few minutes he returned, saying he had been wrong initially. The chopper was not worth salvaging. He showed me where to place a C-4 charge on the fuel tank to destroy what was left.

As I set the charge, several of my men stripped the chopper like an automobile on a dark street back home. Instruments, knobs and handles disappeared from the bird and went into first platoon rucksacks.

The chopper went up in a fireball. Nothing except the engine and transmission was even recognizable. DeForrest handed me the bird's clock as the major flew off into the distance.

Several weeks later I was questioned by the Battalion Adjutant who was working on McGinnis' recommendation that I receive a Soldier's Medal for helping after the crash. He asked, "Was the chopper burning?"

I replied, "Hell, no. What kind of fool do you think I am? You think I'd go near a burning chopper?"

He asked no more questions. It was the last I heard of any medal.

The *Life* magazine cover story on one week's dead in Vietnam filled page after page with pictures of the more than three hundred Americans killed in one week. Many of Charlie Company found pictures of friends from basic training or from their hometowns.

We cursed the media in general and *Life* in particular. We needed no reminder of death. Yet the article was effective, whatever our opinion. It is the only copy of a magazine that I kept of the war.

✈ 10 JULY 1969
Thursday

Black Horse
  Clean up & repair
  Briefings etc.
  S-3 said in briefing—"We can shoot up millions of dollars but we can't replace one man."
  Learned from CO today that he talked to LTC Mess about me for XO—Col said I was needed in field
  SSG Marple, my plat sgt, sent to another Co today—Replaced him with SGT E-5 Collier

Marple had fought bravely and was a good soldier. He did not distinguish himself as a leader, however, and was more like just one of the troops than the head NCO. In another company, he would have a new opportunity to establish himself.

Difficult decisions are what officers get paid for. Marple was a friend. We had arrived in the platoon on the same day and had been through a lot together. The move was based on what I felt was the best for the platoon rather than personal feelings. Later reports were that Marple was doing well in his new job.

🛩 11 JULY 1969
Friday

Black Horse
    Bde CG Brigadier General Bennett presented medals to men who found caches
    My men receiving Army Commendation Medals were
        SP4 Aultman
        SP4 Gancanz
        PFC DeForrest
    Easy day—Good rest

BG Warren K. Bennett had replaced BG Davidson a few weeks before. A story being told in the Brigade said much about the departing General. While visiting a unit in the field, General Davidson saw a soldier whose fatigue trousers were hanging in tatters. The General exchanged trousers with the soldier on the spot.

Days like this at Black Horse were a welcomed rest. Hot chow and a decent night's sleep were luxuries we appreciated. During the day the troops played cards, read and participated in bull sessions, mostly lies about women and booze.

A frequent disagreement was about which brand of P-38 was the best. The one-inch-long can openers, with their collapsible cutting edge, were one of the Army's most functional items. Many soldiers kept their P-38s on their dog tag chains and several old timers proudly noted that they had carried the same opener their entire tour.

P-38s were identical except for the brand name: either Shelby or Speaker was imprinted into the metal. Everyone seemed to have an opinion about which cut faster or was easier to use. In reality the two were indistinguishable. Their merits just offered something to argue about.

Personally, I preferred the Speaker brand because fewer of them were in the C-ration cases. Rarity seemed a positive characteristic to me. I exhibited no loyalty, however. I could never keep up with one of the damned little things. DeForrest knew when I reached for a can my next action would be to ask to borrow his P-38.

12 JULY 1969
Saturday

Black Horse
   Prepare for another mission
   Airmobile out by Chinook—We were first plt in as usual—Married up with tracks and headed out
   In move were informed to go aid Bravo Co in contact—Tracks couldn't go—So we moved on foot—My plt leading through thickest stuff I've seen in RVN—I had to help break point at times—By the time we got there contact was over—Tracks met back with us and we moved out—Tracks dropped us and we moved again—
   Long day—1st plt on point whole time—Covered 7 km—Moved into NDP with B & D Companies to prepare to move to cordon area

Our AO was a plain between Black Horse and Xuan Luc which was dotted by low hills. Its surface was covered by razor-sharp elephant grass about seven feet tall that contained football-field sized thickets of low trees, vines, and brambles.

We pushed as hard as possible when fellow Americans were in contact. Speed could mean lives, both US and enemy. Our route was so thick that at times the point man could mash down the vegetation only by lying on it. The next man in the file would pass by and do likewise. By the time we reached Bravo, we were fortunate the NVA had fled; we were damn near too exhausted to fight.

---

13 JULY 1969
Sunday

Thoi Giao
Moved in at 0300 this morning—Cordon of this village with rest of Bn
My plt picked up 2 suspects
Chaplain came out and had services
A man really depends on his religion here
NDP ambush type night

We moved several kilometers through rubber plantations to seal off the village. Documents captured on 3–4 July had revealed several VC agents were providing the NVA supplies from the small hamlet.

The two suspects, a young man and woman, were caught trying to sneak out of the village. A machine-gun team had almost blown them away before finding they were not armed. We handed them over to camouflaged "tiger" fatigue-clad ARVN interrogators who accented their shouted questions with slaps and kicks before they led the suspects away. If the two were not VC before the interrogation, they probably were afterward.

🦅 14 JULY 1969
Monday

Cam Tam
   Had helicopter visual recon of new AO
   After VR trucked to new location—Working with ARVNs
   This is an old French rubber town
   Had a joint ambush with ARVNs tonight
   My bamboo poisoning is getting better but getting more
boils on my arms and rear-end—Kind of funny but hard to sit
down

In the middle of the rubber plantation was Cam Tam, a village covering about a square kilometer. Laid out in precise rows, its white-washed stucco houses with red tile roofs surrounded a central square. On one side was a long, low building where the raw latex was processed, and nearby a pair of two-story villas, complete with verandas and stables, looked down on the village.

Charlie Company took up residence in abandoned houses near the processing plant. With the exception of a destroyed electrical power plant and a small Ruff Puff compound, it looked like the war had passed the village by: it looked more like a movie set than a town in the middle of a war.

The boils on my ass provided great entertainment for the rest of the platoon. Puss from the sores made the fatigue pants stick to my cheeks and Doc Bass would have to peel them down and apply hydrogen peroxide and alcohol. The filth we lived in, combined with a lack of fresh vegetables in our diet, was hard on our bodies. Doc finally was able to procure some vitamins and penicillin tablets which he thought would help.

Since this was Monday, my morning pills included the small malaria pill, the big orange pill, two of the chalky antiring-worm pills, and the penicillin and vitamin tablets. Along with coffee, they were breakfast.

I tried not to complain. It could have been worse. One of the Company CP troops had been bitten by a rat and was receiving daily shots of antirabies serum in the stomach. The serum powder, mixed with distilled water, allowed us to keep another soldier—and rifle—in the field.

✈ 15 JULY 1969
Tuesday

> Working and training with ARVNs
> In conversation today with my Kit Carson scout on why he didn't carry much ammo, Tom said, "Don't need much—Tom see leaders & shoot them."
> Tom is planning on getting married on his next pass—Last pass he was AWOL for 10 days so he will have to wait another month. CPT McGinnis and myself told him we were away from our wives for 12 months—He could wait 4 weeks

Tom's story was a good one, but not very credible. To the best of my knowledge, he never fired his weapon. Perhaps he was afraid he might kill some of his old NVA buddies. Then, again, maybe he was just afraid. The third platoon also had a Kit Carson, Chico, who had been an NVA sergeant. He had a brother who supposedly was still with the enemy in our AO.

Chico and I did not get along. On loan to us a few weeks earlier, he had not wanted to walk point. When I ordered him to, I heard him flip his M-16 off safety. Grabbing him by his web gear, I told him if he ever did such a thing again, I would kill him. Chico assured me he had taken the weapon off safety so he would be ready to quickly engage the enemy. We both knew better. Chico did not question any more orders.

🛩 16 JULY 1969
Wednesday

> Long hot RIF with ARVNs—No results
> Ambushes night
> Used mortar a little today—But very carefully—Have little
> faith in them

Mortars were good when in experienced hands. Even crews who knew what they were doing still occasionally fired a short round. The safest guideline was never to have the mortars flying directly over you.

🛩 17 JULY 1969
Thursday

> 9 km RIF today through the rubber—
> This village must have really been something 10 years ago—
> Rubber everywhere
> Several French mansions in area—One still has an old
> Frenchman with one arm living there—A hard looking SOB—
> Probably pays VC taxes—
> Got some boiled corn on cob from gooks today—Was
> wonderful

Further inspection of Cam Tam revealed that more than half of the forty houses were empty. The remaining inhabitants were women, children, and a few old men.

Occasionally the villagers loaded onto trucks to travel to various parts of the plantations. A truck carrying a large tank went along to transport the freshly tapped latex. The site manager gave us a map of where his people would be working.

The one-armed Frenchman lived in one of the mansions with his Vietnamese wife and an attractive teenage daughter. We rarely saw her, as she avoided any contact with Americans.

We were constantly warned not to eat any of the locals' food because if it was not deliberately poisoned, it would give us dysentery. I had followed the advice carefully, but after having no fresh vegetables for weeks, the corn on the cob was too tempting. I said to hell with it and ate cob after cob. The old woman with the corn was happy with the bar of soap and cans of C-rations I offered in trade.

The corn neither killed me nor made me sick. From then on I listened to my stomach rather than the warnings of some Saigon desk jockey.

✎ 18 JULY 1969
Friday

> Preparations & move out to FB Marge—Started building and rebuilding as soon as we got there
> S-2 said we would get hit tonight—As we figured we didn't
> I am amazed—I find myself very interested in baby news and looking forward to being a father.

Fire Base Marge, just to the east of Cam Tam, had been occupied and abandoned several times before. The locals hauled away nearly anything of use each time the Americans left.

Building bunkers and filling sandbags was easier than humping the boonies. The AO was quiet despite the warnings of the S-2. Boredom was our most constant companion once again.

Staff Sergeant Harry Hondo reported as my new platoon sergeant. Hondo, a small, wiry man in his mid-twenties, was on his second tour. Collier again returned to squad leader duties. Roy did not complain. Although still on his first enlistment, he was a true professional.

My assessment of approaching fatherhood was candid. I had never cared for children nor had much to do with them. Now that I was soon to be a parent and an uncle, my attitudes were changing.

I did not worry about Linda because she was quite capable of taking care of herself and more, nor did I feel any guilt for leaving her for the war. What I was doing seemed like the right thing. It still did not keep away a yearning to be with her. Boredom and fear were my two constant companions in Vietnam. Loneliness was a strong third.

---

19 JULY 1969
Saturday

Marge
   More building bunkers and laying of barb wire—
   Then back to Black Horse for 24 hours
   Got sniped at on my way back—Not too close
   My old plt sgt—SSG E-6 Flores—received Bronze Star for
Meritorious Service—Goes back to Texas soon—A good man
   Got CIBs sewed on my jungle fatigues—Feel proud to wear
it—Highest award in Army in my opinion

Marge was barely large enough for the six-piece artillery battery that arrived slung under Chinooks.

Infantry companies rotated in and out of Marge. Delta Company, with a temporary commander and many replacements, arrived to take our place when we left for Black Horse. Two of Delta's new lieutenants and I talked briefly and I found them as enthusiastic and curious as I had been what now seemed like long ago. The statement that the eager are not experienced and the experienced are not eager came to mind.

The sniping incident was another of the frustrations of Vietnam. The two rifle shots came from the same village we had cordoned the week before. Since this was a "friendly" village, we could neither return fire nor call in artillery.

As I shook Nat Flores' hand before he left, I gave him Linda's phone number in San Francisco. Word from me was always at least a week old by the time she got my letters. Nat's call to her forty-eight hours later was the most current news she had received.

20 JULY 1969
Sunday

Marge
    Trucked back to Marge
    Ambush at night

Delta went back to the jungle as Charlie took over Marge again. Battalion S-2 had provided intelligence that the area VC leader, reportedly a middle-aged woman, frequently visited Cam Tam for supplies. A younger, one-eyed man was said to be her constant companion. It sounded like a B-movie script rather than fact, but S-2 was convinced the information was correct.

Things continued to be quiet.

Bill Little and I had a long bull session about Vietnam, trying to remember the first time we had heard of this country which was now so important to us. I do not recall any mention of Vietnam in my grammar and high school geography classes. My first awareness of Nam came, appropriately, from television. In one of the weekly episodes of *Route 66* in 1963, Martin Milner and George Maharis befriended a young Green Beret soldier just back from Vietnam. The veteran talked of fighting Viet Cong. At the time I was sixteen and aware of Korea and the World Wars, but this war in Vietnam was news to me. I asked my father if Vietnam was real or just television fantasy. Little did either of us know how important a role that country would play in our lives over the next ten years—and beyond.

I do not recall much of the show's story line. Interestingly enough, I do remember that the young soldier was ridiculed by the locals in a small Route 66 town. I should have paid closer attention to the homecomings of Viet vets.

Bill and I concluded our conversation as time to move out on night ambushes arrived. I had a feeling that the night's mission would somehow be different.

🛩 **21 JULY 1969
Monday**

Marge
    This morning got word we had landed men on moon—My first thought was a big accomplishment like that and I was still lying in ambush trying to kill someone
    A few minutes later LT Jong called on radio and said astronauts were in heavy contact—Saddle up—I told him as usual 1st plt on point—Also asked him if we got travel pay
    Return to Marge

Continue to build bunkers etc
Planning future missions etc

Our ambush position, occupied just before dark the previous evening, had been well-selected. Located four klicks south of Marge, we were on the edge of the rubber plantation. The ground sloped downward across a small stream and then back up to the green-walled jungle about 350 meters to our front. A well-used trail snaked out of the rubber on our left flank, wound around a few banana trees, crossed a log footbridge, and into a cut in the jungle.

Artillery was pre-plotted on the trail. A two-foot high berm provided us protection in as perfect an ambush zone as I had seen. We remained on fifty percent alert all night. As the first sign of light appeared on the horizon, we went to one hundred percent.

It was a beautiful morning. The sky was clear except for a few low clouds turning purple and then red in the rising sun. An hour later, with no sign of the enemy, we were disappointed. Everyone had felt something was going to happen.

A few minutes after I let the men know it was all right to smoke by lighting up myself, the radio squelch broke with our call sign. I immediately recognized McGinnis' North Carolina drawl. It had to be important; usually the old man had his RTO send the company messages.

The CO's transmission about the first men on the moon seemed unbelievable. If someone had tried to make a "giant step for mankind" in our ambush kill zone, we would have blown his foot—and more—off. We realized it was an historic moment, but just where we fit into this great accomplishment, we did not have a clue.

Jong's subsequent transmission helped put it in perspective. We traded comments on the radio until both of us were giggling like children.

A few hours afterward, we were back filling sandbags and stringing wire at Marge.

Linda later sent Polaroid pictures taken directly of her TV

screen of the landing. (Today I still never hear of our first men on the moon without remembering that beautiful calm morning, lying in ambush.)

≈ **22 JULY 1969**
Tuesday

Marge
   Moved out on a long RIF and night ambush with ARVNs—
Saw a lot of signs but no gooks
   Every day that goes by I realize that Communism must be fought but the people (animals) of Vietnam are not worth one drop of American blood
   We are committed however and must do our best

      Sign in latrine at Marge:
         "Fighting for Freedom
            is like
         Fucking for Chastity"

Part of my idealism had been left behind on Butterfly Hill and in the prop wash of the many dust-offs. My journal entry five days before in reference to getting corn from the "gooks" and today's reference to "animals" aptly showed my loss of respect for Vietnamese of both sides.

Soldiers love graffiti as well as anyone. If I had had the forethought, I could have compiled an interesting book by just recording "GI scrawls on shithouse walls" that ranged from the philosophical to the obscene. *Fucking for chastity* seemed to fit both categories.

23 JULY 1969
Wednesday

Marge
   Returned from mission
   Used CS gas for first time—We use it to keep whores and kids away from fire base

Black Horse
   Got word to return to Black Horse to write statement on why SP4 Aultman had malaria
   Returned to Marge by LOH—Good recon of area

After eight months in the paddies and jungle, exposed to swarms of mosquitoes carrying virtually every type of malaria known to man, Aultman had succumbed—even though he had followed the Company SOP of daily and weekly malaria pills, rolled sleeves down at night, and liberally used insect repellent.

I noted in my statement that Aultman was one of my finest soldiers. Verbally I added to the investigators that it was not at all appropriate that I had been taken away from my platoon for over half a day to write their damned fool statements.

After a few weeks, Aultman returned from his in-country hospital stay. His records reflected that he had FUO (fever, unknown origin) rather than malaria. Someone at a higher level had evidently figured out how to keep the malaria rate down.

Vietnamese prostitutes must have had one of the best intelligence networks in Nam. We had barely arrived at Marge when a three-wheeled Lambretta arrived full of whores.

The whores set up business in one of the abandoned houses in Cam Tam. It was all right for the troops to visit them, but we tried to keep the women away from Marge. We never knew when a begging child or a soliciting hooker might be more interested in diagramming our defenses than peddling their wares. The CS tear gas did a fine job of keeping them at a distance.

My letter to Linda noted that I now had more time in the field than any other lieutenant in the Battalion except one. I also told her that I had read in *Army Times* that a friend of ours from Fort Bragg and jump school, 1LT Johnny Davis, had been killed the week before. I knew nothing of the circumstances of Davis' death. The name and rank in small agate type in the *Times* was the only obituary I saw for Davis.

The casuality page was probably the most widely read section in the paper. GIs understood why a tongue-in-cheek parting comment between friends was "see you in the *Army Times*."

---

24 JULY 1969
Thursday

> Moved out in truck convoy to pick up rest of company—After picked up Co. on way back 3rd platoon spotted 5 gooks—2 body count reported—However they were not confirmed
> MAJ Loeffke BN CO came out—My plt & he swept the area with negative results—MAJ Loeffke does everything the troops do—He takes too many chances—Does things that are not his job

McGinnis had taken the rest of the Company on a day-time RIF while my platoon had remained at Marge to secure the artillery. In the late afternoon, I led a truck convoy to the edge of the rubber plantation to pick them up.

The five gooks stepped out of the bordering jungle on our way back in. A jeep-mounted M-60 machine gun, as well as part of the 3d Platoon, engaged the fleeing enemy. I doubt if we did the enemy any damage, though the company was credited with two kills. This was the only contact that I participated in that I felt the reported body count was incorrect.

MAJ Bernard O. Loeffke had assumed command from LTC Mess a few days before. A West Pointer born in Bogota, Columbia, he looked and acted like a true professional soldier. Loeffke was on the Army promotion list to lieutenant colonel and had already been in Vietnam for over two years with the 9th Infantry Division in the Delta. Promised a battalion in the 9th, he had been transferred to the Two-thirds when it was announced that his old division would be the first to be pulled out of Nam.

Loeffke spoke passable Vietnamese and was fluent in Spanish and French. My initial impression and writings about the new Battalion Commander proved accurate. Our association over the next months was close. He worked us harder than any prior commander, but he was without a doubt the bravest individual I have ever met.

Many of us initially thought Loeffke was too agressive—the true "war lover" soldier. We later saw him as a sensitive man dedicated to doing what he thought he should. At times I was convinced he was equally as dedicated to getting me killed. Regardless, I respect him as the finest leader I have ever known.

25 JULY 1969
Friday

Marge
    Went out on a long RIF (Recon in Force)—Only spotted a baby tiger
    MAJ Loeffke came out again to go on an ambush with my

plt—Dropped from moving trucks after dark—MAJ is wild on
new things or ideas—In my opinion he's going to get killed or
get us the same
    Was informed I was going in as XO—Later informed CO
found he could keep me in the field—Guess I am doing a good
job—Have had 4 offers for other jobs—Turned them all
down—CO says he needs me

Many years before, the rich of Vietnam had hunted tigers
in this area. The half-grown cat that ran through our formation
was one of the few survivors of that previous idle pastime.
Tigers that had not been killed by the artillery and bombing
had surely migrated away from the hostile jungle. Why this
tiger had remained or been able to survive, we had no idea.
No one even raised a rifle at the cat. We would not hesitate to
kill a man, but the beauty of the small tiger's run we could
appreciate without bloodshed.

Before Vietnam I hunted regularly. I no longer do so. Since
Vietnam I buy my meat at the supermarket.

The jobs I had been offered were as XO, recon platoon
leader, and other lieutenant positions. I stayed with the first
platoon because it was where I felt needed and could do the
most good. Another strong motive for staying was that I knew
it was the fastest route to gaining a company command. Whenever possible, I watched McGinnis, observing how he ran the
company. If the time came, I would be ready.

26 JULY 1969
Saturday

Marge
    Prepared for another mission. MAJ Loeffke says he wants

me as Recon Plt Ldr—I told him my plt was better and that
I'd rather stay with Co.—CO says he will not let me go—
Time will tell

Trucked to mission—Then changed to airmobile—No
briefing—They dropped 2 plts in an area I didn't know—Didn't
even know mission—Finally CO came in after his briefing—
We had 30 minutes to search—Then airmobile out—Then
we lost choppers—Had to walk out—Made 5 km in 50 minutes—I was on point—A Ranger walk—Thoroughly a confused mission—Back to Black Horse

When the choppers picked us up we had no idea where we
were going. As usual I had my map out while in the air to
remain oriented. If the chopper went down or landed in the
wrong LZ, I would have to know the six-digit map coordinates
so artillery and other help could be called for on the radio.

Our flight was to the east. In a few minutes we had flown
over the landmarks I could recognize. Shortly we were over
an area that was off my map. Across fifty meters of open sky
I could see Bill Little in another chopper as he turned his map
in several directions. When I waved to him, he smiled,
shrugged his shoulders, and placed the now-useless map back
in his pocket.

On the ground Bill and I quickly consolidated our two platoons into a single perimeter. Our RTOs tried every push (frequency) in their code books. They got no answer. We told the
platoons to dig in. With no commo and without knowing where
we were, the best course of action was just to stay put.

A long half-hour later, McGinnis arrived with an ARVN
propaganda team and explained there were supposed to be
gooks in the area who wanted to surrender. After half an hour
of the ARVNs shouting over loudspeakers, it was obvious that
the mission was another wild goose chase.

We established commo with the Battalion S-3's C & C ship
and were informed the choppers for our extraction had been
cancelled. We saddled up and headed due west with the objective of getting back to areas covered on our maps as soon
as possible.

Days like this made me wonder why in the hell I wanted to stay in the field.

═══════════════════════════════

✈ 27 JULY 1969
Sunday

Black Horse
   Clean up etc
   Was chosen Old Guard Plt Ldr of Week
   Dined with CG Bennett tonight at General's mess—Attended Bde briefing—Certainly large scale
   MAJ Loeffke comments on my uniform before meeting General were kind of funny—Said I looked like a field troop
   Co party—Lot of hell raising
   Lt Sassner now XO

Loeffke had begun a program of sending a platoon leader to spend a brief time with the Brigade Commander. Before I left Black Horse, Loeffke called me into his office, sparsely furnished with a field desk and a cot. Rather than a friendly greeting, the Battalion CO returned my salute with an ass-chewing. He criticized my wrinkled uniform and dusty boots, saying I was in no way satisfactory for seeing the Brigade Commander.

Before I could tell him that this was the only set of jungle fatigues I owned that had rank sewed on, or that I had not seen a can of boot polish in three months, his demeanor changed. With a smile he made the quip about "field soldier." He then had his RTO iron my fatigues as I shined my boots with the polish he provided while we discussed my platoon.

Upon arrival at the Brigade compound in Xuan Luc, I went to the Tactical Operations Center (TOC). Just outside the sandbagged bunker were a major and a sergeant marking a straight line in front of the structure by using a long piece of white string. Curiosity finally got the best of me. In answer to my question about what they were doing, the sergeant said that the General wanted flowers. With military precision, they were ensuring that they would be in a straight line.

Inside the TOC, I met the Brigade S-3 and his staff. After brief talk about the 3 July battle, the S-3 took me into a room in an adjoining building. Maps of the Brigade AO filled the front wall. Colored pins and grease pencil markings noted the positions of various units and suspected enemy locations.

Directly in front of the map was an overstuffed leather chair. Thirty metal folding chairs occupied the floor and an equal number of the Brigade staff were milling around.

We were called to attention at the General's entry and after Bennett sat in the easy chair, the rest of us found our seats.

A major and a captain, dressed in sharply creased uniforms and spit-shined boots, briefed Huntley-Brinkley style for the next hour covering the activities of the day and future operations. I noticed several of the staff wrote letters while another read a book. No one except the general and S-3 paid much attention.

When the briefing concluded, a lieutenant who was the General's aide directed me to the General's mess. He was nervous and preoccupied. Thinking there must be a fire fight going on in the Brigade AO, I asked him what was going on. He explained that the General had been wanting blue cheese dressing and that he had tried all over Vietnam to locate some with no success.

In the dining room I met the General, who was surprisingly polite. His knowledge about my platoon and Charlie Company was so vast that despite the surroundings, I found him likable and obviously a strong leader.

I was glad to return to Black Horse. Loeffke and McGinnis asked about the visit over a bottle of bourbon. After a few drinks, I mentioned flower beds, easy chairs and blue cheese dressing. Their laughter let me know they, too, had visited Brigade.

✈ 28 JULY 1969
Monday

Black Horse
    Ambush classes
    Prepare to move out
    NDP in rubber plantation

> "I cry warning
>   Night is falling
>   Sleep not, least there be
>   No dawning."
>
>   Pat Frank
> HOLD BACK THE NIGHT

Everyone resented the new Battalion policy of having classes during our brief time at Black Horse, although they were good for breaking in replacements.

Linda and I had earlier discussed in letters that the best time for our R&R reunion in Hawaii would be a month or so after the baby was born. I decided this was too long to wait. The Battalion had received a number of R&R allocations for October. My letter to Linda asked her to check with her doctor about the latest date he would allow her to travel.

My reason for the R&R date change was twofold. First, of course, I wanted to see my wife. Second, now that I was remaining in the field, I was aware I might not live until January.

🖎 29 JULY 1969
Tuesday

> Trucked to Long Binh-Bien Hoa area—Secure these areas from rocket attack
>
> Later learned we were in that area to secure for landing of President Nixon

> "When the enemy advances, we retreat. When he escapes, we harass. When he retreats, we pursue. When he is tired, we attack."
>
> Mao-Tse-Tung

Most of our AO west of the Long Binh complex had been worked by large bulldozers while other parts had trees still standing but completely without foliage. Airplanes spraying defoliants had turned the landscape from green to brown. (It would be well over a decade later before I heard the term Agent Orange. Even if we had known of its alleged cancer-causing effects, I doubt if we would have been very concerned. Our interest was in short-term survival rather than in long-range health.)

We found no sign of enemy activity, either present or past. Until we learned that President Nixon was landing at Bien Hoa, the mission made no sense at all.

Nixon's visit was the source of more rumors about an end to US involvement. It had already been announced that the 9th Infantry Division and the 3rd Brigade 82d Airborne would be pulled out. The most popular conjecture was that the 199th would be next.

30 JULY 1969
Wednesday

Long Binh-Bien Hoa
    Continue air base security
    Only contact was with a deer—Negative results

> "Guerrillas should be as cautious as virgins and as quick as rabbits."
>
> Mao Tse-Tung

The small red deer was the only sign of life in the AO. I suppose our security plan for the President's visit worked; no rockets nor mortars endangererd his stay.

Our resupply contained a surprise passenger. SP4 Jerry Woody, wounded in the May booby trap incident, returned to the Company. I was delighted to see my old RTO. The last I had heard from Woody had been a brief letter from an evac hospital in Long Binh stating that he was going to Japan and hopefully on home to recover from his leg injuries. Woody had added a postscript that now seemed most appropriate. He had said, "I hope to be sent home, but with my luck I will probably see you all again in the boonies."

As I introduced Woody to half of the platoon who had arrived since his departure, he told me about his last couple of months. He admitted it had been "easy duty" at the convalescent center in Japan. He concluded with an ironic laugh that his plane load of recovered from Japan would be the last. According to new directives, all soldiers injured seriously enough to be evacuated to Japan would now be returned to the US.

Jerry did not complain about being back in the war. All he asked was to get back his old job of carrying my radio. After a brief talk with McGinnis we decided Woody should now be one of the two men to carry radios for the Company Commander.

The quotes from Mao came from several books I had been reading on communism. I thought if I was willing to fight something, I should at least know about it.

✒ **31 JULY 1969**
Thursday

Camp Frenzell-Jones
    Went to BMB for a few hours for pay, resupply, cleanup etc
    Trucked then walked—Night ambush—Received light fire—Nothing close—Never figured if we were sighted or source of fire
    Made plans for 4th time to go up hill in that area—Mission was changed—We now call that mission Mission Impossible or Mission Improbable

Our night platoon ambush position was near the village we had received sniper fire from a few days before. A hard rain began shortly before midnight. The downpour soon had the ground covered several inches in water.

The rain finally stopped about 0200. A few minutes later several bursts of automatic rifle fire cracked through the trees just above our heads. Familiar green tracers came from the general direction of the village, but we could not see their exact point of origin.

We did not return fire since we could not identify a target. I thought that if the enemy knew our general location, the probing fire might be an attempt to pinpoint our position by our own muzzle flashes. We spent another restless night.

🛩 **I AUGUST 1969**
Friday

Marge
  Walked to Marge
  No one has been here since we left—Of course, as usual
C Co had to rebuild

> "A man's greatest joy in life is to break his ene-
> mies, and to take from them all the things that
> have been theirs."
>
> Genghis Khan

It was frustrating to see much of our previous work at Marge
now in ruins. The entire Brigade, including the artillery, had
been pulled out to secure the President's visit. During our
absence most of our building materials had been carted off by
the locals.

🛩 **2 AUGUST 1969**
Saturday

Marge
  Continue day & night ambushes—I do most of ambush planning for entire Co now—
  2nd plt OPCONed to 11th Cav

> "He had decided to live forever or die in the attempt."
>
> Yossarian in CATCH 22
> Joseph Heller

McGinnis and I sat down daily and went over our maps to select the best ambush positions. There was never any doubt about who was in command of the Company. McGinnis made the decisions. Still, I greatly appreciated his ability to take recommendations and to rely on my experience.

Letters to Linda continued to discuss R&R in October. I also wrote that when I got home there should be little trouble getting up at night to help with the baby. I had not slept over two hours at a time in months.

---

3 AUGUST 1969
Sunday

Marge
    Continue day & night ambushes
    Co got 12 replacements today—I got one of them, PFC Morford from California
    Co got new 3rd plt ldr in today—2LT Harold Steward—OCS from Illinois
    Took a light observation helicopter visual recon of next area we are going to—approx. 30 minutes
    Sign on gook cig lighter for sale to GIs:

    "When I die bury me face down so the world can kiss my ass."

Our AO, as well as the rest of the Battalion's, was quiet. Intelligence said the enemy was there, but we put limited faith in these reports. Except for the occasional CIA-supported Project Phoenix analysis of the NVA and VC, we paid little attention to other opinions on the enemy locations. Our best information on the gooks was what we found ourselves.

LT Sassner was now the Company XO. He or Top would bring a supply convoy into Marge about once a week with clean uniforms. Except for US Army cloth tapes above the left pocket and a 199th patch on the left shoulder, they were void of adornments.

I could usually tell when we were due a change of uniforms by looking at DeForrest's fatigues. Like most RTOs he wrote incoming codes and grid coordinates on the green cotton cloth of his trousers with a ballpoint pen because dry paper was hard to find and difficult to manage even when not holding a radio hand set. When the thighs of Roger's pants were so filled with numbers and letters that there was no space remaining, it was time.

The twelve replacements brought the Company strength up to over 110. 2LT Steward, who took Sassner's old platoon leader job, made a good first impression. Although the same age as myself, he seemed extremely young and naive. Four months in Vietnam aged one's mind as well as body.

PFC Larry Morford was an unusual soldier. Muscular and medium height, he readily looked like the gymnast he had been in high school. Before being drafted, he had been a member of a professional dance troupe. He showed us pictures of himself in top hat and tails with a cane dancing onstage in Los Angeles and Las Vegas revues.

Morford's obvious pride in his dance profession, as well as his bulging physique, prevented any harassment about his non-soldierly past. We recognized that his agility and quick reactions would be assets for a point man. Over the next months the California dancer would become one of my best soldiers.

✈ 4 AUGUST 1969
Monday

Marge

Today CO, myself and a few troops took a look at the French mansions in the village—None occupied but one—All very nice

Night—Visited and ate supper with the one-armed old Frenchman whose nice home is next to Marge—A very interesting evening—He served wine, soup and C-rations which we supplied—Felt funny to see a tablecloth, dishes etc

Frenchman showed us his military record—From 1938 to 1949 he was in nearly every action the French were—Also highly decorated—As of now he is married to a VN—Has a very good-looking daughter—Only saw her when she served table—Old man is truly very lonesome—Seems to be a man without a country—Wish we could have communicated with him better—Am sure he pays VC taxes—Still good time

Windows and doors of the largest vacant villa in the village were boarded up. We broke in on the pretext of looking for enemy supplies. Our real reasons were curiosity and just a desire to have something to do.

The mansion was dark and musty. Our footsteps echoed on the parquet floors of the empty rooms. It felt strange to be in a real house after living in holes in the ground. By the time we started up the ornate spiral staircase, we were feeling more spooked than adventuresome.

At the top of the landing, we heard a rustling noise behind a door. McGinnis took a hand grenade from his web gear. I flipped my M-16 safety to full automatic and kicked the door open, diving in, ready to fire. I realized I was in a bathroom at the same time I saw a shadowy figure on the far wall. Just before I squeezed the trigger, my eyes focused and details of the figure became clearer. A smiling Donald Duck decal, complete with blue-billed cap stared back at me. I had damned near blown away a Disney character.

A rat scurried from the room, making more of the rustling noise. McGinnis laughed as he removed his finger from the pin and returned the grenade to its carrying place.

That night at dinner with the Frenchman we made no mention of our afternoon visit to the other mansion. He said nothing about our radios and weapons leaned against his dining room wall. Neither did he acknowledge our RTOs on guard just outside his front porch.

We could understand little of our host's conversation, although his pride in his military service was obvious. McGinnis could speak a little Vietnamese and, as best as he could understand, the old man claimed he had lost his arm in an accident and not in battle. He had come to the rubber plantation in the early 50s. His first home had been a wagon with a wooden top that still stood in his yard. When the French owners departed, he had moved up from a minor worker to caretaker. We figured the Michelin Rubber Company must be paying high taxes to the VC for the mansion and the old soldier's safety.

It was an exotic evening. Fine French wine served in bright crystal and C-rations eaten with real silverware made even our daily fare taste good. A pet mongoose eyed us from under a side table.

I do not think I ever met a man more lonely than our host.

✍ 5 AUGUST 1969
Tuesday

Marge
    Had a 2 plt airmobile—On a wild goose chase—Neg re-

sults—In AM on way back forced down by weather at Black
Horse—Finally back to Marge—Met Delta Co there—Found
out C Co was moving out to new AO tomorrow
    Night—About dark Delta ambushes moved out—About
15 minutes later we heard a loud explosion—Delta ambush
had hit a mine—CPT McGinnis and I went and helped—I KIA
4 WIA—KIA throat cut—2LT in charge hit very bad in legs—
LT had been in country less than a month—Married—Wife
expecting—Believe he will make it—I am tired of seeing death
& blood—The smell of blood is something hard to forget—
Especially in these circumstances

Lack of results from our airmobile and other operations were
beginning to convince me that the rumors of the enemy's no
longer being in our area were true. Some of the Intelligence
officers were saying the NVA had pulled back into War Zone
D or even all the way back to Cambodia to regroup for an
offensive when the dry season returned.

Delta Company dropped their heavier equipment at Marge
before moving out on night platoon-size ambush. They were
to take over responsibility for Marge the next morning.

Several of the old-timers in Delta stopped by my bunker to
bullshit before they left for their NDPs. They reported that
some of their buddies who had been through the fights of the
last few months had finally found their way out of the field.
Their method was to re-enlist for six more years. With these
extensions of their service commitments, they were allowed
to change MOSs from Infantry to Supply Clerk, or Mechanic,
or whatever. They now had safe, secure jobs back in Long
Binh and Saigon. It seemed like a hell of a way to get out of
combat. Still, a six-year extension sounded better than the fi-
nality of death which seemed the Infantryman's fate in Delta
Company.

One of the Delta platoons stayed back for several hours after
the rest of the company departed because their NDP was
nearby. I had talked with the eager new platoon leader a few
weeks before when most of our conversation centered around

our both having pregnant wives back home. His was supposed to deliver a month after Linda. We exchanged updates.

McGinnis, Steward, and I were in the CP bunker when we heard the dull explosion a half a klick from the fire base. The black cloud of smoke rising in the rubber trees was accompanied by screams of the wounded. McGinnis told Stew to crank up a medivac as he, Doc Bass, and I ran toward the Delta platoon.

We were at the scene in a few minutes. The platoon sergeant was trying to get security set up as his RTO was making reports on the radio. Blood was still pumping in bright red jets from the cut jugular of one soldier. His buddy was trying with both hands to stop the blood flow. It ceased only when the heart had pumped all the liquid from the body. McGinnis and I walked past the body to the other wounded.

The platoon leader I had been talking to only a few minutes before was clutching at what was left of his legs. A medic was trying to tighten a tourniquet on the limb that was hit the worst, but when he tightened the cord, the lieutenant screamed. The young medic released the pressure with each outburst. McGinnis grabbed the tourniquet while I held the man to the ground. Placing his foot on the bloody thigh for leverage, McGinnis added pressure on the tourniquet until the blood flow mostly stopped.

Taking a tube of morphine from the medic, I place a needle on the tip of the syrette. It was difficult to find a piece of skin not already punctured by shrapnel. As I pushed the needle in, the officer grimaced in pain. I could not believe with all the holes already in him that he could feel the small needle. Seconds after I rolled the tube downward, forcing the morphine into him, he relaxed.

As I marked an M in blood on his forehead so the medivac would know he had already had morphine, he began to talk. He inquired about his men, followed immediately by asking if his balls were all right. We were cutting his trousers away at the time, so I checked. I told him his balls were okay but I did not tell him that he would obviously lose one leg if not both. He continued to talk as I cradled him in my arms while keeping pressure on the tourniquet.

Darkness and low clouds slowed the dust-off's descent into the yard of an abandoned church at the edge of Cam Tam. The medivac must have had a busy day; its floor was covered with blood. We added more when we put the wounded and the poncho-wrapped corpse on board.

As the bird lifted off, McGinnis and I walked back with the Delta platoon sergeant to the blast area. The sergeant said the platoon leader had been helping the soldier who was killed to cross a shallow ditch when the explosion occurred. He thought it was a booby trap or maybe an old French mine. I could find no evidence of a trip wire or any indication of a mine field. The lieutenant's web gear was lying nearby. One of the grenades usually carried on the upper strap was missing. Had the dead soldier slipped and somehow pulled the grenade loose? We reported that it must have been a pressure booby trap or an old mine and took the rest of the platoon back to Marge.

The Artillery battery had a large water trailer near its fire direction center. Their head NCO, called the "chief of smoke" for good reasons, always raised hell when the water meant for drinking was used for washing. As I crouched under one of the trailer spigots, he ran over, hollering and asking what the hell I was doing. When he saw the blood that covered me from neck to boots, he mumbled he was sorry and left.

My wrist compass was so caked in blood that it no longer worked. Blood does not wash off easily. The smell seems never to go away.

6 AUGUST 1969
Wednesday

Marge
    RIFed out of Marge—Took a sqd about 500 m in front of
the Co.—Ran into one hot trail—Checked it out—Neg results
    Set NDP in a VC base camp—2 wks old—Not com-
pleted—No one home—Glad there wasn't as we were in the
middle of it before we detected it
    I always walk in the first 5 men—Sometimes even point—
I feel that this is the only way to properly ensure we get to
the right place—Also this is the best point from which to
control the plt in contact

I had become convinced that an entire company simply could
not move quietly enough through the thick vegetation to surprise the enemy. A small group could be much more successful. If we did find anything, the company trailing behind could
quickly reinforce us. I would soon learn the merits and hazards
of the technique.

I took a recon group of eight and headed north out of Cam
Tam. After a few klicks of rubber trees, we were in the jungle.
DeForrest made frequent checks with the CO's RTO to be sure
they were able to follow our path.

This was our first operation without LT Jong as the Company FO. After six months with Charlie, he had returned to
his artillery battery as an XO. No replacement had yet arrived
so the artillery sergeant was acting as the FO. Don's ability to
put steel on the target, as well as his friendship, would be
missed.

Fresh trails showed recent enemy activity; however, except
for leeches, no contact was made. When we halted for a break,
I found one of the bloodgorged creatures on my back. I
squeezed my blood from his body as thoughts of all the blood
the day before came to mind.

My confidence was somewhat shaken by our walking into the abandoned bunkers. Ten of the fortifications had been dug out but not yet covered with logs and dirt. Work appeared to have ceased about a week before. A well-beaten path led to the southwest.

I decided the half-completed bunkers were a good location for the NDP. McGinnis, with the rest of the Company, caught up a few minutes later. He agreed with my recommendation that we change our route the next morning to follow the trail and to let me continue the point with my recon squad.

🐊 7 AUGUST 1969
Thursday

Moved out, first plt still on point—went approx 800 m— Found another trial—100 m later SGT Ito on point, me second, heard more gook voices to our front—Informed CO and went on line as we thought gooks were coming toward us—At this time thought we had 4 or 5 on a trail—Tried to get arty and couldn't—Finally got word to open up—Terrain very thick— We opened up—Quite a surprise—We started receiving much more fire than we were putting out—Also heard gooks screaming as if shot—Then commands—We started taking fire from both flanks—Called CO for help—Rest of Co. also pinned down by fire and terrain—We continued firing till nearly out of ammo (approx 15 min)—Gave word to pull back—Just as we did RPG hit out position—Somehow Thank God no casualties—SGT Ito and myself covered withdrawal—Worst fire fight I've seen— Then called in Air, arty, gunships, etc

After strikes went back in—1st leading—Found many bunkers, clothing, food, ammo etc—We got credit for 3 body count—Echo Co. reinforced by blocking got 5 body count—Later learned air & arty possibly got 30–40 VC— Delta also maneuvered to help

The recon element was composed of myself, Deforrest, and six men of SGT Elroy Ito's squad. Ito, a Hawaiian of Japanese ancestry was a short, stocky soldier the same age as I. A man of few words, Ito had only been in the platoon a month but had demonstrated that he was a man who could be relied upon.

Our ability to move quietly was aided by the sounds of raindrops on the trees. I stopped our advance when SP4 Ben Estep, carrying the M-60, became entangled in some vegetation. In his attempt to free himself from "wait a minute" vines, he made more noise than necessary. Estep, at five-feet-six-inches tall, was the shortest soldier in the platoon. He was strongly built, however, and had been carrying the machine gun for several months. Ben was a fine soldier. As I motioned for him to be quiet with a finger to my lips, he nodded and glanced downward, acknowledging his mistake.

We were about to move again when Ito cupped his hand to his ear. We froze. Seconds later I also heard the dim sing-songy, chirpy sounds of Vietnamese. I could not pinpoint the sounds but estimated them not to be more than two hundred meters away. On the radio I whispered a report to the CO. We briefly discussed artillery but decided that the heavy clouds just above the trees would prevent our seeing a marking round.

Over the next hour we crept forward, covering a hundred meters. The voices slowly got louder. My assessment to McGinnis was that there were only four or five enemy and that possibly they were taking a break. I told the CO that we would get as close as we could and zap them. Another half an hour of crawling and we could see movement twenty-five meters away.

We were on a small rise no more than a meter higher than our prey. When everyone was in position, I nodded and squeezed the trigger on full automatic. By the time my first bullet left the muzzle, the entire group had opened up in one big roar.

After two magazines, I stopped shooting. On my hand signal the rest also ceased firing. Amid the screams of pain to our front, suddenly a very calm voice started shouting what were obviously orders in Vietnamese. The jungle exploded on three sides with far more fire power than we had been delivering. I did not need to give any orders to return fire.

The enemy fire was so heavy that tree limbs began to fall on us. Our only protection was the slight rise that seemed to be causing the zinging bullets to go slightly over our heads.

I frequently fired with one hand while holding the radio handset with the other, shouting to McGinnis about what was happening. The enemy was so near that the artillery now firing was doing little good. With every call, I dropped it fifty meters closer until it was nearly on top of us.

McGinnis and the Company were only four hundred meters away. However, he told me on the horn that they were pinned down by the bullets which were going over our heads.

Gunships were in route, and Loeffke had diverted Delta Company, already in flight on an airmobile operation, to an LZ three klicks away. The Battalion recon platoon was moving into a blocking position to try to get any escaping enemy.

On the radio I told McGinnis that I did not think the enemy had any plans of going anywhere. The CO's response was lost as the radio, propped in front of DeForrest, took a hit. We were now without commo.

I had been firing less than the other men, but, still, I was on my last bandoleer of magazines.

Something hit me in the back, nearly knocking the wind from my lungs. At first I thought I was wounded but then discovered the 100-round belt of M-60 ammo that had been thrown to Estep just to my right. Estep alternated between firing and pouring oil on his now red-hot barrel to cool the metal. He had already fired a thousand rounds in less than a quarter of an hour. As he reached for the belt, Estep shouted that this was the last one.

I had no time for any great decision making process. As our fire diminished, the gooks' increased. It became obvious that they were maneuvering to surround us. My estimate now was that the eight of us were fighting seventy-five to one hundred of them.

No one at Fort Benning had taught me what to do when I ran out of ammo. The idea that commo would be lost at the same time was a never-discussed possibility. Fixing bayonets was an option but not a realistic course of action because the gooks evidently still had plenty of ammo.

Ben Estep suddenly hollered at me. Through the battle sounds and the now painful ringing in my ears, all I could understand was, "Why in the hell don't we run?"

I damned near smiled. Estep was a better tactician than I. I crawled over to SGT Ito and told him to send his men in pairs two hundred meters to our rear, and for them to find a concealed position where they could wait for the rest of us.

Estep's machine gun was now out of ammo. He calmly took the base section apart. By taking the critical butt part with him, he could ensure that the gun would be useless to the enemy.

As the groups of two readied themselves to crawl to the rear, they threw any remaining magazines of ammo to SGT Ito and me. They also left us their frag and smoke grenades.

After a few meters of crawling, they sprang to their feet and ran, breaking through the thick foliage. As one pair got out of sight, the next pair followed. DeForrest was in the last group. He handed me a magazine as he patted me on the shoulder.

At least fifty gooks were still firing wildly in our direction. For twenty minutes, the roar had not ceased nor let up.

Ito and I were down to our last magazines when we both pulled pins on several smoke grenades. As soon as the green, yellow and purple smoke surrounded us, we threw a few frag grenades. We had just begun our run when three RPG rounds whistled in behind us, nearly blowing us back to the ground. We did not slow down. Every few steps we tossed more grenades over our shoulders until they, too, were gone.

Fifty or so meters into our sprint, the firing behind us began to diminish. Another hundred meters and it ceased. My hope now was that the enemy, too, was running—in a different direction from us.

The trail the other six men had left was fairly easy to follow. As Ito and I neared a large, fallen, vine-covered tree, De-

Forrest stuck his head out of the greenery and waved. We nestled into the thick vegetation with the other men. A couple of them were bandaging cuts received from bamboo in their flight. Another was applying rifle oil to his hand, blistered from clutching a hot gun barrel. Except for one man with minor shrapnel wounds in the arm, no one was injured.

Ito began to count M-16 bullets and redistribute the brass cartridges equally. There were only eight or nine per man. Estep had no weapon at all. DeForrest looked strange without his radio.

Our predicament was far from over. We had withdrawn at a right angle to the original route of march and I was unsure of the Company's location. If they heard us moving through the jungle now, they might shoot first and ask questions later.

It had been nearly an hour since our last radio contact. The artillery had stopped with our loss of commo. When and where it would start again, I did not know. I instructed the men to stay hidden. Surely McGinnis would have patrols out looking for us now that the firing had stopped.

A long ten minutes later, we heard movement in the jungle. The only sound from our hide-away was deep breathing and the clicks of M-16s being taken off safety.

Through the matted vegetation a figure slowly emerged. I felt like shouting. Instead, as calmly as possible, I said, "Sergeant Breeckner, it's us. Please don't shoot."

Breeckner hit the dirt as he brought his M-16 around in my direction. I slowly stood up from my hiding place. A grin broke over Breeckner's face as he said, "Hello, One-six. How are you doing?"

I wanted to hug him. Instead, I answered, "Fuck you, give me some ammo."

SGT Greggory Breeckner was a squad leader in the third platoon. Nearing ten months in the field, he was as good as they came. He and his squad had volunteered to look for us. Greg said he figured if we were alive, we would head in the only direction from which the enemy had not been shooting.

After splitting his squad's ammo with us, he led us back to the Company.

Even though Breeckner's RTO had radioed the Company that we were all right, the soldiers in McGinnis' perimeter stared at us as if we had returned from the dead.

When I approached the CO, he smiled and said, "Welcome back."

My response was quick and angry. "Where in the hell were you? Why didn't you come to help?"

A hurt look came to his eyes. He pointed to the bullet pocked trees around him and responded, "We tried. We couldn't."

No one overheard our exchange. I said, "Okay." We never discussed it again.

Many choppers were circling our area while the Company RTOs kept continuous smoke out to mark our position. Cobra gunships had started working the contact area as soon as we had returned to the perimeter. The clouds had lifted enough for fairly good observation.

A slick hovered over a nearby bomb crater as crates of ammo and grenades were kicked out. After the last crate hit the ground, the chopper hovered to about twelve feet above the brush. A lone figure jumped to the ground. As he walked over to me, I recognized Don Jong—even in his rear-area clean fatigues. Don smiled and said, "I heard you were dead." With no further comment, he went to the FO radio and began to coordinate the artillery's alternating fire with the gunships'.

Another fire fight erupted a few klicks to our south. It was over in minutes. The radio soon squelched with a report from the Battalion recon platoon that they had killed five. They said the dinks were running so hard that they had had no security out and never knew what hit them.

A few minutes later we headed back into the contact area taking the route via our previous hiding position. When we reached the rise on which we had made our stand, I saw part of my rucksack hanging in a tree. My poncho liner was filled with holes. I retrieved it anyway.

Thirty minutes later, after reconning by fire, we moved in

to find bunkers. The area into which we had initially fired was covered in blood. Although no bodies were present, we later claimed a three-body count. No one argued.

The enemy had indeed fled. We began our search of the complex as a radio message said Delta Company was nearing our position. After shouts of recognition, we linked up.

Delta was exhausted. They had been moving toward us for the last two hours. Their sweat-soaked uniforms showed they had come to help with all due speed. Near the head of the column was CPT Jim Lewis. When he saw me, he said, "What the hell are you doing here? You're supposed to be dead."

I laughed as I replied, "I thought you were dead a month ago."

Lewis said he had rejoined Delta the day before. Except for a scarred lip, he did not look much different.

Later, the events of 7 August would be used throughout the Brigade as an example of piling on the enemy once he had been located. Loeffke had orchestrated the Battalion like a master.

The official reports were brief and in the usual Army language. Intelligence Summary 219–69 from the Battalion headquarters, classified Confidential until twelve years after the battle, simply stated:

070920 Vic YT36024 Co C eng unk size en force with org wpns. TAC Air, HKT and ARTY in spt. En rtn fire with SA/AW and RPG. Results: 3 en KIA (BC), 1 US WIA, 20 bunkers 8X8X6' w/2 OHC, 2X60mm mortar rds, 5 CC gren and 100 lbs rice dest. D/O was completed to 93rd Evac at 1830 hrs.

As for me and the seven others, the day was a little more remarkable. Since that time, I have done little to commemorate my 18 September birthday. August 7 has been a date celebrated as a new beginning.

🪶 **8 AUGUST 1969**
Friday

> CG Bennett came out today and pinned a Bronze Star with
> "V" device on me—I feel proud—But also very fortunate—
> God was certainly with us
> ABC News was also on LZ taking pictures—
> Everybody still a little shaky
> CG says the way we handled this contact was classic—That
> it will be used as an example to the other units

Ito's squad and I were lined up in the center of a clearing
we had moved to the evening before. Four Cobras orbited
overhead to add to the security.

General Bennett was accompanied by the ABC News crew.
The Brigade Public Information Officer seemed quite concerned that the circling gunships not be included in the background of any film footage.

I do not recall nor did I record any of the CG's comments
as he shook my hand. I felt proud, but the good feeling of just
being alive was my overwhelming reaction. I did not feel brave
or heroic. I had made a mistake in not detecting the bunker
complex and in my inaccurate estimate of the enemy strength.
We had fought well. However, we had fought for our lives
rather than for any other motive.

After the General pinned the medal on my chest, I glanced
down at it. The bronze star, suspended from its bright red,
white and blue striped ribbon, looked unbelievingly clean
against my torn, filthy fatigue shirt.

Everything seemed even more intense for the next few days.
Food tasted better. The air smelled cleaner. Each cigarette was
as satisfying as the one I lit shortly after SGT Breeckner found
us in the jungle. Except for the dull, painful ringing in my
ears, I felt wonderfully alive.

I made no journal entries until several days later when I sat down to re-create the events. I need not have worried. They are as vivid today as they were then.

➤ 9 AUGUST 1969
Saturday

> Moved on to rubber and jungle—Nothing during day
>
> Night ambush—Much movement—Either a gook or a large animal almost ran through our ambush position—Everybody still shaky but we definitely heard something
>
> Things finally got quieted down about midnight—At this time SP4 Clayton on my other sqd ambush cracked up—Started screaming—Completely out of his head—I could hear him at my position 500 m away—I phoned sqd ldr and had him tie and gag the man
>
> Clayton all right next morning—Dusted him off anyway
>
> We need a break
>
> Have been finding much evidence of elephants in this area

My comments of "Nothing during day" was far from accurate. I had made another mistake. My error was so bad that I did not want the story recorded in my journal.

First Platoon was securing the Company CP in the rubber plantation while the other platoons were conducting cloverleafs looking for fresh trails. McGinnis, Jong, and I were brewing coffee when Ito whispered over the radio that he could see movement from his observation post. Running and crawling, I was by his side in seconds.

Just beyond an old elevated roadway, and beneath the trees four hundred meters away, I could see figures slowly walking from our right to left. With no hesitation, I sighted on the lead man and opened fire. Ito and his squad followed in an instant.

We had only fired a few rounds when shouts of "Check fire! Check fire!" rang out from McGinnis and several RTOs.

Their order for us to stop shooting was based on a screaming call by the fourth platoon leader, Sergeant First Class Joe Bender. Bender had somehow gotten turned around on his cloverleaf and was several thousand meters out of his sector.

After Bender's location was confirmed by popping smoke, I walked over to him. The NCO and his men were still flat on the ground behind the roadway. From his position I could tell that Bender himself had been my target. All I could do was to say that I was sorry. Bender's glare softened to a smile as he said, "Sir, I'm glad you are a piss poor shot—and I wish I was a better map reader."

When I returned to the CP, McGinnis handed me his cup of coffee and said, "Lee, you can't kill them all."

Nothing else was said except Bender frequently introduced me to new arrivals with a warning, "Watch this guy. He'll try to kill you."

By dark a light rain was falling. The canopy of rubber trees, combined with the low clouds, made it so dark that our star-lite scopes were useless. Even with the ringing still in my ears, I could distinguish the sounds of something approaching our position. I was about to order a Claymore fired in the direction of the noise when something—or somebody—suddenly ran past us. DeForrest said perhaps it was a ghost of some gook coming back to haunt us. The night was endless.

Clayton was calm when I saw him the next morning. He could not recall anything beyond going to sleep. Waking up hours later tied and gagged, he had no idea what had happened. He repeated apologies to everyone, as he fully realized the danger he had placed the entire squad in. Clay went back in for various medical checks, including a visit to a shrink. He returned a few days later and went back to doing his job with no problems.

🚁 **10 AUGUST 1969**
Sunday

> Decorations on LZ on 8 Aug for action on 7 Aug:
>   Bronze Star "V"
>   CPT McGinnis
>   LT Lanning
>   SGT Ito
>   Army Commendation "V"
>   SP4 Estep
>   SP4 DeForrest
>   SP4 Pecorard
>   SP4 Drenth
>   SP4 Clayton
>   PFC Morford—four days in the field
> I am damned proud of my men
> I now have one of the most decorated plts in 199th LIB

I was not sure why McGinnis received his medal. I still
thought that he could have done more to help us on the 7th. I
did not doubt his courage, however, because he had always
done what was right for the Company. If the award was not
deserved for this particular action, he earned it on many other
days.

PFC Morford was no longer a FNG. He had been on the
far right flank when we made our stand and his calm actions
were those of a veteran. Morford was soon volunteering to
walk point. The young dancer was an unlikely hero, but he
would repeatedly perform acts of bravery over the next months.

11 AUGUST 1969
Monday

> Co NDP—1st plt getting it a little easier now—Not like on the 9th when my plt nearly blew the 4th away—They were in wrong place
> Night ambush tonight
> Any time someone starts complaining, someone else will tell him, "It's a hardship tour."
> About got my ringworm cleared up—Got another boil on my jaw—No sweat
> On 8 Aug dusted off SP4 Hines—Learned today he has hepatitis

Matter-of-factly, I had finally made mention in my journal about the incident with the fourth platoon. My justification of their being in the wrong place had placated my thoughts about being too quick on the trigger. Although happy I had missed, I still could not understand how I had failed to drop Bender. Even at four hundred meters, I should have hit him.

When SP4 Hines was medivaced, we thought he had malaria. Hepatitis was an illness we had not seen before. Every day the dangers of the jungle seemed to increase. The only dangers that went away were the ones we killed.

Hines, like many others we put on dust-offs, eventually returned to the platoon. For the grunts, the field was always there. You could leave for awhile but the meat-grinder boonies were always waiting for your return.

My letters to Linda answered her recent concerns that she might not be too appealing in her advanced stages of pregnancy by R&R in October. I wrote that she would look beautiful. The one who would look bad would be me with my boils and the loss of over twenty pounds.

✒ 12 AUGUST 1969
Tuesday

> Walked out to Highway 1 to be trucked back to Black Horse—Many civilians trying to trade MPC for anything—It is evident it is change day for currency
>
> When back at Black Horse all our money was taken up—Be replaced with new currency tomorrow—So first day and night at BH in 2½ weeks and we have no money
>
> Attended Bn briefing
>
> Lot of people on sick call

Every six months to a year, "funny money" certificates were replaced by currency of different design and color. Only authorized personnel were allowed to exchange the old for the new, leaving many of the Vietnamese stuck with stacks of the now-valueless paper.

We attempted to keep the civilians away from the Company as we waited for trucks. I learned later that one of my soldiers did manage to trade his wrist watch for a few minutes' liaison behind a rubber tree with a moped-riding prostitute. He seemed quite proud that he had received favors and "funny money" for his cheap time piece.

Top, as usual, had planned ahead, securing a trailer-load of beer before the PX and other facilities closed their doors for the 48-hour exchange period.

When our new MPC was finally issued, it pictured B-52 bombers, Infantrymen, and tanks. Even our money had gone to war.

Most of the sick calls were for ringworm and colds. We had not gone a day for over two months without being wet. The constant damp, combined with sleeping on the bare ground, caused almost everyone to have respiratory problems.

✈ 13 AUGUST 1969
Wednesday

Black Horse

PFC Johnson today told Bn CO that C Co had been in no contact on 7 Aug—Trying to get a psycho out of field—Plt found out about it—Found Johnson in shower hooch tonight—Broke nose and jaw—Men said they guessed he slipped—These men are proud of their plt—Also found pot in Johnson's possession—So this ends any problems with Johnson I am sure—Was up late talking with MPs—First problem with pot I've had—Will bring the max on the man

Bn briefing tonight—Bn CO & S-3 talked to me & CO about new techniques—Many of my suggestions will be tried

PFC Johnson had been one of the few soldiers in my platoon who was a persistent problem. He complained constantly and avoided doing anything more than the minimum. Months earlier in the rice paddies, he had tried to fake a heat injury. Johnson looked for every excuse not to carry his share of the load, literally and figuratively. The tall, lanky soldier had become a loner, as few would have much to do with him.

MAJ Loeffke ignored Johnson's story about no contact. The platoon did not do likewise.

I accepted the report about Johnson's fall in the showers but, of course, knew better.

Johnson was not charged with possession of the marijuana. It seemed likely that it had been planted in his pack to add to his problems. There was no proof that it was his.

The perception back home was that drug use was widespread in Vietnam. Drugs were common in the rear areas—however, not much more so than on the streets in the States. In the field, drugs of any type were not tolerated. Everyone recognized that safety depended upon the actions of everyone's working as a team.

I was not so naive as to assume that no drugs were used on

our occasional return to Long Binh. There is little doubt that the grunts obtained joints from the REMFs or local workers. I never checked because I had confidence that the soldiers would be clean when we returned to the boonies. More importantly, I was not going to court-martial a soldier whose rifle or machine gun was badly needed on future operations.

☞ **14 AUGUST 1969**
Thursday

Black Horse
   Pictures for ⅔ yearbooks
   Good break—Got drunk with CO & 1st SGT

Two Korean photographers fabricated a studio by hanging camouflage cloth in a corner of one of the hooches. A "mug shot" of each individual was made, followed by squad photos where the troops posed fierce-looking scenes with crossed bandoleers of ammo and fixed bayonets.

Over the next week the entire battalion was recorded on film. Loeffke had managed to fund the yearbook through the Brigade Welfare Fund and a free copy for each man was promised.

(A couple of months later the books were delivered. The only problem was that by the time the year book arrived, well over a quarter of the Battalion personnel were dead, evacuated with wounds, or—in all too few instances—had completed their tours.)

I was amazed by just how young we all looked. Except for the uniforms, the final product could have passed for the annual of any small high school in the world.

🛩 15 AUGUST 1969
Friday

> CH-47 to back near Long Binh/Saigon
> Operations to see if there was VC force consolidating for attack on Saigon—Moved south—Neg results

Every time we were getting familiar with an area, we moved to a new one. The enemy always knew the territory. We were strangers wherever we went.

It did not take long in the new AO for me to know the enemy was not present. I am not sure precisely what sense develops after months in the field. Whatever it is, the longer I stayed in the bush, the more accurate my prediction of enemy action became.

🛩 16 AUGUST 1969
Saturday

> Continued looking for VC force—Found no trails, no signs, nothing
> Rain as usual—It is really something "The GI Infantry-man"—Food terrible, walking constantly—Life often in danger—Still he goes on—The comradeship a LT feels for his men in this situation—Also the disgust you feel for rear area troops

REMFs cursed civilians for not being in uniform while Infantrymen felt a total disdain for all who did not carry the rifle. Yet, we, too, profaned the circumstances that made our days so unforgettable and dangerous—particularly on missions so useless as the one in which we were now engaged.

There was no talk, however, of noble causes, sense of duty, or of the lack of recognition. The soldiers cursed the Army, Vietnam, and God Himself for their circumstances. As a leader, I did not verbally join in their grumbling, but under my breath and in my mind, my lamentations were the same as theirs.

✈ 17 AUGUST 1969
Sunday

> Continue same mission—Terrain is very thick and wet—
> Everyone in bad spirits—They realize how useless this mis-
> sion is
> Only contact—Leeches—From every angle

The terrain and living conditions were taking their toll. Colds, infections, fungus, and malaria continued to lessen our morale as well as our numbers.

Bill Little had been battling immersion foot for weeks. With his usual stubbornness, he refused to stay back for treatment until the infection got so bad that he could hardly walk. Over his objections, he was sent to an in-country convalescent center at Cam Ranh Bay.

Personal hygiene was difficult in Vietnam. When time permitted, we secured both sides of a stream or a water-filled bomb crater and took turns bathing. Occasionally a soldier would strip his shirt off and wash in the punctual afternoon showers. Otherwise washing had to wait until we returned to Black Horse.

We soon learned that in the jungle a smooth face was not worth the risk, for even a minor razor cut would become infected. Several of the men were able to grow fairly respectable beards between shaves; however, most of the platoon were so young that pale peach fuss was all that needed to be scraped off.

Haircuts were available at Black Horse and at BMB. Our visits to those areas were so widely spaced that our hair frequently grew down over our ears. When a barber was available, we had our hair cut back to an inch or so on top with close-cut "white side-walls" on the sides.

✈ 18 AUGUST 1969
Monday

> Same, same
> At least this mission nearly over—Most interesting thing we saw was animal snares as we returned to near Highway 1—Strong enough to catch wild pigs or deer
> Sayings on helmets I've seen:
> "Caution: VC may be hazardous to your health."
> "VC—Don't shoot me in the back. Face me like a man."
> "God be with us."
> Many home states or city
> Girls' names
> Crosses
> Many of them have ETS and/or DEROS dates, also dust-off line numbers

The cloth camouflage cover of the helmet was the GI's graffito board. Most commonly scribbled on them were the dates of estimated return from overseas (DEROS)—the magic date ending the year's tour in Nam—and estimated termination of service (ETS) dates.

Along with the names of sweethearts and home towns was

one sober notation that even we example-setting officers were required to have on our pots—our dust-off line numbers. Each man was assigned a number when he reported in-country, and lists of these numbers were kept on rosters at the Company and Battalion headquarters. If we were killed or wounded, the report on the horn listed us by our line numbers rather than by formal names. Numbers were reused. When I had arrived in Charlie Company, the First Sergeant had assigned me mine saying, "You are 773. The last guy who had it doesn't need it anymore."

We all hated the damn steel pots. Heavy, hot, and uncomfortable, mine was the first thing I took off every opportunity I had. But we all recognized the helmet's ability to stop shrapnel, and that made the pot as close a companion as a weapon.

We used the helmets for much more than protection. We sat on them and carried our cigarettes in the webbing at the top of the inside liner—the only place we could keep them dry. The elastic bands securing the pots' camouflage covers served as convenient holders for P-38s, insect repellent, and crosses.

Peace signs adorned some of the helmets. They were not statements of protest against the war but rather expressions of desire for a real peace that only soldiers can appreciate.

✌ 19 AUGUST 1969
Tuesday

Walked out to Highway 1 at original insertion point—CO had to go to BMB for meeting—I took Co back to BH by truck—Resupply there and got order for Co

Always good to be in charge—Wish I could get a Co.

CPT McGinnis returned—Moved by truck from Black Horse—Co NDP

DeForrest pretty well summed up our attitude toward the jungle and the country as we moved toward Highway 1. According to the RTO, Vietnam should be leveled and a six-inch slab of concrete poured from border to border.

From Black Horse we moved to the southwest, to another new area. My brief time as acting company commander spurred me to continue my campaign with McGinnis and Loeffke for a command of my own.

---

20 AUGUST 1969
Wednesday

> Moved south
> Day ambushes—Co NDP—NVA Bn supposed to be in area—If they are we can't find them

Again we tramped through the jungle, but the only deadly thing we found was an occasional bamboo viper. The small green snakes were better known as "two steppers," as two steps was as far as a person lived if one bit him. Fortunately, the vipers were not aggressive.

I noted in my letter to Linda on this day that I had received several letters from old college friends. One was in graduate school, putting off the Army for as long as possible. Another wrote from Ranger School about how he was looking forward to Nam.

I enclosed their addresses for Linda, telling her to write them if she wished. My only letters now were to her, my brother and parents. Everything and everybody else seemed so long ago. Beyond family and war, I thought of little else.

I also expressed concern over the impending arrival of my

brother's child. Judy was due any time, and her measles in early pregnancy was still much in my mind.

✎ **21 AUGUST 1969**
Thursday

> Moved further west—1st plt on point as usual—We were supposed to find an NVA base camp—Only thing we found was the thickest jungle, biggest leeches, worst swamp in RVN
>
> Was in swamp so long CPT McGinnis called me and asked if I was starting my own Ranger School—I always receive a lot of jokes about being Airborne-Ranger—All just jokes—The Ranger tab is respected by all—I am almost as proud of my tab as my CIB—Purpose of going through swamp was to reach a PZ for airmobile to BH tomorrow—We got word tonight to walk 2–3 klicks to road for trucks—Everyone "got the ass"—Those damn rear people have no understanding of the foot soldier

Vietnam was a lieutenant's war. One-year tours and heavy casualties required a constant flow of new officers. The demand was met by waiving the stringent peace-time commissioning requirements, by increasing the number of Officer Candidate School graduates, and by awarding direct commissions for NCOs.

Rapid officer training, followed by immediate orders for the war, allowed few lieutenants the "luxury" of attending the eight-week Ranger course. It was unusual for more than one Ranger-qualified individual to be in a company.

1LT Tom Fallon, who replaced Don Jong as the Company artillery forward observer when Jong was ordered back to his XO job after the 7 August fight, was one of the few with the tab. An archetypal New Yorker, Fallon was an immediate

asset. Jong's boots would be hard to fill, but if anyone could
do so, the Brooklyn native appeared to be the man.

Tom's first words to McGinnis were that he did not want to
be an FO or even in the Artillery. His request for transfer to
the Infantry was already being processed. Fallon had raised so
much hell with the Artillery battalion commander that he had
sent Fallon to an FO job to get him off his back. McGinnis
told Tom he thought he would find the action he was looking
for in Charlie Company.

---

22 AUGUST 1969
Friday

> Ready to move to road for trucks—Got word to go to
> PZ—Not to airmobile to BH but to another mission—I had
> to organize airmobile as CO was picked up by C&C ship—
> Inserted us at "Decoration LZ" (see 8 Aug)—Went in behind
> arty prep, gunships etc—Kind of exciting—But scary
>
> Hit LZ—rejoined by CO—Intel said NVA Bn in area—
> Swept to northeast—very hot—and hilly—I told CO it looked
> like from Ranger Florida phase to mountain phase—Once
> again found nothing
>
> As we say Bn "needs to get their shit together"
>
> Finally picked up by truck and back to Bravo Hotel (Black
> Horse)

Perceptions of the Battalion operations differed between the
platoon leader and those who had an understanding of the "big
picture." The apparent indiscriminate missions we were sent
on actually fit in the overall plans of the Battalion and Brigade,
but for those of us who were sweating and confused, it seemed
at times that no one had any idea what was going on.

In the jungle, there was no typical day, though most of the

time one day was pretty much the same as the one before and the one after. Each morning the platoon leaders met with the company commander to receive instructions on the day's mission that had come over the radio from Battalion during the night. Orders were brief and included any updates on intelligence on the enemy, our route of march for the day, and the sequence of the platoons in the company formation. We platoon leaders then passed along the same information to our squad leaders, who briefed their men.

The point platoon was responsible for keeping the company headed in the right direction, but McGinnis, his FO, and all of us platoon leaders carefully kept up on our maps so we would know our exact location at all times. All leaders—down to the squad leaders—carried compasses, and many of us supplemented the hand-sized Army issue lensactic compass with wrist compasses for quick confirmation that our direction was true.

At the lead of the company was the point man. He not only had to make the initial break through the thick foliage but also, as the man most vulnerable to an enemy ambush, had to constantly watch for booby traps and signs of enemy activity.

The point man was followed by the soldier called "the slack" whose sole purpose was to guard the lead soldier. Frequently the men in these two slots traded positions, allowing the point a little rest and ensuring that the most alert man was first.

Point and slack were followed by the squad leader and his RTO. The squad leader directed the two front men by hand signals to keep them on the proper azimuth. Another soldier trailed the squad leader's RTO, counting each step. This "pace man" was experienced in knowing how many of his steps equalled one hundred meters, and he would inform his sergeant as he completed each count.

By knowing how far and in what direction we had proceeded, we could accurately determine our location for reports and calls for artillery and air support.

All the soldiers except the RTOs and machine gunners rotated frequently in each of the positions of point, slack, and pace man. Some were better than others at one job or the other, and men like Morford, who possessed a keen sense of direction, lightening-swift reactions, and a personal pride in his reputation, did the same duty much more often than others.

The thick jungle restricted us to a single-file formation that snaked several hundred meters from the point to the trail man. The dense vegetation prevented our maintaining an interval of more than five meters because any greater distance caused us to lose visual contact with the man in front of us. Yet we could not follow too closely, as one enemy sniper could get two instead of one. The jungle itself helped us maintain our proper proximity to one another; after being hit in the face by thorny bamboo brush as it broke free from the man ahead, even the newest FNG learned not to follow too closely.

When the point man stopped because of suspicious sounds or signs of the gooks, the company spread out in alternating positions a few meters to each side of the file, forming a long, slender oval perimeter. Each man sought out a log, tree trunk, or depression in the ground for protection in case the bullets began to fly. We also used this procedure every hour or so for a ten to fifteen minute break.

Around noon we halted and spread out the oval a little more than usual, and again used the buddy system of one man on alert, one eating. Frequently we skipped this break and pushed on until the heaviest rainfall of the day and took a longer break while we waited for it to abate.

An hour or two before dark, we formed our NDP. The officers met with the CO and FO so each man could report his evaluation of where we were. The FO called in an artillery air burst smoke round on a known point. When the shell exploded, we could calcuate our exact position by checking the compass direction and the number of seconds between seeing and hearing the blast.

We bet a beer on who could predict our location the closest each night, though we never paid off because it was too difficult to remember who had won what after weeks in the jungle.

It was fun matching our navigational skills but quite embarrassing to be certain the marking round would light up the sky in the south only to have it explode hundreds of meters to the north.

Administrative actions for the platoon provided a constant workload when I was not humping the boonies or waiting in ambush. Reorganization of the squads caused by evacuation of wounded or sick, R&Rs, completion of tours, and breaking in replacements were daily concerns.

A major problem was the selection of squad leaders. Few NCO s arrived through the replacement chain, so Specialists Fourth Class or corporals frequently took over squads when no sergeants were available. We pinned sergeant stripes on them, but because we had no authority to promote the men, they wore the rank without the additional pay. These "acting jacks" got nothing for their extra responsibilities except more work.

When authorizations were received for promotions, another problem often occurred. Many of the men did their best to turn down the new NCO rank because an unwritten policy in the Battalion allowed the enlisted men to complete the last month of their tour in rear jobs while those wearing stripes stayed in the boonies up until the last ten days before they rotated home.

None of the soldiers ever mentioned the possibility of reenlisting to stay in uniform. Everyone always claimed that he would soon be a civilian again. At the separation stations back in Oakland, California, and Fort Lewis, Washington, many changed their minds and stayed in the Army. For some it was a sudden decision. Others had planned to reenlist all along. By waiting until they got to the separation point, they avoided the harassment they would have received from their buddies back in the platoon.

Regardless of rank or future intents, leaders surfaced. Some were better than others. All were as good as any our country has ever depended upon on the battlefields of the past.

23 AUGUST 1969
Saturday

Black Horse
    Typical break—Drink—Eat, etc.
    Rumors I've heard recently:
        1. 199th home by Christmas
        2. 199th back to paddies in 6 weeks
        3. 199th to become part of Big Red One
        4. 199th further north
    Etc. Etc. Etc.
    Took CO's place at meeting—Discussed missions with Bn CO
    Learned today that Delta LT that hit mine of 5 Aug lost a leg—Bad shit

The news that the Delta lieutenant had lost his leg was no surprise. It was almost in the category of good news, as I had feared he would lose both, or might not live at all.

Loss of limbs, genitals, or senses was never far from our minds. Fear of such wounds seemed at times to rival that of death itself. Yet I never saw anyone not fight for the last gasp of breath. We were warriors; we did not give up on anything easily.

Everyone had a fear of some particular wound. I never told anyone about mine, though at one time or another I thought of all the different possibilities. My recurring fear was a burst of automatic rifle fire stitching me across the chest. Another frequent vision was a bullet penetrating my steal pot and going straight into the top of my skull, a fear based on the fact that during fire fights we were in prone positions on the ground.

Oddly, these thoughts never occurred during the fire fights themselves because during a battle I had too many other things to think about and do. After the fight, the mind had time to focus on the possibilities.

(Some visions have remained all these years. Occasionally

I have a sudden feeling of bullets striking me in the chest in the seconds after a close-call in a car or after an unexpected loud noise. Perhaps there are no new fears, just old ones we keep remembering.)

✎ **24 AUGUST 1969**
Sunday

Black Horse
    From Black Horse airmobiled northwest to LZ Swamp as we call it—Headed east—Bad humping—Found an old base camp—No one at home
    As SP4 Vito Lovecchio, Co RTO, said about the jungle: "Sure is bad, but good training if we ever go to a combat zone." Sarcasm is GI's strike back

Vito Lovecchio, a nineteen-year old draftee from Ohio, told me that when he had received his draft notice his father had offered to drive him to Canada and support him until the war was over. Vito said that he had regretted many times not taking the offer.

His father had supported the young man's decision somewhat reluctantly. As Vito packed for Nam at the end of his leave, Mr. Lovecchio had given his son a snub-nosed 32 caliber automatic which Vito carried in a holster inside his fatigue shirt. Although personally owned weapons were against regulations, nothing was said or done about his carrying it. The size of the weapon made it virtually useless as a battlefield tool. Its only purpose seemed to be as a reminder to Vito of his father's love.

Other companies in the Battalion and Brigade had much the same success as Charlie Company during the month of August. Except for a few radio transmissions we overheard and the occasional chance to read the Brigade newspaper, we were hardly aware of the Redcatchers' mounting body count.

A priority message from General Bennett put our part of the war in a little better perspective. The message stated in part:

> "With one week still to go, August 1969 is already the fourth most productive month in Redcatcher history, in terms of the number of enemy eliminated from the battlefield. Only in the months of January, February, and May 1968 (months of enemy TET and "mini—TET" offensives) were larger numbers of enemy eliminated. Further, the enemy now being eliminated are being found, captured, destroyed or induced to chieu hoi in very small groups, normally no more than one to four or five at a time. This means that Redcatcher units are becoming increasingly more proficient in the demanding and time-consuming tasks that must be carried out with imagination and precision if our mission is to be accomplished; by this I mean digging out hard intelligence concerning the VC local forces; conducting wide-ranging but detailed search operations with small units to locate the elusive enemy; and getting positive results from each contact through aggressive and imaginative operations which confuse the enemy, keep him off balance and make him more and more vulnerable to our superior mobility and firepower. We are becoming increasingly successful in accomplishing these difficult tasks. However, real success will come when we have developed a degree of momentum that will allow us to dominate our AO; keep the enemy continually off balance, hungry and without access to the population, and cause the ARVN, RF and PF units with which we work to gain improved capabilities and self-confidence."

The Brigade Commander concluded:

> "All Redcatchers are doing a tremendous job. Commanders will pass to all personnel my congratulations and appreciation for the significant progress already made, and my confidence that this progress will continue and gain greater momentum,

so that 1969 will indeed be a year of decision in the Redcatcher AO. Keep up the good work."

Several of us placed copies of the document in our rucksacks
as mementos. A pat on the back is always nice, but the message brought mixed reactions. We all knew that the General's
words about increasing "a degree of momentum" meant longer
RIFs and more continuous days in the bush.

---

25 AUGUST 1969
Monday

> Moved out to rubber to east ready to go to FB Marge—
> New mission—Airmobile to north—Moved and set up NDP
> in old NVA base camp—Very scary area—One of men
> dropped a grenade—Everyone hit dirt—Nervous
> Seems as if Bn is trying to make a recon element out of
> us—We only have 2 plts in this mission—One at Xuan Luc,
> one at FB Marge

McGinnis had platoons spread out over a twenty-five-kilo-
meter area. One platoon was securing the Brigade TOC at
Xuan Luc and another was guarding the artillery at Marge.
The CO was with the other two platoons of us that were beating the brush, by far the hardest of the missions. But the captain went where he knew he was needed.

My inner senses had been telling me all day that the enemy
was nearby. Our route, which followed a well-used trail, carried us into a narrow valley where thickly foliaged cliffs surrounded a small stream. It was a prime ambush position, and
if the enemy were occupying the high ground around us, we
could not have been in a worse location.

I halted the point and walked back to McGinnis' CP. He agreed to hold the company in place while I took a small recon element forward.

Collier, DeForrest, two riflemen, and I proceeded cautiously. We paralleled the trail, frequently moving in the shallow stream. A few hundred meters later, the trail made a hard right to the base of a hundred-foot cliff where footholds reinforced with small logs formed stairs up the incline.

Collier went first. At the top of the cliff he signaled that all was clear so we quickly joined him. We had gone only a few meters more when a hand grenade rolled past me and stopped at DeForrest's feet. In an instant everyone dove for cover.

I waited seconds that seemed like hours for the explosion that would preceed a gook ambush. Nothing happened. All was quiet.

Then to my front I could hear Collier in muffled conversation with one of his men, after which he picked up the grenade. In his other hand he held the firing mechanism—complete with blasting cap, handle, and pin. I watched from my still prone position as he screwed the device back into the grenade. Roy explained that the grenade had come unscrewed from the detonator on one of his men's web gear, a thing we checked for often but evidently not often enough.

There had never been any danger. Continuing the mission, we spotted a small bunker complex a hundred meters later. After carefully moving around its circumference, we determined it was unoccupied. My premonitions of the enemy's proximity had not been completely accurate, but they were close enough for me.

🚁 26 AUGUST 1969
Tuesday

> Moved—Set up Co NDP—Everyone is really tired
> Airmobile operation: Co CO is picked up by C&C bird—
> Gives me my instructions by radio—I am in charge on ground
> Usually have a fake pass at another LZ—Go in with M-60s
> shooting, rockets, etc to clear LZ—Really something—I go
> in on 1st lift, 2nd bird

On an air assault everyone was pumped up with the mixture
of flying, firing, and fear. We waited out on the skids in the
90-knot wind as the choppers made their descent. Jumping to
the ground, we were running for the nearest wood line before
the birds touched down. The quiet of the jungle after the tur-
moil of the airmobile was always frightening because it held
the unknown.

🚁 27 AUGUST 1969
Wednesday

> Moved south—Finally got trucks—26 klicks in 5 days—
> Moved to FB Marge—Top came out—From him I learned
> two things:
>> 1. I have been put in for another medal—Some VN
>> award
>> 2. I go back in with him—Bn has to have someone pay
>> troops in hospital at Cam Ranh Bay—Bn CO said since
>> I had the most time in field of any of the officers I would
>> get the break

> Am looking forward to break and seeing more of the coun
try
>   Chopper to BMB
>   "Screw them all but six—and save them for pallbearers"
>
>   Old Airborne Saying

The news about the Vietnamese medal was interesting. Top said it was a valor award for the action back on 7 August. I was to hear several more times about the medal, but it was never awarded. Weeks later Loeffke explained to me what occurred.

About the time Top was telling me about the medal, an ARVN colonel visited the Battalion TOC at Black Horse. He had come to get information about whom the "Two-thirds" recommended for the decoration. Upon arrival at the TOC, the first thing the colonel saw was a soldier cleaning map boards. Instead of a rag, the soldier had been using a small yellow and red striped Republic of Vietnam flag. The flag, which was one of the many made to give the villagers in our AO, was well-stained with grease pencil residue that had been wiped from the acetate-covered boards. The Vietnamese colonel left immediately and with him all mention of the award.

Loeffke apologized to me, adding that the flag problem had been resolved and would not happen again. The story of how the VN medal was lost made a better tale than one about receiving a piece of colored ribbon.

I was pleased at the news of my going to Cam Ranh Bay, knowing that it would be a good break and a chance to see something beyond the jungle, and knowing, too, that the trip was a reward for my extended time in the field. At the same time, I wondered if the incident of my shooting at SGT Bender three weeks before had had anything to do with it.

The story of the near-miss had made the rounds in the Battalion, seeming to confirm beliefs that anyone who stayed in the field longer than he had to was a bit crazy. I wondered the same occasionally but not very much or often. I damn sure was not crazy enough to turn down the chance to see Cam Ranh.

✍ **28 AUGUST 1969**
Thursday

> Camp Frenzell-Jones
> More BMB time—Even had to go to a formation this morn-
> ing—These BMB people are really something
> Ran into a couple of Aggies at club tonight—Good time
> talking to them

Leaving the platoon was difficult even though I would be
gone only a few days. I felt much better when McGinnis put
Tom Fallon in as acting platoon leader during my absence.
The frustrated FO would get to be an Infantryman for awhile,
at least.

BMB never ceased to amaze me with its adherence to routine
Army procedures. Formations, regular duty hours, and the "eye
wash" of spit-shined boots and painted rocks made the concertina
wire compound an island of REMFs in a sea of war.

✍ **29 AUGUST 1969**
Friday

> BMB, Bien-Hoa, Phan Rang, Cam Ranh Bay
> Picked up money and guard SGT E-5 Peter Fryar and went
> to Bien Hoa—Boarded a C130—Went to CRB by way of
> Phan Rang—Arrived CRB after dark—Went into 6th Con-
> valescent Hospital—Am sleeping between sheets in an aircon-
> ditioned room—Unbelievable
> At Bien Hoa many troops were going home—Must be quite
> a feeling

My guard was a Finance sergeant who had never been outside BMB. As I reviewed weapon safety procedures with SGT Fryar, who wore thick glasses and was a bit overweight, I began to wonder just what kind of break Loeffke had awarded me.

However, when I signed for the ammo box containing $5,000 in funny money, I began to realize that Pete Fryar and I might be a pretty good team after all. Pete told me he thoroughly understood the forms and pay procedures. His assurance that he would keep the records straight so we would not have to make up any losses made me feel better.

Our journey to Cam Ranh was the usual noisy, hot-on-the-ground, cold-in-the-air flight, courtesy of the US Air Force. The flight crew looked "movie tough" in their camouflaged fatigues adorned with assorted knives and pistols.

Throughout Vietnam it seemed that everyone enjoyed looking the part of the combat soldier. The problem was that damn few ever got closer to the war than the PX.

Camn Ranh Bay was so large that I could not see the wire and guard towers of its perimeter from the airfield. When I asked the NCO at Flight Operations how to get to the 6th Convalescent Center, he curtly answered, "Take the bus," and pointed to a stop in front of the terminal.

At the bus stop was a schedule indicating a bus would be by every 15 minutes. I wondered what kind of war stories the Transportation officer told about his duties when he got home. Probably his favorites would be about seeing that the line of six stops was made in 15 minutes, or maybe about the difficulty of scheduling during the monsoon rains. What a hell of a war.

When we finally reached our destination, the 6th Convalescent Center night duty officer placed my box of money in a safe. He wanted to lock up my .45 caliber pistol as well, but I refused. I felt naked enough without my M-16.

The duty officer found a room in the NCO barracks for SGT Fryar. For me he had only an apology because all the officer billets were occupied. I told him not to sweat the situation, for I could sleep on a couch in the adjoining day room. He asked if I minded sleeping in a patient ward. I explained to him that I had not slept on a real bed in over four months and the idea of having air-conditioning as an added benefit made the offer more than attractive.

I slept my most restful night in months. The only distractions were the hard .45 under my pillow and a slight longing for my poncho liner.

✎ **30 AUGUST 1969**
Saturday

> 6th CC Cam Ranh Bay
> Started paying troops—Found LT Little—Good talk with him
> Really beautiful country
> Went to several O clubs tonight—CRB is not at all like being in VN—All the MSC officers wanted to hear "war stories"—Felt like telling them all to go to hell

SGT Fryar put up signs in the mess hall of the hospital announcing we were in the day room to pay soldiers of the 199th. Anyone who came in and claimed to be in the Brigade received a "casual pay" of $50. Fryar would take the vouchers with the soldiers' signatures, ranks, and service numbers back to BMB to update their finance records because with the frequent transfers between hospitals, convalescent centers, and evacuation to Japan, no one at BMB had been able to tell us just who would be at the 6th CC. The payments we made were to see the men through until they returned to the Brigade.

Bill Little came into the day room about mid-morning. Surprised to see me so far from the jungle, he eagerly asked about what had been going on during his two-week absence. The infection in his feet was almost well, and he was looking forward to returning to Charlie Company.

Except for the occasional troop who came in to get paid, Bill and I had the day room to ourselves. Our conversation then turned to our lives before Vietnam. While Bill and I had lived, sweated and fought together for over three months and knew each other extremely well as soldiers, we had never discussed our pasts to any extent. I told Bill about growing up on a farm, about my parents, brother, and Linda and our expected child. He talked about his childhood in New Jersey, his parents' divorce and his days as a cadet at West Point.

We laughed a lot about the rigors of Ranger School. Bill was proud of having completed the course but was obviously bothered about not having received his Ranger tab.

Of the two hundred or more students who started each Ranger class, only an average of 120 finished the entire eight weeks, and about twenty of those finishing did not receive the coveted tab.

Bill explained that several of his graded patrols had not gone well. The more we talked, the better I understood why Bill was so aggressive in the field. He might not have had his Ranger tab, but he thoroughly intended to have several rows of ribbons for valor awards when he went home and to West Point.

That night Bill went AWOL from the Center and we visited the various officers' clubs in Cam Ranh where we had some good arguments and a few near-fights with the Air Force officers. At one point when things were getting heated, a group of fighter pilots came in. Spotting the Infantry rifles on our collars, they bought us drinks and told the REMF "blue suiters" to back off. We closed the club, exchanging stories about the differences between killing from the air and killing on the ground.

🚁 31 AUGUST 1969
Sunday

CRB
    Another good resting day—Went swimming in the South China Sea—Very clear—Very beautiful
    Saw movie "Romeo and Juliet" tonight
    Birds taking 9th and Marines home early are called Golden Dustoffs

Cam Ranh Bay had the clearest water and the whitest beaches I had ever seen. High mountains looming in the background provided a tranquil, majestic setting. I spent most of the day in the water and on the beach thinking how seldom I stopped to realize what a beautiful country this was.

🚁 I SEPTEMBER 1969
Monday

CRB, Bien Hoa, BMB
    Flew back by C130—Very good time
    Learned that while I was gone my plt on mission got a gook—Point man PFC Morford turned a bend in a trail—Came face to face with him—My man shot first—Only hit him once—In calf of leg—M-16 nearly tore his leg off—A body count always raises morale
    PFC Morford taught modern dance and ballet in world—Strange person but oddly a good Infantryman

My first news at BMB was of Morford's kill, convincing me that I had been correct about the California dancer's quick reactions. It had been just like the Old West gunfights where one man was a little faster.

M-16 bullets have an extremely high velocity. Morford's round had entered near the man's knee and exited at the ankle and the tumbling bullet had stripped most of the calf from the enemy soldier's leg. He bled to death in minutes. Tom Fallon later told me that one of the NCOs had taken a machete to the body. Tom had not actually seen the mutilation take place, but he had seen the results. Neither of us condoned the action, yet we well understood why it had occurred. The frustration of constantly humping the boonies and losing fellow Americans had been vented on the enemy's lifeless body.

Tom and I let the NCO know that we would not tolerate another such incident. At the same time we agreed not to let the information about the mutilation get outside the platoon.

The captured AK47 was almost new. Papers in the dead NVA soldier's rucksack showed that he was a replacement from the North joining the 33rd NVA Regiment—the regiment we had encountered on 3 July. FNGs on both sides were prone to make fatal mistakes.

Also waiting for me when I got back to the Charlie Company rear orderly room was a stack of mail. Three letters from Linda and one from Jim were mostly about the now past-due date of Judy's baby.

My letter to Linda told her I had weighed on scales at the 6th CC and found that I had lost over twenty-five pounds since my arrival in Nam. I liked to think that the present 187 pounds on my six-foot, five-inch frame made me look lean and mean. Actually, like most veterans, I probably appeared skinny and gaunt.

✈ 2 SEPTEMBER 1969
Tuesday

BMB to Black Horse to Boonies
    Talked with Bn CO MAJ Loeffke—He said I had good chance for general's aide—I told him I wanted a Co.—This seemed to be what he wanted to hear—He said that most likely I would stay with C Co for another month or so then go to TOC for a month or so—Then a Co—I definitely hope so—There are damn few Co CO LTs—6 months from CPT—23 years old
    Met Co coming in from mission at BH—Then trucked to area of Marge—Set up in ARVN compound as Marge has been abandoned

When Loeffke asked if I wanted the aide's job, I replied, "I did not come to Vietnam to look for blue cheese dressing for the general's mess." He made no more mention about the job. His outline of my future, leading to a company command, was the first concrete promise I had had about attaining my goal. I was ecstatic. There was nothing I wanted more.

✈ 3 SEPTEMBER 1969
Wednesday

ARVN Compound—Cam Tam
    Talked to CPT McGinnis about my chances to get a Co—He said he would recommend me and help all he could
    Took plt to old area of Marge and finished tearing it down and cleaning up
    Night ambush tonight

1st Plt

Plt SGT	SGT Hondo—Washington
1st SL	SGT Ito—Hawaii
2nd SL	Acting SGT Drenth—Minnesota
3rd SL	SP4 Estep—Ohio

The ARVN camp, smaller than Marge, was manned by a platoon of the South Vietnamese. Except for an occasional walk through the streets of Cam Tam, they never seemed to leave their barbed-wire perimeter.

Several of the ARVN soldiers had their wives and children living with them in their small bunkers. They kept their women out of sight the first few days we used the compound, but the longer we stayed, the friendlier they became and the women began to appear. For a can of C-rations, one woman provided bowls of excellent noodle soup with finely cut fresh onion.

Beyond having limited space, the compound's biggest problem was the rat population. McGinnis and his RTOs got quite proficient at throwing rocks, cans, and even knives at the scurrying rats. After a night of waking up with the large rodents running across my face and body, I decided I much preferred to spend my evenings in the jungle.

My listing the squad leaders in my journal was to note the absence of SGT Collier. Roy was nearing the completion of his year, and he would spend the last weeks in the relative safety of Black Horse.

Traditionally in Charlie Company, the departing soldier popped a smoke grenade in final salute to the company as he lifted off on the resupply bird. Other than that, no dramatic departure scenes occurred when a soldier finally got out of the field. Brief handshakes and perhaps an exchange of awkward "good lucks" were the extent of the farewells. No one was sad to see a friend and comrade go. We all felt good that another soldier had finished his tour rather than have left on a dust-off.

✈ 4 SEPTEMBER 1969
Thursday

Moved out on 2 day mission pulling day and night ambushes—Area shows little activity—Resupply by Rat Patrol

The day before I got letter from Linda saying she was pregnant, the Red Cross advertisement, "When a baby is born in NY and the waiting room is in VN," came to mind—Had the same thought this morning

The Battalion Rat Patrol was a new experiment by MAJ Loeffke. Jeeps mounted with M-60 machine guns ran the roads in the rubber plantations trying to catch the enemy, escorting convoys in and out of Black Horse, and delivering supplies to places like Cam Tam.

To the best of my knowledge, the Rat Patrol only produced one body count. It was just another of the gimmicks that did not work. The only way to consistently find the enemy was to go into the jungle and hunt for him. Sooner or later we found the gooks—and on occasion, they found us first.

✈ 5 SEPTEMBER 1969
Friday

Continued the same mission

B Co had contact west of here today—Ran into a large triangular NVA base camp—Had 7 KIA 22 WIA—Gooks popped a 40 lb Claymore on point element—They found over 135 large bunkers in the area

Other companies in the Battalion were doing pretty much the same type of missions as Charlie Company. McGinnis' RTOs maintained one radio on the Battalion frequency at all times, and, as a result, they kept up with the contacts and body counts of our sister companies.

At the platoon level we maintained only the Company push, making our world much smaller than the Company's. Unless I was at the Company CP or later talked to one of the RTOs, I was usually not aware of small engagements by the other units.

Bravo's fire fight was of such a magnitude that everyone soon heard about it. We were genuinely surprised at the news. "No contact Bravo," as most of the troops called B Company, was not known for finding the enemy. In the entire time we had been in the jungle, I could recall only one previous incident of their being in a fight. This battle made up for Bravo's earlier inactivity, but their inexperience demanded a heavy price in dead and wounded.

B Company had been following a jungle trail when the point man reported seeing something unusual to his front. His squad leader had gone to investigate, and his last report on the radio was, "It looks like a big Claymore. . . ."

A forty pound anti-vehicular mine designed to destroy trucks was detonated and the ambush sprung. The first five men in the Bravo lead element were blown to pieces. Automatic rifle and machine gun fire, along with grenades, did the rest of the damage before the gooks withdrew.

Although Bravo captured a large amount of supplies as well as eventually destroying the bunkers, there was little evidence of any enemy killed or wounded. Loeffke told me later that he was not at all satisfied with the way the Bravo Company Commander had handled the action. I did not realize it at the time, but this day's contact would have a great influence on my future.

Our war went on in the jungle. The conflicts that were dividing our country at home continued as well.

A letter from Linda included news that she had gone to the Presidio to see President Nixon. There the crowd was friendlier than in the streets of San Francisco, where the protestors received him as a traitor rather than the nation's leader.

She related her feelings about being a waiting wife in a city that was synonymous with antiwar sentiment. Except for a few friends of Susan's mother who had been waiting wives during World War II, no one understood nor cared about their situation. Vietnam was a different kind of war on the home front as well as on the battlefield.

☙ 6 SEPTEMBER 1969
Saturday

> Returned to ARVN base camp—On way back in had light contact with a flock of peacocks—No casualties on either side
>
> My morale at a fairly low point—Will change I'm sure
>
> Received a letter from Uncle McKee—Good letter—Also picture of Confederate Monument in Hamilton, Ga.—It reads: "Fate destined them Victory but crowned them with Glorious Immortality."

We were moving through an area of tall elephant grass when a human-like scream, followed instantaneously by an eruption of M-16 automatic fire, filled the air.

As I raised my head from a prone position, I could see a dozen beautiful peacocks and pea hens flying away over the top of the grass. Morford, on point as usual, rather sheepishly explained that he had seen movement and fired before recognizing his target as birds. With the exception of a few long, colorful tail feathers lost, the flock had escaped unharmed.

Morford suffered good-natured harassment for several days

after the incident. The teasing did not bother him and he wore one of the feathers on his helmet for weeks afterward.

This was the first time that my own morale had been so low that I commented on it in my journal. Even the peacock fire fight did little to improve my humor. Vietnam was either boring or frightening, yet at the same time, it provided an excitement and intensity like no other environment. A year was a long time, however, and nearly five months of missing my wife and family, as well as the creature comforts of regular food and sleep, made it difficult to feel good.

The letter from my uncle helped a little in boosting my morale. At the same time I wondered if there would ever be any monuments to our war—and if there were, just what would they say.

===

⌘ 7 SEPTEMBER 1969
Sunday

> Still working around ARVN base camp—Ambushes etc
> Things a little boring—CPT and I went out on a Rat jeep
> today—Looking for enemy—Dangerous—Stupid for officers
> to do this—Still sometimes doing things like that breaks the
> monotony a little

A few minutes after the resupply convoy arrived, I saw McGinnis talking to the NCO with the Rat Patrol escort. The CO called me over and, with a grin, asked if I would rather drive or be the gunner. I answered by climbing into the rear of the jeep and loading the M-60 machine gun.

We were soon zooming along the narrow roads of the rubber plantation at fifty miles an hour. My initial fears of running into a large enemy force were overridden by the more immediate danger of McGinnis' driving. After half an hour of running the trails, we were both exhilarated. Our laughter, as we ducked tree branches and jumped pot holes, was even louder than the straining jeep motor.

When we returned the Rat jeep to its worried sergeant, McGinnis was as happy as I had seen him since the last time we had gotten a body count, and I felt better than I had in days. The NCO remarked that if Loeffke had known what we were doing he would have fired us both—or else joined in the fun himself.

Whether the CO had recognized I needed a morale boost or just needed a gunner, I did not know. It was not the first, nor the last, time that we did insane things to keep our sanity.

✈ 8 SEPTEMBER 1969
Monday

> Rains picking up again—Raining about 6–8 hours a day now—Just stay wet all the damn time
> Continue ambushes
> C Co Officers:
> CPT James McGinnis—N.C.—CO
> 1LT Tom Fallon—N.Y.—FO
> 1LT Bill Little—N.J.—Two-six
> 2LT Errol Stewart—Ill.—Three-six

Being wet all the time did not dampen the GI's humor. DeForrest frequently whispered, "Quack, quack," as we moved through the rainy jungle.

Bill Little had returned from Cam Ranh Bay bringing news that he had heard Pete Petrosilli had been transferred from

Japan to Letterman Hospital in San Francisco to further recover from his wounds.

My next letter to Linda relayed this information, and she was soon visiting Pete after her prenatal check-ups at the same facility. She later told me that she had felt a responsibility to visit my friend, but more importantly, she felt closer to me when she talked to him because he had seen me more recently than she had.

Vietnam was a small war, bringing together people of all backgrounds and origins who would otherwise never have crossed paths. Those who participated by either fighting or waiting felt a kinship. Linda and Pete's acquaintance provided a connection in a fragmented time and brought a semblance of normalcy to the confusion of the war.

🖎 9 SEPTEMBER 1969
Tuesday

> Got a VR in a LOH of first base camp we hit in this area—
> Low and fast—Saw several fresh trails—Looks as if gooks may
> be back in there—Which means we will go back after them

Our orders were to remain near fire bases and to "slow operations" due to the death of Ho Chi Minh. Negotiations for a cease-fire had been undertaken but none had been declared. We had no idea what "slow operations" meant nor did we have any idea if the enemy was following a similar guideline. It seemed strange as hell to stop or slow down trying to kill the gooks just because their leader had died.

We had no orders limiting reconnaissance so McGinnis arranged for a light observation helicopter (LOH), a chopper that looked like a large football with rotors. It had a pilot, a door gunner, and a space for one observer—in this instance, me.

Through a headset, I could direct the pilot to various parts of our AO. I had difficulty seeing through the triple-canopy, but an occasional clearing or break in the foliage showed new trails in the areas we had already been through.

My pilot, a nineteen-year old warrant officer, enjoyed his trade. He maneuvered the small bird just above the tree tops at one hundred miles per hour, popping over ridges and hugging the contours of the land as he told me about driving stock cars back in Alabama before the war. His skills at the bird's stick were truly remarkable, especially considering that he never stopped talking during the entire flight.

At times the gyrations through the air had me on the verge of throwing up. Fortunately, I was able to hold everything down, relieved that I did not embarrass myself nor the Infantry in front of a goddamn aviator.

Cursing the pilots was easy. Every night they returned to sheets and clubs while I hunkered beneath a poncho in the jungle. I really felt no malice, however, for many pilots and crewmen never finished their tours because of the chances they took to help us. In earlier wars these young men flew bi-planes and Spitfires and went home aces and heroes rather than just more unappreciated Vietnam vets.

🛩 10 SEPTEMBER 1969
Wednesday

Still ambushing around ARVN base camp—Operations curtailed due to cease fire

Some ARVN showed up with a whore—Supposedly clean—Several of plt visited her—Stood in line—Crazy GIs

Letter today that James David Lanning has arrived—Thank
God he seems to be okay

Almost as important I received my first letter ever from
my father—Good news to hear a good way

While Uncle Ho received his state funeral in Hanoi, we sat
around still trying to decide what a cease fire or "slow operations" meant. The best we could understand, it provided an
excuse to have an easy day of sitting in a platoon perimeter
doing nothing.

Our position, just behind the abandoned French mansion in
Cam Tam, was adjacent to the main road, a one-lane dirt path.
Except for a few people on guard, we spent the early part of
the day sleeping and reading, rousing ourselves only to check
ID cards of the few foot, bicycle, and lambretta travelers.

A break in the otherwise boring day was provided by an
ARVN soldier and his "companion." No such diversions had
been available for the troops in the Cam Tam area since Marge
had been closed down.

I was not comfortable with the prostitute-delivery service, but
many of the troops were interested in her favors and eagerly
awaited my decision. A radio call to McGinnis brought instructions for me to bring the couple to the nearby ARVN compound.
Upon our arrival, the CO said that the compound commander
wanted to "check out" the woman before she began to peddle
her wares. His "inspection" took place in a nearby bunker where
a poncho-covered entrance offered privacy as well as a reminder
that rank has its privileges in all armies.

When the prostitute returned from delivering her "freebie,"
she went back to the first platoon under the escort of one of
my NCOs. I told the sergeant that I would stay with McGinnis
for two hours and that when I returned to the platoon, I expected the whore to be gone.

The rest of my instructions to him were graphic but designed
to keep the platoon healthy. I told him that the woman could
set up business in the old stable at the back of the mansion.
No man was to visit her without first being issued a prophy-

lactic by Doc Bass. Each man was to report to the sergeant after his visit with a used rubber as proof of his VD protection procedures. As the prostitute and NCO turned to walk back to the platoon, I told him to make sure she got paid.

(I suppose there are some who would question an officer's allowing his men to temporarily establish their own bordello, but I reasoned that if they were old enough to fight, they were old enough to decide about their sexual activities. My job was to keep them alive, not worry about their morals.)

When I returned to the platoon, the woman was gone. The NCO who had been in charge reported that the VD prevention measures had been followed. He did not tell me how many of the men, nor who, had participated, and I did not ask. His only complaint was that because he had been in charge, he had had to go last.

Several of the men were teasing an FNG who had made the mistake of admitting that the prostitute had been his first woman. His ears were bright red from embarrassment but his smile indicated he felt the harassment was worth it. He had nearly a year left in the jungle, and I figured this would not be his last encounter with a Vietnamese hooker—that is, if he lived long enough and kept the necessary equipment from being blown off.

Except for the kidding of the FNG, the platoon was strangely quiet. As I went over to my rucksack, which I had left in the perimeter while I waited at the compound, the men began to smile, and then there were a few muffled laughs. Suspicious, I asked the NCO what the hell was going on. He reluctantly explained that when setting up the prostitute in the stable, someone suggested that One-six, as the platoon leader, should make some contribution to the effort—and my contribution seemed obvious when one of them spotted the rucksack that contained my air mattress. They thought it extremely funny that One-six's mattress had provided the foundation for their fun.

Whether it really pissed me off or whether I was reacting according to the expectations of the platoon, I am not sure. But all laughter subsided as I none too calmly told the sergeant that he would be walking point until we both rotated or were dead. He mumbled that he had washed off the mattress before returning it to my rucksack, an explanation which only made matters worse. I told him, in no uncertain terms, that he and I had just traded air mattresses.

My final words brought an outburst of laughter from the platoon. For days afterward, GIs asked me—with straight faces and all the innocence they could muster—if they could borrow my air mattress.

Later in the afternoon supplies and mail arrived for the platoon. The news that my brother's son had been born with no apparent ill effects was an answer to many prayers. The birth date of 4 September made me recall my journal entry about the Red Cross commercial. I kept thinking that if I could just figure out how to continue these premonitions, the horse tracks would not be solvent long after I got back to the world.

How I found out about my nephew was almost as good as the news itself. Precise, neat printing by my father's hand resembled more the style of an engineer or architect than a farmer. I had never seen his writing except when I occasionally glanced over his shoulder as he made entries into his farm records when I was a boy. I had never received any correspondence from him in the five years since I had left home. He simply did not write to anyone—never had before and never has since.

Dad spent the two and a half years my brother and I were in Vietnam doing what he always did—working in the fields and pastures. The only difference was that he worked harder and longer when we were in the war zone. His only interruption came from a transistor radio he carried in the pocket of his khaki work shirt. Every hour on the hour, he stopped and listened for news of a war half a world away.

Not many cars traveled the dirt road that ran by his farm. When they did happen by, they left a long trail of thick red dust resembling the vapor trails made by high flying planes in the skies above me in Vietnam. I often wondered what motorists thought when they saw the lone figure of my father standing in the middle of the field with a radio held to his ear.

⚒ 11 SEPTEMBER 1969
Thursday

> Bn CO told Co CO today that after standdown I go to recon plt for 1 to 1½ months—Then to TOC for about same length of time—Then a company—Looks as if things are going my way
>
> Airmobiled south—Joint operation with ARVN, Thais, US and Aussies
>
> Mission today—Rain rain—Very thick jungle—Lots of trails—No contact
>
> M-79 buckshot round fired accidentally—Lucky soldier didn't kill someone—Discipline will be taken care of
>
> Observed many monkeys on mission

Loeffke's news brought the first realization that I would soon be leaving the first platoon and Charlie Company. That I would have a three-day standdown at BMB with the Company before my departure did little to quell the rising sadness.

Before we departed Cam Tam, Loeffke had also told me that my R&R dates were confirmed. I quickly wrote Linda and gave the letter to a door-gunner on the airmobile to mail for me when he returned to base. One of my shorter—but more important—notes to my wife, it read in total: "R&R, 13–19 Oct. Details later."

My previous long-range goal of surviving till 18 April 1970 had been put aside in favor of the dates the next month. R&R was now my objective. If I could make it that long, I would worry about April later.

But before standdown and R&R, it was work as usual.

Safety was one of my constant concerns. Hourly, or more often, I passed the word for the men to check the safeties on their weapons. Everyone carried his M-16 with one hand on the front hand-grip and the other wrapped around the lower stock and trigger housing. A finger rested on the trigger while the thumb rested on the safety lever, making the soldier instantly ready to flip it to semi- or full-automatic.

The majority of soldiers in our one hundred-man company had never held, much less fired, a rifle before joining the Army. With such a large group of heavily armed men, accidents were always a possibility. Checks and reminders about safety were continuous chores of leaders at all levels.

The M-79 was particularly dangerous. Its safety was located on top of the stock, just behind the breech. It could easily be knocked into the fire position by a vine or a careless hand. Even worse was the fact that the safety did not work dependably, sometimes allowing the weapon to fire even in the "safe" position. As a result, our SOP called for the M-79 to be carried in the breech-open position with a round in the chamber. If needed, the gun could quickly be snapped closed.

Another precaution was never letting the FNGs carry the weapon. I assigned the M-79 only to the more experienced soldiers who had learned to be conscious of the dangers of its erratic safety device and who were cool enough in combat to be sure its grenades would have a clear path to the target before discharge.

During movement through the jungle, the M-79 gunner loaded the weapon with buckshot rounds rather than the high explosive grenades. In close quarters, the large shotgunlike cartridges were safer for us and just as lethal to a close-in enemy.

Careful supervision, combined with a lot of luck, had prevented any accidental weapon discharges in the first platoon until this date, when we were skirting the edge of a large bomb crater. I heard the booming shot a short distance behind me and saw dirt kicked up by the lead slugs just a few meters to my right. We all hit the ground. As my mind caught up with my reactions, I quickly understood that the danger had passed.

The M-79 gunner, who had been in the platoon almost as long as I had, explained that he had tripped on a vine and had accidentally closed the weapon breech in trying to regain his balance.

The specialist was one of my best soldiers. It had been only luck that had sent the buckshot into the ground instead of into the back of the man to the gunner's front.

The realization that he had nearly killed a fellow soldier might be punishment enough for the guilty troop. However, I let the soldier, as well as every man in the platoon, know that the errant shot had cost the man seven days' pay. No one had to tell them that the shame about the accident outweighed the loss of dollars.

✈ 12 SEPTEMBER 1969
Friday

> Moved north for extraction by CH-47
> On way spotted 4 gooks—Engaged with neg results—Gooks returned fire—No sweat
> Finally back to BMB—Caught up on a little drinking & card playing

> "Soldier, Soldier, come from the wars,
> Did ye see no more o' my true love?"
> "I seed 'im running by when the shots begun to fly—
> But you'd best go look for a new love."
>
> Rudyard Kipling

Morale was high as we headed to the LZ and standdown. Little's platoon had the point, followed by the first platoon, the Company CP and the other two platoons.

In our rush to meet the helicopters, we failed to spot the four camouflaged gooks although we had moved within twenty-five meters of their position.

Our numbers must have frightened them because half of the Company had passed their position when they tried to sneak away. McGinnis' RTOs saw their movement and fired. SGT Ito, Morford, DeForrest, and I were only a few steps in front of the CO. As we half crawled, half ran back to McGinnis' position, Ito, with a big grin, said, "Let's go get the sons of bitches." I yelled at Tom Fallon to get some artillery going to block the enemy's escape route, and the chase was on.

With Morford and Ito in the lead, the four of us set out at a dead run. Our path was a small trail where we could see fresh tracks in the mud. A hundred meters later, we came across a dropped, loaded AK47 magazine—evidence that the gooks were running scared. For some reason my team and I did not share their fear. We laughed and shouted obscenities about what we were going to do to the gooks when we caught them as we huffed and puffed in pursuit.

Morford got close enough a couple of times to see movement in the thick jungle ahead. He sprayed the area with his M-16 while still on the run. DeForrest was by now cussing the heavy radio as much as the gooks, but he managed to keep up so I could talk to Fallon on the horn and adjust the artillery.

After the chase had covered a klick, our excitement and good humor began turning into fatigue. The realization that the gooks might be running back to a large force or a bunker complex slowed our pace. A fork in the trail provided a good excuse to stop.

It had been a crazy pursuit with more dangers than we admitted. Our smiles returned, though, as our lungs began to recover and we headed back to the Company. My last fire fight with Charlie Company, no matter how brief, had been fun.

We were quickly on the move again, and a short time later we were airborne on our way to Black Horse.

The trucks, taking us to BMB were late as usual, so we had an hour or so to wait. A couple of Donut Dollies entertained the troops with ridiculously childish games and skits which, much to my surprise, everyone seemed to enjoy. I noticed the round-eyed Donut Dollies were getting better looking with every month I spent in the jungle.

By the time the trucks arrived, one of the women had been convinced to ride to BMB with the first platoon rather than wait for the late afternoon courier helicopter. I wondered about her sense of smell as she climbed into the open truck with the twenty-five members of the platoon who had not bathed nor changed clothes for over a week. Whatever her sensitivities, her heart was in the right place. More than one of the soldiers fell in love with her during the two-hour ride back to BMB. The unbecoming name of "Biscuit Bitches"—often substituted for Donut Dollies—certainly did not apply to her.

The convoy back to BMB with a Donut Dolly aboard was a good reminder of the difference in danger levels in Vietnam. As grunts we were always alert, yet we felt little danger in a heavily armed convoy.

Black Horse and BMB received occasional rocket and mortar rounds, but there was absolutely no comparison between the hazards there and the dangers a field soldier faced every day. The Donut Dolly experienced more danger on this single convoy than many of the Saigon warrior types did on their entire tours.

Today I realized even better the small number of Vietnam veterans who faced the true hardships and dangers of the war. Nam has seemingly become the excuse for erratic actions by anyone who participated, regardless of his or her real involvement. I can only shake my head when I read or hear of a "former Long Binh supply clerk" who blames his present problems on the war.

➤ 13 SEPTEMBER 1969
Saturday

Camp Frenzell-Jones
    MARS call finally went through to Linda Ann—Good to
talk to her but sure seemed a long way away
    Party tonight—We raised hell
    My plt gave me a plaque—They said I was best plt ldr in
world—I nearly got sentimental

Units on standdown had priority on placing the MARS calls,
so mine took "only" five hours to get through. I called from
the Charlie Company orderly room around midnight after the
standdown party and spent the wait sleeping next to the telephone. By the time the MARS station rang me back, my head
was fairly clear from the evening's merriment.

In her excitement, Linda had trouble remembering to say
"over" when she finished speaking. The most memorable part
of the call was my "I love you, over," and her response, "I
love you, too, over." Five months and eleven thousand miles
made her and R&R seem so far away.

Sassner and Top had the usual band, steaks, and trailer loads
of beer ready for the standdown. The party was an excellent
method for everyone to unwind, for it allowed troops, NCOs,
and officers to interact as individuals rather than as the leaders
and the followers that field discipline demanded.

The plaque, combined with the sentiments of my men, made
the months of hardship, boredom, and terror worthwhile. I was
proud—as proud as I had ever been, and what I did not realize
at the time—as proud as I would ever be. My feelings were at
a peak that would, on rare occasions in the later months in
Nam and in future years in other locales, be equalled but never
exceeded. I had no regrets beyond the fact that Charlie Company was now part of my past rather than my present.

✎ **14 SEPTEMBER 1969**
Sunday

> BMB
>> Party at NCO Club
>> Rest & booze—That's a standdown

My final night in Charlie Company was spent with the sergeants and officers in the NCO Club. I shook some hands but said few good-byes. Farewells were part of the tour, and the turnover rate was so high that everyone knew there would be many new faces by the next standdown three months down the road.

Most of the talk around the beer-can and shot-glass laden table was about past fights. Brags of body counts accompanied by hysterical laughter about humorous incidents filled the smoky room. We depleted the club's supply of Michelob beer after SGT Ito discovered that the Vietnamese waitress pronounced the brand "make love." She did not understand the laughter each time she asked if we wanted another round of "make love."

The party ended when one of the men grabbed a mini-skirted waitress and threw her on top of the table. He was almost successful in burying his head between her brown thighs before the club bouncers and MPs arrived. The club manager expressed concern that none of us around the table had tried to stop the activities and had, instead, only laughed at the girl's shrieks. McGinnis explained with a reasonably straight face that he thought it was part of the floor show.

The CO, Fallon, Stewart, and I stopped by the officers' club on our way back to the Company. No swinging doors graced the entrance to the club but the following minutes closely resembled the Western saloon scenes on the silver screen. McGinnis partially shoved, mostly kicked, the club's door open. He entered first with the three of us spread out close behind. Charlie Company was the only grunt outfit on standdown at BMB at the time, and except for a table of well-oiled aviators in one corner, the room was full of REMFs.

Our noisy entrance quieted the club. The band, between songs, waited to see what was going to happen before starting their next number. McGinnis walked to a table occupied by lieutenants and captains wearing the "shields of shame" of the Adjutant General Corps. Politely, the CO thanked them for reserving our table. In seconds the clerk-types finished their drinks and exited.

As we took the now-vacant chairs, drinks arrived, courtesy of the aviators. We recognized several who had flown ammo in to us on 7 August. While we had no great love for anyone not in the Infantry, the helicopter jocks were as good company as we could find in the land of the REMFs.

After things quieted, McGinnis told me Tom Fallon would be the next first platoon leader. His transfer from the Artillery was not yet official, but the CO said no one would be out in the jungle to see how he used his officers.

———————————————————————————
———————————————————————————

🛩 15 SEPTEMBER 1969
Monday

BMB
    Ready to go to boonies in Echo Recon
    Back to BH by truck convoy—strange to drop C Co and not go with them

    "Duty is the sublimest word in the language; you can never do more than your duty; you shall never wish to do less."

                          Gen Robert E. Lee

Before departing BMB, I sent Linda a letter which pretty well summed up how I felt about the last five months. I wrote:

> "Honey, you asked how the war is affecting me and what I value. Have no worries. I love life—My love for you and ours could not be any more. I am careful. However, you have to realize that there is very much of a war going on. When the shit starts flying, I have to make the best decisions possible. My first consideration is how not to take any casualties—including myself. Second is how best to eliminate the enemy entirely. We have done well in both.
>
> Besides being 25 pounds lighter, much tanner and blonder, I'm still me. Don't worry."

Tom Fallon and I both rode with the first platoon back to Black Horse. The convoy stopped at the base only long enough to drop me off.

I told Tom to take care of the platoon, and he warned me to be careful in recon as I jumped out of the truck and stood beside the road while the rest of the Company passed by. I waved a farewell to the men who had played such an important role in my life the last months. McGinnis gave me a "thumbs up" as they disappeared down the road.

I turned and began walking slowly to the Echo Company headquarters and the recon platoon. By the time I got there, I was looking forward, not backward.

🐾 16 SEPTEMBER 1969
Tuesday

Black Horse
  Recon is out on a mission—No way to get out to them—
They had a small contact last night
  Mostly just got more rest.

Echo Company was smaller than the other units in the Battalion, having only the recon platoon, a 4.2-inch heavy mortar platoon, and a section of ground surveillance radar operators. The Company Commander, 1LT Hank Billings, held a position I did not covet, for I had no desire to command from a fire base.

Recon worked directly for the Battalions Operations officer and MAJ Loeffke. According to the Battalion Commander, our mission was to find the enemy, destroy them when we found them in small enough numbers, or direct the other units to the gooks' location if their numbers were too large for us to engage alone.

I was disappointed that I could not immediately join the platoon. However, I understood that my insertion by helicopter would compromise their mission. The key to recon's success and survival was stealth. As a single platoon operating far from other friendly units, the unit had to "see without being seen."

My prior association with the platoon had been minimal. My most vivid memory of the platoon had been a few weeks earlier when they briefly stopped at Marge.

At that time the platoon leader's radio had been adorned with a gleaming white skull which had many colored ribbons attached to the forehead. Each piece of cloth had a date and a number, chronicling the date and body count of each contact over the past year.

When I asked about the skull, Hank Billings told me it had "been found in the paddies" long before we came north. He said the platoon no longer carried the trophy after a picture of it had appeared in *Stars and Stripes*. It seemed that several of the high ranking folks in Saigon had objected to the platoon's method of maintaining historical records. Hank added that the skull "may have been buried in the jungle or sent home by one of the troops." He laughed, saying he did not want to know the method of disposition.

✈ 17 SEPTEMBER 1969
Wednesday

Black Horse
    Recon returned
    Met the men and talked to them—Seem to be a damn good
bunch
    Understand now I am to have recon for 1½ to 2 months

I met the platoon at the landing strip and rode back to Echo Company with the platoon sergeant, Staff Sergeant Robert Standard. Standard, about six feet tall and weighing more than 240 pounds, was an unusual Infantryman. His weight and physique did not match his reputation as one of the most professional NCOs in the Battalion. Standard was the type of soldier whom the peace-time Army would not allow to reenlist because of his extra pounds. In Vietnam, however, his leadership and ability to gain body count were far more important than his personal appearance.

Standard briefed me on the platoon's recent actions, beginning by showing me the two AK47s they had captured and the man responsible for the two-body count. PFC Joe Johnson, a massive black from Forth Worth, Texas was credited with both kills. He cradled his M-60 machine gun as if it were a toy. I learned over the next weeks that Johnson was a bright, gentle man, but my first impression of him was that he was the meanest, toughest looking individual I had ever seen. His fatigue shirt sleeves bulged from seam-splitting arms that rippled with muscles.

Johnson told the story of killing the two gooks with the calmness of describing a walk through a city park. His squad had just reached an ambush position at dusk two nights earlier. Before they had had a chance to set their Claymores out, Joe had spotted the two dinks approaching directly toward him. Opening fire with the M-60 in deliberate six-round bursts, he dropped both of the men, killing them before anyone else fired a shot. Johnson's accuracy with the machine gun was fantastic. He had fired only twelve shots. Four of the bullets from the first burst had struck the chest of the lead dink, and several of the rounds from the second burst had found their mark in the following dink's head, leaving nothing but a bloody mess of skull fragments and brains.

Standard joked that he guessed he would have to talk with Johnson about wasting bullets.

Johnson's squad had grabbed the gooks' weapons and moved quickly to another site because recon was too small to stay in a contact area for any length of time.

At the conclusion of the debriefing, I gave Standard the chance to clean up before we talked further. In less than an hour he approached me wearing nothing but a towel and shower shoes. As he headed for the showers, he handed me a piece of paper with notes that would help acquaint me with the members of the platoon.

I lay back on a cot and carefully studied the sergeant's comments. After only a few lines, I even better appreciated the wide-spread reputation of my new platoon sergeant. His hurried printing revealed that he knew his men's experience, capabilities, and personal problems as well. It would be several days before I knew the platoon well enough to thoroughly evaluate Standard's comments, but in every case he proved to be right on target.

Standard's synopsis was a good start. I placed the notes between the pages of my journal for reference. I am glad I did, as this profile list of the men in recon is one of my best keepsakes of the platoon and the war.

The notes included these comments:

> PFC Plescia—Good soldier but hasn't yet totally grasped duties of RTO—Field 2½ months
> SGT (acting) Brown—Outstanding soldier, with more experience, outstanding sqd ldr, but is lonely—Field 6 mo.

SGT (acting) McKinney—Same as Brown, but sometimes is too inquisitive and voices opinion very often—
Field 8 mo.

SP4 Nyman—Quiet, reliable soldier. Very competent
and willing to do his job—5 mo.

PFC Grayson—Very reliable, but so far knows only his
job well—2½ mo.

PFC Johnson—Good soldier, lacks enthusiasm but does
his job—2 mo.

PFC Knudsen—A bit hot-tempered, but controlled and
cool in field—2 mo.

SGT (acting) Smith—Understands his duties very well
and can be completely relied on, sometimes seems
less a leader than he is—8 mo.

SGT Harrison—Seems very good so far. Perhaps a bit
overzealous, but with age comes caution—1 mo.

SP4 Young—Pointman. Does good job, but goofs off
some in rear. Is tired of field, and is "only child"—6
mo.

SGT Mobley—Outstanding in field. Sometimes gets
overly bull-headed in rear—6 mo.

PFC Spuriel—Just a good soldier, no more, no less—2
mo.

PFC Lowrey—Very intelligent and capable, a potential
leader—2 mo.

PFC Johnson, J—A good all-round man, one of the platoon's morale builders—2 mo.

SGT McHaffey—Very cool and reliable, but needs a bit
more field duty—2 mo.

PFC Smith JR—Extremely reliable. One of the best men
you have—8 mo.

PFC Hexam—I don't know. Has been gone over a
month to sniper school—2 mo.

PFC Binda—An average soldier doing his best—2 mo.

SP4 McKown—Outstanding and intelligent. Good leader
material—5 mo.

Interspersed between the lines were the names of PFCs Gib-
son, Rankin, Rash, R. Young, Felty, Prescott, Clarke and
Matterand—each followed by the notation FNG. Standard and
I would learn together what these men could do.

The platoon sergeant returned a few minutes after I finished studying the list. I thanked him for his thoroughness, told him I was looking forward to being part of recon, and commented that I had heard good things about him.

My initial talk to the platoon was brief. Beyond sketching my background and telling them I was proud to be their leader, I said little. During the rest of the day I wandered through the barracks talking to each man individually, which confirmed my feelings that they were a closely knit, confident group.

SSG Standard accompanied me on my rounds. He now wore jungle fatigues rather than his towel, but his footwear was still shower shoes. When I made comment on his Ho Chi Minh sandals, made of pieces of truck tire and leather straps, one of the soldiers laughed and said, ''We had to kill a hell of a lot of gooks to finally find one whose sandals fit Big Sarge.''

🪰 18 SEPTEMBER 1969
Thursday

> Supposed to have a day off for recon today—However A Co got in contact—We airmobiled in to help—Everything over by the time we got there—A Co got 1 gook and 1 AK47
> We swept south—Sighted some bunkers
> Rained like hell most of day—Very cold tonight
> Recon is good
> Hell of a birthday

Recon was organized into three squads, each containing two teams capable of operating independently under the leadership of a sergeant. However, we rarely broke down to less than squad size and most often kept the entire platoon together.

Instead of one RTO in my headquarters, I now had two, as I had to maintain commo with the squads as well as the Battalion TOC. Standard, the RTOs and I spent the morning going over the platoon's SOPs. As much as possible, communications between me and the subordinate leaders were by arm and hand signals. A hand waved in a circular motion meant for the squad leaders to come to my position; a fist pumped up and down signaled the men to move out or speed up; a hand to the ear indicated sounds detected; and a snap of the fingers alerted the unit that gooks had been spotted.

The Battalion TOC called hourly for situation reports. If recon's position was unchanged, the RTO broke squelch twice by pushing the radio handset button. When the platoon changed locations, the RTO converted the numbered grid coordinates into letters from our code books and whispered the information into the handset.

Spoken words were kept to a minimum. Over the next weeks I would often go for days without saying anything aloud beyond a few whispered coded coordinates.

Recon's day off came to a quick end with word of Alpha Company's contact. We scrambled to grab rucksacks and were at the air strip waiting for helicopters within ten minutes.

As we waited, I noticed that many of the men tied the loose legs of their fatigue trousers around their calfs with NVA belts or strips of OD cloth. My RTO, PFC Plescia, explained that this prevented the pant legs from making noise while moving through the jungle. Besides serving as a precautionary measure, the brown belts—and there were many—also represented symbols of kills, much like the notches on gun butts. Plescia added what I had already learned in Charlie Company—the damn gook belts were too small for even the tiniest GI's waist.

Another practice followed to keep down noise was not wearing the steel helmets. The risk of the pinging and scraping of tree branches against the metal headgear outweighed the protective advantage of the pots. Instead, we all wore full-brimmed, round floppy ''boonie hats'' made of heavy cloth which offered protection only from the sun.

We landed in an area where Alpha Company had reported the gooks were headed. The driving rain made finding trails difficult, but SP4 Young proved he was as good as Standard had noted in his profile. Darkness was nearly upon us when Young picked up a trail and led us far enough to detect bunkers. We pulled back, as we were far too few in numbers to go up against an enemy base camp.

Carrying no ponchos because the rubber made too much noise, we huddled under our poncho liners throughout the rainy night. It was a wet, cold, miserable twenty-third birthday.

✈ 19 SEPTEMBER 1969
Friday

> Called in artillery on bunkers—After careful recon found no enemy present
> Arty of this morning was terrible—Must have had guns laid in wrong
> Finally airmobiled back to BH
> Rained most of the day again

> "Whenever we stroll there are always three—
> You and I and the next war."
>
> Contemporary Israeli Poem

No artillery FO accompanied the recon platoon, so I communicated directly with the artillery battery. As usual, I first called in a smoke round to be sure I was correct in the target's location. Everything worked well until the entire battery of six tubes fired. Four rounds landed on target, but two rounds landed in the distant jungle.

I immediately called a check fire and, as angrily as one can whisper on a radio, demanded they check their guns. The artillery's fire direction center called back minutes later and said the problem was fixed without explaining what had gone wrong. My journal entry later in the day still reflected my anger, as the misguided rounds could just as easily have landed on us.

I was mad as hell. But at the same time, I would have readily admitted, if asked, that the redlegs had pulled me out of more than one bad spot. Yet it was hard to be tolerant of mistakes—even though we all made them.

Our recon of the bunkers revealed that they had not been occupied in some time. We followed a trail out of the camp but lost it in the continuous rain. During a brief weather clearing in the afternoon, helicopters picked us up and returned the platoon to Black Horse.

---

20 SEPTEMBER 1969
Saturday

Black Horse
   A day at BH
   Usual—Drank and slept

Over a few beers Standard and I discussed the platoon. His recommendations for various personnel changes and promotions were well-thought-out, and I approved them without question.

Recon was at Black Horse more than the regular Infantry companies. Missions usually were shorter but more intense with constant movement and little rest. Since the men managed to get little sleep in the jungle, they spent much of their time at the base camp "catching Zs."

Recon's soldiers had had the same training before Nam as

the rest of the grunts. When replacements arrived in the Battalion, they were offered the opportunity to volunteer for recon. If no one stepped forward, we got whoever the personnel officer "recruited" for us. If a soldier tried recon and wanted a transfer to a regular platoon, we let him go. Few ever made the choice of leaving, however, because the platoon was a tight unit where the men took care of each other.

Standard, a few years older than I and the oldest in the platoon, often talked of staying in the service, but he knew he would have to lose many pounds to get along in the Stateside Army. I did not care what the Army expected a man to look like. Standard could soldier with the best of them, for I had watched him move in the jungle as quietly as a lizard without seeming to tire or slow down. The men responded to his orders with respect. That was enough for me.

🐟 21 SEPTEMBER 1969
Sunday

> Moved out with K Troop 2nd Plt ACR—A damn good outfit—Of course, they ride, we walk
> Still a pretty good operation
> Set up NDP and AP
> Only contacts were with a deer (missed) and a big lizard (hit)
> Got VR of area prior to mission

K Troop, one of the last units of the 11th Armored Cavalry Regiment at Black Horse, joined us in the mission. Our operation was designed to take advantage of the stealth of the recon platoon in coordination with the fire power of the Cavalry.

The K Troop platoon had five M-113 armored personnel

carriers, each mounted with one 50-caliber and two M-60 machine guns. Augmenting the unit were two Sheridan light tanks, each armed with a 152mm main gun—capable of firing HE or fleshette-filled canister rounds—and one heavy and one light machine gun. One of the personnel carriers sported a 4.2-inch mortar and pulled a trailer full of HE and illumination rounds.

We spent the day in several ambush positions while the Cav vehicles moved toward us through the elephant-grass plains and along the edges of the jungle. The idea was that the enemy would flee from the loud, heavily armed Cav platoon into our ambush. Although the plan was well-executed, the results were negative.

The K Troop platoon was well-disciplined and easy to work with. Their platoon leader was accurate in his map-reading as well as careful to ensure his men were always aware of our locations to prevent any misguided firing.

My only problem with the Cavalrymen was their complete lack of noise discipline—a philosophy diametrically opposite ours. Since the roar of their huge diesel engines drowned out any other sounds, they were not at all concerned about loud talking or firing their weapons. I was surprised when the Cav lieutenant opened fire on a small deer. Then just before dark another Cav soldier shot a three-foot lizard out of a tree. Recon did not appreciate the noise—nor the flying guts of the splattered reptile.

I never saw an Infantryman show any concern over killing enemy soldiers. Lizards, regardless of size, were a different matter. Their abilities to move quietly and blend into the colors of the foliage had gained our admiration. One smaller species of lizard we found especially endearing. It frequently broke the stillness of the boonies with a croaking sound that closely resembled, "Fuck you." FNGs were told that the "fuck you" lizards were NVA taunting us. Grunts thought that any creature with such a foul mouth must be kin to the Infantryman.

22 SEPTEMBER 1969
Monday

> Chased sensor readings with Cav—Neg results—Tonight
> set up on a heavy VC trail—Tracks' trip flare ignited—They
> opened up with 50s, 60s and Sheridan canister rounds—These
> boys really have the fire power—They didn't want to sweep
> area with tracks—I did with 6 grunts—Kind of funny

Intelligence gathering efforts by Brigade included a gambit of Buck Rogers devices that ranged from infrared radar to aerial photography. Sensitive microphones, imbedded in the ground along trails and monitored at stations in the larger fire bases, supposedly had the capability to "hear" an enemy.

We spent the entire day racing from site to site where the intel folks were sure the enemy was located. Most of the time we rode the Cav tracks, but several of the sensor hot spots were in jungle too thick for the iron monsters to penetrate. On those occasions, it was back to beating the bush for recon.

A couple of the spots indicated by the sensor reports showed recent enemy activity. Another was occupied by a large troop of monkeys that obviously did not realize that their warm bodies had assured some intel officer that his millions of dollars worth of electronics had pinpointed the enemy for us bumbling Infantrymen. Regardless, we found no gooks. Except for the track platoon's mongrel dog mascot that seemed to enjoy the bumpy ride atop the platoon leader's track, it was not a good day for the Cavalrymen or the grunts.

Riding the tracks surely beat walking, but it had its disadvantages as well. On more than one occasion while cracking through trees and vines, we hit nests of red ants which broke open and covered everyone in the track carrier. The half-inch-long insects built their homes in branches by sticking together leaves and twigs into fist-size balls. When disturbed, the damn ants stung everything and everybody they could reach.

After the second ant attack resulted in the vehicle's stopping while the troops slapped at themselves and tore off their clothing, the Cav lieutenant remarked that if the ants were twice the size they were, no one—American nor Vietnamese—would be able to go into the jungle.

Our last sensor chase of the day brought us to a well-used trail in an area of high grass with thickets of small trees. The Cav platoon made overlapping circles until the vegetation was flattened for several hundred meters on both sides of the trail. We set up a tight perimeter in the center of the newly made clearing with the majority of the tracks' weapons oriented to the trail's entrances. Across the well-worn path, the Cav placed wires leading to flares that would illuminate an area fifteen meters wide when tripped.

A couple of hours after dark one of the trip flares suddenly lit up the trail. In an instant a Sheridan fired a canister round, then machine gun tracers, toward the flare. Soon the entire perimeter was blazing away.

My soldiers were crouched on the ground beside the tracks. None were firing, as I had not told them to. I could see no enemy, and the Cav was not receiving any return fire.

I had the 4.2-inch mortar crew drop a couple of illumination rounds over the tripped flare. The Cav ceased fire when they could find no targets in the now well-lit clearing.

After darkness returned, I asked the Cav platoon leader what his people had seen. Just as I reached him, another flare—near the first—went off and the entire perimeter of the Cav opened fire once more. Again, illumination rounds from the mortar revealed nothing.

When I reported the incident, Battalion told us to check out the area. I suggested to the Cav lieutenant that he send a track to investigate. When he replied that it was too risky, I told him that recon would handle it. My bravado was based far more on my doubts that the enemy was anywhere near than on bravery.

Precautions were still in order, however. While we waited for our eyes to adjust to the darkness a second time, I walked to each of the Cav vehicles. I told the soldier in charge of each that six grunts and I were going outside the perimeter and that if they so much as fired a single shot while we were out, no matter for what reason, they would answer to the rest of recon.

One of the Sheridan crewmen assured me there would be no problem, explaining that the big 152 gun's electrical firing device did not work anyway. He said the only way they could shoot was to run a wire from an interior dome light to the breech. As he rolled up the wire and put it in his pocket, I commended him for his ingenuity.

SGT McHaffey's team and I quickly covered the two hundred meters to the burnt-out flares, where we were welcomed, not by dink bodies, but by the Cav's mongrel dog shivering behind a small log. Except for being frightened, he was unhurt. I noticed that several of the small trees that had been run over in making the clearing were slowly regaining their vertical posture in the cool night air.

I carried the dog back to the Cav lieutenant and told him he was lucky that recon had not joined his platoon in the firing or he would have had one dead dog.

We reported the negative findings to Battalion without noting the possibilities that either the dog or Mother Nature might have been responsible for tripping the flares.

I slept well the rest of the night. Every gook in a ten-mile radius knew our location and fire power. I figured no enemy in the entire country was dumb enough to attack such a force. If they were, they were not worth losing sleep over.

✇ 23 SEPTEMBER 1969
Tuesday

Moved by track back to Black Horse—Hope to work with them again—First track outfit I've had any respect for

Working with the Armored Cavalry had been a good change of pace. My complimentary comments for K Troop were more significant than they may appear, as I was well past the point of respecting to any degree anyone who was not an Infantryman.

A stack of mail and late-arriving birthday packages greeted me on return to Black Horse. Along with various foods, Linda had enclosed a 12- by 18-inch hand-knitted American flag she had made. The platoon and I quickly consumed the chow. I carried the flag the rest of my tour.

A letter from my brother said that his son was healthy in every respect. The accompanying birthday package showed Jim's awareness of what I would be hungry for. A large container of pickled sausages and a can of green English peas provided a wonderful late birthday dinner.

24 SEPTEMBER 1969
Wednesday

> Moved from BH to Cam Tam by truck—Saw CPT Mc-Ginnis at Cam Tam—His morale seems low also—Then moved southwest for nighttime position

Charlie Company was back working out of the ARVN compound. I missed seeing my old platoon, as they were in the jungle, but it was good to talk to McGinnis.

I called Tom Fallon on the Charlie Company radio, violating most of the communications-security procedures in the process. Our personal conversation might have been against the regulations, but we had been in the field long enough that we mostly went by our own rules rather than by those made by the non-warriors. After all, what were they going to do, send us to Vietnam?

🛩 25 SEPTEMBER 1969
Thursday

Moved south—Long, long hump with negative results

"Bravery is the capacity to perform properly when scared half to death."

General Omar Bradley

The long patrol through the rubber plantation and on into the jungle gave me plenty of time to think. I tried to concentrate on the mission, but my mind often wandered. I thought about the prospects of my getting my own company, and the count down of days to R&R was never far from my thoughts, although the idea of six days with Linda in Hawaii was difficult to picture or believe.

In the years that have passed since I was in Vietnam, I have ventured far from the fundamentalist religious beliefs of my youth. Those days in the jungle, however, I carried a belief that prayer would help see us through. It never crossed my mind that the enemy soldiers might also be praying to their god with the same fervor for their preservation and our destruction.

My soldiers wore crosses, crucifixes or, occasionally, the Star of David while the Asians wore small figures of Buddha strung around their necks. We laughed at their habit of clenching the charms in their teeth when they went into battle against us. Their metal or wooden Buddha, found still clenched in dead jaws, made good souvenirs for the GIs.

Our religious beliefs (and lack of respect for theirs) did not stop us from taking what we could from those for whom the rites of protection had not worked. Some of the troops found satisfaction in extracting gold teeth with bayonets and later selling them for additional platoon beer money. FNGs were instructed that to get to the gold treasures they had to force the dead dinks' jaw bones downward, for the top of the mouth was immobile.

I prayed often in the jungle for Divine protection for my men as well as myself. Close brushes with death brought not a feeling that I was invulnerable but rather that my number might be due to turn up at any time.

As the days passed, my prayers became simpler. All I asked for was to make it to R&R and have a week with Linda. I promised whoever was hearing my prayers that I would ask nothing else if I could just have this.

26 SEPTEMBER 1969
Friday

> Moved south—Set up night ambush on well used trail—
> Once again no results
> Getting damn hot again

If you live in an abnormal environment long enough, you adjust so that the abnormal becomes normal. I rarely thought any more about the constant conditions of being wet, dirty and physically exhausted. An extreme change, such as an unusually hot day, might merit brief notation in my journal, but as often as not, I made the entry for lack of anything else to say rather than because it was really important.

A shower in a base camp or a bath in a cold stream had

become a real pleasure instead of a daily routine. When the silent hand signal of a single finger extended in a wiggling motion was passed along our column as a warning that we were entering an area heavily infested with leeches, I felt no real concern. I had picked dozens of the slimy blood suckers off my body, and they had ceased to bother me.

Long ago days of soft beds, regular meals, and nights lit with flashing neon lights were in a past that seemed neither real nor important. I had not driven an automobile nor sat in a bath tub in nearly half a year. I spent my days with the burdens of keeping my men alive and of seeking out the goddamn gooks who were the cause of our hardships. Beyond those objectives, I lived for more of the same, a company command and R&R.

---

27 SEPTEMBER 1969
Saturday

Airmobiled near Highway 1—Moved southeast and began checking hills—Lots of hard climbing with negative results

The helicopters carried us back to the north to check out the hills McGinnis and I had wanted to recon several months earlier. We moved fast after hitting the LZ, as the swarm of choppers would let the gooks know GIs were in the area.

Because many of my men were on R&R or had been left back at Black Horse with respiratory problems, recon was down to a field strength of twenty-one. Some of the sick men could have kept up without difficulty, but the coughs from their colds would have endangered our ability to move silently through the jungle.

Our rucksacks were a little lighter now because we were carrying the new freeze-dried rations called LURPs instead of the Cs. The plastic-bagged chow weighed only ounces and was designed to be eaten dry or reconstituted with water. Initial issue of the packets went to Long Range Reconnaissance Patrols (LRRPs) of the Ranger units and to recon platoons like ourselves.

Water heated in a canteen cup over a small piece of burning C-4 explosive made the dry chunks of beef and the chicken mixed with vegetables look like a real meal. We soon found, however, that the chili and beans could never be soaked thoroughly enough. Even Standard, who could eat anything, said that the rock-hard beans would make good shrapnel for the home-made gook hand grenades.

The LURPs were a tasty change from our meager diets, but they got monotonous far quicker than the C-rats, even with the additives of hot pepper and Heinz 57 sauce. Recon platoon was soon referring to the LURPs as "wet sawdust" and "sawdust with rocks." We went back to carrying the heavier C-rations and a LURP or two to break the routine.

Both types of rations were accompanied by a small brown foil accessory pack containing instant coffee, sugar, salt, chewing gum, and toilet paper. It also contained a packet of four stale cigarettes that were usually Chesterfield or Lucky Strike. These cigarettes provided a good way to cut back on our smoking, for most of us were accustomed to the filtered brands.

Another item each accessory pack contained was a sanitary-wrapped white plastic spoon which I threw away as I unwrapped each ration. I reused the same spoon for weeks at a time. After each use I wiped it on my filthy jungle fatigue trousers and returned it to my shirt pocket. My spoon was dirty, stained, and, of course, not very healthful. Nonetheless, it was my spoon, and I would be damned if I used a new one each time just because one came with each meal. In a war where everything was in a constant

state of change, including the men who fought it, my spoon
was my one bit of permanency.

_____

🛩 **28 SEPTEMBER 1969**
Sunday

> Finished up search of hill mass with negative results—Was
> told we would go in today—However Bn had us move 2 klicks
> to the NW—Hard moving—Bad jungle
> Rained like hell

According to the calendar, the monsoon season was supposed to be ending. Regardless of the ''supposed to's,'' it
rained every day.

Rumors were abundant that the enemy would pick up its
activities as soon as the rain stopped. We hoped that the reports
were accurate, as we were far more prepared to fight men than
we were prepared to endure any more of the constant wet. In
our present conditions we faced a better chance of rusting to
death than suffering any ills from the dinks.

Our unending movement through the jungle brought me to
a point where I promised myself that if I ever got out of Vietnam, I would never walk another step not absolutely necessary. Months before in El Paso, while shopping for my journal
with my brother, I noticed that he returned to his car and drove
as little as a block to the next shop rather than walk. He told
me that after Vietnam I would never enjoy walking again. As
recon humped through the jungle, I knew that Jim was right.

✄ 29 SEPTEMBER 1969
Monday

> Moved to Tan Lap—Rat Patrol got 1 body count there last
> night
> Rain again last night
> Tonight moved into cordon position
> Bn is pushing really hard—I am the most run-down I've
> been in a long time—Not long till R&R
> Talked with Bn CO again today—Once again he promised
> me a company

Tan Lap, a village of several hundred residents just south
of Highway 1 between Long Binh and Xuan Luc, had houses
quite similar to those in Cam Tam, as it also had originally
been built as a company town by Michelin. A rubber processing plant, a small general store, and a district government
office were its only enterprises. Many shacks, made of corru-
gated iron and flattened tin cans, were on the edge of the
village. Their occupants were apparently farmers who had
moved into the village for the protection offered by a platoon
of RF/PF soldiers. A soccer field on the outer perimeter of the
hamlet served as an excellent helicopter landing zone.

Several kilometers to the north across the highway was a compound of French villas surrounded by a broken-glass and con-
certina-wire topped wall. The complex housed the management
officials of the Michelin Company which owned the rubber plantations in the entire area. We were told the compound was off-
limits to all US personnel. Reports from helicopter pilots, who
overflew the complex, saying that it had a swimming pool fre-
quented by a blonde added to the mystery of the place.

Except for an armed guard at the compound gate, the
Frenchmen seemed unconcerned with security. Dressed in im-
maculate white linen suits, complete with matching white Pan-
ama hats, they toured the rubber plantation and drove the roads

in their long black 1950's vintage limousines with no apparent regard for the war. One of the primary functions of the Frenchmen seemed to be the filing of claims against the governments of South Vietnam and the United States for damages done to their property. Rumor had it that most of the money from the settlements went to the VC as taxes for the security the French obviously felt—and took advantage of.

The Frenchmen totally ignored our presence and always directed any questions or inquiries to the local ARVNs rather than any US Forces—even Loeffke, who spoke French and was one of the senior officers in the area. It seemed strange that they lived so comfortably, and profitably, in the midst of a war zone.

Tan Lap had been a stop on the railroad that ran along Highway 1 until VC sappers destroyed the tracks and bridges. The abandoned train station now served as a base of operations for our troops.

When Loeffke met me at the depot upon our arrival at Tan Lap, I noticed the new rank of lieutenant colonel on his collar and congratulated him on his promotion. He reassured me that I was still to get a company and then briefed me on the battalion-sized cordon that recon would be joining that night. He was optimistic about the mission because the Rat Patrol's body count the previous evening had indicated that a nearby village was providing supplies to the enemy.

Loeffke did not elaborate on the body count, and it was not until later in the day that I learned that he had been in the middle of the contact. A sergeant in charge of the two Rat jeeps said that they had planned to stay with the mortar platoon the night before until Loeffke arrived at dusk and took the sergeant and his two jeep teams into the rubber. They had pulled off the road, put out Claymores, and stacked brush to hide the jeeps.

About midnight they had heard a gook walking down the middle of the road. Detonating a Claymore and opening up with machine gun fire, they had zapped him before he could raise his gun. But seconds later they had realized the dink must have been the point man for a large force because suddenly green tracers filled the air around them.

The sergeant laughed as he told of pulling Claymores into the jeep by their wires and of racing wildly down the road in retreat. Except for a few bullet holes in one vehicle, they had gotten away clean. The NCO and his men had been terrified but said that Loeffke had been totally calm and not at all concerned that, as the Battalion Commander, he had been out on a five-man ambush. With a final laugh, the sergeant concluded that the jeep had likely set a land speed record for a Vietnamese rubber plantation road. As I walked away, he mumbled, more to himself than to me, "But it really wasn't funny at the time."

✎ 30 SEPTEMBER 1969
Tuesday

Tan Lap
    Finished cordon—Understand it went badly—Returned to Tan Lap—Finally got trucked back to Black Horse—Learned our 2–3 day break was cancelled—Prepared to move out tomorrow
    The "Old Guard" is not what it used to be—Bn CO and XO pushing too hard—S-3 and Hq Co CO and S-5 all requested transfers—There is very little cooperation—I will endure it in hopes of getting a company
    Pay day

We had moved into our position in the cordon the evening before. For the next several hours I had listened on the Battalion radio to the confusion of the rest of the units. Several companies were late getting into place while another set up in the wrong location, leaving a gap in the encirclement of the village.

I was disappointed about the cancellation of the promised break for recon, and my evaluations in my journal about the declining effectiveness of the Battalion reflected my attitude.

Loeffke commanded on the ground instead of from helicopters, and he shared the hardships and dangers with complete disregard for his own comfort. As Battalion Commander he was out to accomplish the Infantry's sole mission: to destroy the enemy. If he had a fault, it was one imposed by calendar rather than character. Loeffke knew that he had only six months to command the Old Guard before the Army gave command to another officer. At times we all cursed the CO for pushing us so relentlessly, but, except for the few officers who requested transfers to less demanding units, most, like me, found him to be the best commander we ever worked for.

In my letter to Linda I made no mention of the Battalion nor recon's operations. I concentrated instead on writing about how happy I was that there were only thirteen days left until R&R.

In the "Remarks" column of a pay voucher I sent to Linda I noticed that subsistence entitlements were being deducted for meals at a rate of 27 cents for breakfast, 45 cents for lunch and 60 cents for dinner. A footnote explained that reimbursement for any "missed meals" could be claimed through finance channels. Since all my meals were either C- or LURP-rations, I thought it a little ridiculous that one could cost more than another depending on when I ate it.

Obviously set up for the REMFs who slept in and missed their mess hall breakfasts, the procedure at least obligated Finance to accept our claims. These we submitted on any kind of paper we had, and, surprisingly, the water-smudged pieces of notebook paper and mud-splattered scraps of stationery we sent in listing missed meals somehow made their way back to BMB to eventually reappear in the dollars-added column of the next month's voucher.

I would gladly have given up the few bucks to free some clerk from his record keeping duties at Finance so he could have gotten an honest job with the Infantry.

❧ 1 OCTOBER 1969
Wednesday

Black Horse
  Prepared to move out
  This morning at 0400 was alerted to move out—Didn't materialize
  Later moved to Tan Lap by truck—Had accident with 11 ACR truck on way out—No sweat
  Truck stuck tonight
  I am feeling very bad

Some days nothing went according to plans. After rushing to move out in response to the 0400 alert, we stood by for several hours while our mission was changed, and then changed again.

Finally, we were directed to return to Tan Lap by truck. Only a few kilometers out of Black Horse, our vehicle slid on the rain-drenched road into an on-coming truck. The damage to both trucks was minimal.

In the Stateside Army, a similar accident, no matter how minor the damage, would have required an investigation involving stacks of paperwork. Bureaucracy took a back seat in the war zone, though, and beyond instructing both of the drivers to be more careful, I took no further action.

Several of my soldiers complained of back injuries, whiplash, loss of memory and even mental anguish as they threatened to sue both drivers, the Army, the Saigon government and Ho Chi Minh. I told them that if they did not quiet down that I was going to send them to Vietnam. We then continued our journey.

Our luck followed us toward Tan Lap. When we reached the drop-off point the truck again lost traction, and we ended up in a ditch. After establishing security, we tried but failed to get the vehicle back on the road.

I radioed Battalion to request a recovery vehicle, but because darkness was approaching, I was told we would not get help until the next morning. Instead of looking for the enemy, we spent the night securing the truck—pleasing at least the driver who thought this was a great adventure because he had never been outside a fire base after sunset.

Besides the problems of having nothing go according to plan, I was sick. A burning fever, alternating with cold chills, kept me awake most of the night. I could do little to ease my discomfort except take a few aspirin and cuss the rain, truck drivers, and the war in general.

✒ 2 OCTOBER 1969
Thursday

Tan Lap
  Feeling a little better

> "Water shapes its course according to the ground over which it flows—As water retains no constant shape, so in warfare there are no constant conditions. He who can modify his tactics in relation to his opponent can achieve the victory."
>
> Sun Tzu   500 B. C.

By the time we got the truck on its way back to Black Horse, the sun made a brief appearance through the monsoon clouds. I began to feel better as we scouted the jungle for signs of the gooks that the Rat Patrol had engaged a few nights earlier. We worked the jungle all day but found nothing.

The only excitement was offered about midnight by one of

Alpha Company's ambushes that was securing Tan Lap. One of the squads covering the railroad bed between the depot and a village to the west had selected their site well, for a lone gook walked into the edge of their kill zone. Obviously not too smart about his choice of routes or in his ability to recognize danger, the enemy soldier spotted one of Alpha's Claymores and, instead of running, curiously picked it up. As he brought it up to study, an Alpha troop pressed the detonator. The blast cut the dink in two, leaving little that was recognizable as human.

It was encouraging to know the enemy had bad days, too.

☛ 3 OCTOBER 1969
Friday

> Another short break
> Typical VC-NVA bunker in base camp type area: Thick jungle—Slightly high ground—Using crest of hill—Lay-out zigzag or semi-circle or even perimeter
> Bunkers often connected by trench line—All so well camouflaged—Can't be seen from air—Got to be on ground within 10–15 meters to see them
> Means of detection:
>   1. Smell   4. Combat feeling
>   2. Cut   5. Litter
>   trees
>   3. Trails

SSG Standard reported to me in the late afternoon that one of our men was missing. Shortly before disappearing, he had told a buddy that he had had enough of the war and was taking LT Billings' jeep. When last seen he was headed for Highway 1 with a couple of rapidly emptying whiskey bottles.

I had been aware of the soldier's problems since Standard briefed me my first day in recon. The missing soldier had been in the Army for over five years and was on his second tour in Nam. He was a tremendous soldier in the field but had a drinking problem in the rear. Some of the men thought he was a bit crazy but I did not find that bothersome, for many thought the same thing about me for staying in the field.

If the man was a little weird, he had good reasons to be. On his first tour with the 1st Cavalry Division, he had been the sole survivor of his platoon when his unit had been ambushed by an NVA force. He had lain under dead comrades while the gooks had searched the bodies. Hours later when US soldiers arrived, the man was still feigning death beneath his lifeless buddies.

Evidently, the soldier felt he had done his part in the war or maybe he just could not forget all the dead. I reported his absence to Battalion, which passed the information along to the various Military Police units. Several days later he was picked up by the MPs in a Saigon bar while trying to trade the jeep for more whiskey. He was hospitalized in a psychiatric ward before being sent back to the States. I was glad he was not jailed, as the man obviously needed help. I thought about how we had been more interested in his helping us kill gooks than in trying to understand what was bothering him. Yet the man had never seemed happier than when he was in pursuit of the enemy. Whatever his past, his physical participation in Vietnam was over, but I doubt if his war will ever end.

✈ 4 OCTOBER 1969
Saturday

Airmobiled to another swampy LZ
Move out

Airmobile insertions of the recon platoon were different from the artillery- and gunship-supported air assaults of the regular Infantry companies. The four helicopters that picked us up never raised above the tree tops more than a hundred feet. Flying at top speed, they made low passes over several LZs before dropping down into the proper clearing.

Our best means of survival was to out-guerrilla the guerrillas themselves by moving quietly, engaging the gooks on our terms, and fighting when the odds were stacked in our favor. Standard and I added a factor to tip the scales of chance more our direction. At Black Horse, we had located several cases of CS canisters. These cylinders, about the size of beer cans, produced a large cloud of a tear-gas-like substance when the pin was pulled. I had briefed the platoon, telling them that if we were in contact with more gooks than we could handle, we would withdraw up-wind, popping the canisters as we went. The tear gas would not kill the gooks, but it surely would slow them down.

I was not certain, nor did I care, if the use of the chemical agent was in accordance with the laws of land warfare. According to the newspapers, tear gas was being used regularly against anti-war rioters in the streets back home. What was good enough for the protestors was good enough for the gooks.

✄ 5 OCTOBER 1969
Sunday

> Followed VC trail most of day—Once again no results—
> Found a bunker complex of 50 + —No VC there in approx.
> 3 months—Highers wanted us to blow them—18 men, 6
> klicks from friendlies—Tore them up by hand

One of the great advantages of being a ground commander
in Vietnam was that no one was looking over your shoulder to
ensure you did what you were told. Higher headquarters could
tell me on the radio to destroy bunkers with explosives, and I
could just as easily tell them to go to hell.

There was no way I was letting demolitions advertise our
location. It never ceased to amaze me that someone sitting in
a safe bunker in a fire base would order us to do dumb things
that would place our lives in danger.

When I refused to blow the bunkers, the Operations Officer
countered that it was a direct order. I answered that I took my
orders from the Battalion Commander. Because our radio conversation was monitored by every company RTO in the Battalion, I allowed him to save face by agreeing that we would
destroy the bunkers—but our way, not his.

Several of the recon troops overheard my radio transmission
and nodded in agreement with my responses. They were well
aware that the man on the other end of the radio was a major
and that I was only a lieutenant. I had done no more than what
they expected of their platoon leader, but they seemed to appreciate it nonetheless.

Over the next hour we caved in many of the fortifications
and, with the help of a log as a fulcrum, prized off much of
the overhead cover. We could have done more if we had stayed
longer, but an hour was already too much time in such a place.

6 OCTOBER 1969
Monday

> Airmobiled back to BH—Usual break—Getting ready to go back out
>
> New plt sgt looks good
>
> R&R gets closer and closer—And time goes slower and slower
>
> Good news—Texas A&M 20, West Point 13—Won 2 cases of beer, 1 qt bourbon, $5—Also moral victory

On our return to Black Horse, I was met by a Sergeant First Class who had just reported into the Battalion. A veteran of two tours with Special Forces and Ranger units, he had asked LTC Loeffke for assignment in the recon platoon. I was reluctant to agree with the assignment because the new sergeant was senior in rank to SSG Standard and would have to assume the duties of platoon sergeant.

The problem was solved when Loeffke told me that I had no choice. He wanted the new NCO in recon and Standard reassigned to Delta Company where CPT Lewis was badly in need of experienced leaders.

The new sergeant, a career NCO in his mid-30's with more than fifteen years service, assumed his duties efficiently. The men were a little slow in accepting him, but they soon recognized his abilities to take care of problems and read maps as well as occasionally walk point.

My initial respect for the new sergeant was tempered with a feeling that something about him was just not right. Although he did nothing to make me doubt his skills, the rest of my time with recon I continued to harbor a feeling that the decision to replace Standard had not been a good one.

Back home it was Fall and football. Texas A & M was having an even worse year than usual, so I was not surprised at the bets the Battalion West Pointers offered me. Loeffke, his XO, the Alpha Company Commander and Bill Little all sought me out as an easy mark when the Aggie-Cadet game rolled around.

The good news of the Aggie victory did not reach me in the field. When we were extracted from the jungle LZ, my first question to the chopper pilots was about the game. Their report on the score was confirmed by a case of beer from Loeffke waiting for me at Black Horse. While most of the members of recon had assured me that they were for West Point, they did not hesitate to share in the winnings provided by the Aggies.

🛩 7 OCTOBER 1969
Tuesday

> Out on mission with K Troop—11th ACR—Got VR of area—Found a very heavy trail—Followed it nearly all day—Nothing
> Have been feeling like hell—Believe I have a touch of malaria

I was surprised to find K Troop still in our AO. Their move to the north had again been delayed and once more they thought they were on their last mission out of Black Horse. The tracks dropped us off at the jungle's edge after we coordinated a location for link-up the next day.

By mid-afternoon we had followed the trail to a hillside overlooking a wide valley. I was running a high fever and was feeling so weak I could barely keep pace with the platoon. Our position offered good observation across the valley so I used it as an excuse to halt. I radioed Battalion that the platoon was holding its present position until the next day. After receiving a reluctant agreement, I told my RTO not to disturb me unless gooks were sighted. I then crawled into a depression in the ground, covered myself from the rain as well as I could with my poncho liner and fell into a deep sleep.

Over the next sixteen hours, I awoke with alternating bouts of cold chills and sweating fever. Dreams of talking to men whom I later realized were dead and of seeing piles of rotting corpses made me wonder if I was losing my mind. A vision of being surrounded by the enemy and trying to run but not being able to get my legs to move snapped me awake with a terror I had never before experienced.

Several times in the night I woke up with no memory of where I was. My mind raced as I peered through the darkness and rainfall trying to orient myself. Each time, a hand gently touched my shoulder and a voice whispered words of assurance. Sometimes I recognized the voice as that of my RTO or one of the squad leaders. Other times the voice was strange, distant and may not have existed at all.

✒ 8 OCTOBER 1969
Wednesday

> Took tracks back into BH—Recon party tonight—No. I Country and Western band—Many of recon said they hated to see me go—A good bunch of men—Good soldiers
> Recon's motto: "Death before dishonor."
> Recon's saying: "If you ain't recon, you ain't shit."
> Good news—Received word that when I return from R&R I will be CO of Bravo Co—Possibly the youngest company CO in RVN

Shortly after daybreak, PFC Pleseia woke me saying Battalion wanted to know why we were not moving to our rendezvous with the track platoon. I felt extremely weak, but the fevers and chills seemed to have passed. Several of the sergeants came to me with worried questions about how I was feeling. With embarrassment I told them I was all right and for them to saddle up. By the time we reached the tracks, I was feeling much better.

Over the next months and for several years afterward, each time I experienced a major change in the weather, the fever returned. Later tests for malaria came out negative. The doctors said I had been a victim of "fever, unknown origin."

Loeffke met us upon our return to Black Horse with the news that recon would have a few days off. He then called me over to one side and said that I would be taking over command of Bravo Company. Loeffke said that he wanted me to assume command immediately and asked if I would consider cancelling my R&R.

I told him I would if that was what he wanted but that after six months in the field, it would be better for me and Bravo if I had a break first. The Battalion Commander placed his arm around my shoulder and said I looked like I needed an R&R. He concluded by telling me to let my wife know her husband would likely be the junior ranking company commander in Vietnam.

Recon's party that night was a good opportunity to tell the soldiers goodbye and to let them know about my new assignment. My stay with recon had been short but satisfying.

The platoon presented me with a cloth patch—a narrow, three-inch long tab proudly appliqued with "Old Guard Recon." Below, a two-by-three inch shield sported a skull and cross bones with the code of the recon warrior, "Death before dishonor." As they pinned the patch to my jungle fatigue shirt pocket, they chanted the recon slogan, "If you ain't recon, you ain't shit." I could not have agreed more.

✎ 9 OCTOBER 1969
Thursday

> Returned by truck to BMB—Road from BH to BMB is
> about as dangerous as the jungle
> Played a little poker tonight—Lost—Money means little

The threat of an ambush on the road to BMB did not worry me. If the enemy attacked, at least I could shoot back. But I felt totally helpless in protecting myself from the crazy American and Vietnamese truck drivers on Highway 1.

For the first time in six months, I had no responsibilities to occupy my mind. During the next four days I slept long, ate and drank well and watched the calendar. My fever recurred a few times, but my strength was returning with the rest and sleep.

I counted the days and hours with an intensity similar to waiting for Christmas as a small boy. Of all the things I had learned in the past half year, patience was not one of them.

✎ 10 OCTOBER 1969
Friday

> Started getting things ready for R&R—Uniform etc.—
> When I put these khakis away 6 months ago the thought of
> R&R was unreal—Many times I didn't think I would make it—
> It's so damn good to be alive

Six months before I had arrived in Vietnam wearing a khaki uniform and carrying a duffel bag with a change of underwear and a shaving kit. After being issued my jungle fatigues, I had stuffed the travel uniform into the bag and placed it in the Charlie Company supply room. The supply room clerk now had little trouble finding it, as each duffel bag was labeled with name and line number. He explained that part of his job was keeping everything in order so he could send personal effects home to the next-of-kin. To help me get ready, the clerk told me he would have the Company hooch maid wash and iron my uniform as well as shine my shoes.

I had forgotten about shoes. I had worn nothing but canvas-topped jungle boots or shower shoes since my arrival.

My next stop was at the uniform shop to purchase the proper decorations, rank and Combat Infantryman's Badge that I was now entitled to wear. The colored ribbons and badge that I had envied on veterans back at Fort Bragg did not seem so important now. I felt more gratitude that I was alive to wear them than any pride in the acts of valor or service they represented.

✈ II OCTOBER 1969
Saturday

BMB
 Finished getting uniform ready
 Talked with old B Co CO—CPT Rees—Looks as if B Co will be a challenge
 Tonight went to club where they had a good all-girl band from the Philippines

CPT Steve Rees had returned to BMB before reassignment to the Battalion staff. 1LT Steve Beig, Company Executive Officer, was in charge of the Company in the field, but Rees was technically still the commander until I returned from R&R. Rees was friendly and showed deep feelings for the men of Bravo as he briefed me on the unit. I did my best not to make any pre-judgments on the Company, but by the time Rees concluded, I sensed that the unit had not been aggressively seeking out the enemy. The blame for casualties was chalked up to bad luck or superior enemy forces rather than a lack of alertness, stealth and morale.

Rees ended our conversation with an emotional plea for me "to take care of the troops." I told him not to worry, but I departed with the thought that a great challenge awaited me. Yet, I did not dwell on the future beyond the next week. Linda and Hawaii were rapidly approaching. Whatever was to come afterwards could wait.

12 OCTOBER 1969
Sunday

More BMB time—Drink—Rest
*R&R nearly here
Saw good movie at club

R&R eve I spent sleeping, reading, watching a movie and doing anything else I could do to pass the time. The only consolation was that my countdown was now measured in hours rather than weeks or days.

At the mess hall and club everyone was quick to relate stories they had heard of men going on R&R only to be met by wives asking for divorce—or not met at all when wives did not show up. Other personal accounts ranged from graphic descriptions of six days of continuous sex to tales of wives who cried the entire time because the husbands were going back to the war.

I realized that it would be impossible for R&R to be as wonderful as I had anticipated for the last six months, but, at the same time, I could not remotely guess how it could be any less. The only bothersome thought was the occasional recall of my prayers that if God would let me live to R&R that I would ask for nothing on my return to Nam.

✈ 13 OCTOBER 1969
Monday

> Trucked from BMB to Camp Alpha at Tan Son Nhut AFB for R&R—Received instructions, money change, customs, etc.
> Left 1700 on Pan Am 208A—Arrived Guam 0100 then Hawaii at 1230—Still the 13th
> Flight and bus to Ft. DeRussey seemed to take forever
> Staying at Colony Surf Hotel—Room 1105—Nice, large place
> Hawaii is not too impressive—But it's damn good to be with Linda
> Called my folks, Jim, and Linda's parents

It seems that nothing good ever happens quickly—especially in the Army. My impatience grew during the hour-long truck ride to the Camp Alpha R&R Center and the five-hour processing and waiting for our flight. Everything was well-organized but seemed to proceed at a snail's pace. I finally realized I could do nothing to expedite the process so I just relaxed.

During the wait I wandered around part of the Tan Son Nhut Air Base. Air-conditioned mobile homes for senior officers, swimming pools and snack bars again reminded me of the vast differences between REMFs and field soldiers. At a small PX, I picked up a *Stars and Stripes* and was amazed when stopped at the door by a clerk informing me that I owed ten cents for the newspaper. For six months the *Stripes* had been delivered with our mail with no charge ever mentioned. The clerk laughed at my embarrassment, explaining that it was a lesson learned frequently by grunts passing through Camp Alpha. I enjoyed paying the dime, knowing that at least there was something the Infantry was getting for free that the REMFs had to pay for.

An hour before departure, we were checked through customs and isolated in a large room. Of the two hundred passengers, only three of us were wearing Combat Infantryman's Badges. The other two besides me, a full colonel and a sergeant major, were commenting on the lack of CIBs when I introduced myself. They were both friendly and rank was put aside in favor of our commonality of combat. The colonel remarked just before our flight, "Looks like we're flying Air REMF instead of Pan Am."

According to military protocol, colonels were called to board the aircraft first. My new-found friend went to the head of the line with the sergeant major and me in tow. He walked past the airman checking the manifests and said, "Change that to 'Infantry will board first.' "

After the three of us were seated, the airman returned to his usual procedure of loading by rank. Minutes later the plane lifted off to a joint cheer by all and headed east.

The twelve-hour flight to Honolulu included a one-hour refueling stop on Guam where the duty-free shop offered up to a gallon of the finest brand spirits for a dollar or two a quart. Most of the passengers re-boarded the plane carrying their full quota, but I passed up the bargain. Drinking was not a priority on my R&R agenda, as I had seen the bottom of enough bottles in the past half year.

By the clock, we arrived in Hawaii hours before we departed Tan Son Nhut because we crossed the International Dateline. In reality, the trip seemed to take forever.

Upon arrival at Honolulu International Airport, our plane taxied to the edge of the terminal. An Air Force sergeant boarded and directed us to a baggage pick-up point. From there, we boarded buses which transported us to Fort De-Russey where our wives were waiting.

The scramble to find bags and get on the six buses was anything but orderly. As the others surged to get on the lead vehicle, I decided that if I had waited this long, I was not going to worry about a few more minutes.

Twenty minutes later we arrived at Ford DeRussey. The buses unloaded one at a time, letting the men file between the two columns of waiting wives.

Most of the men had already found their mates when I finally stepped off the bus. Linda was easy to pick out of the crowd. Only an inch less than six-feet tall, she had had the figure and cheekbones of a fashion model when I had last seen her. Now, dressed in yellow with her long reddish-brown hair tied back, she looked the same—the radiant beauty still there—even with her seven-month pregnant figure.

As we grasped each other in our arms, tears rolled down her cheeks as she said, "I knew you would be the last one off the damn bus."

I could only reply, "You sure look pregnant."

A loudspeaker announcement asked us to move into a briefing area. As the crowd moved to seats, Linda told me she had flown in the night before and then arrived at the Center three hours early to be sure she did not miss a minute of my time there.

The briefing included only a welcome to Hawaii and a card issued noting that I was to report to the airport no later than 0700 on 19 October for my return flight. Along with the card was a bottle of malaria pills. Another card contained emergency phone numbers on one side while the other side said that the bearer was on R&R from Vietnam and had been exposed to plague, malaria, yellow fever, typhus, smallpox and other diseases I had never heard of. The card seemed funny rather than threatening since I felt the best I had in months.

Minutes later Linda and I were in a taxi on our way to the hotel. We had so much to say to each other that we could not really talk much on the ride or in the first few hours in the hotel room. During the ride we just got used to being together again. In the hotel room we re-acquainted ourselves with one another, proving that Linda's doctor had been right in saying that we could do anything that was comfortable. The old barracks saying that "sex is what you get the furthest behind in and catch up on the quickest" was true, but a hell of a lot of fun to discover for ourselves. Finally spent, we began to talk—and never really stopped, except to reconfirm the barracks saying and occasionally to sleep, for the next six days.

Before leaving San Francisco, Linda had calculated time differences between the islands and Texas. She had written my parents approximately what time to expect a call from me so they could be at a neighbor's house that night. The war had reached their remote ranch home by taking two sons, but the telephone wires still stopped twelve miles down the road.

Mother and Dad were proud that I was getting a company, but their voices betrayed their worry over my staying in the field.

When I called my brother, I expected him to be excited over my good news. He congratulated me on cue. When I told him how much I appreciated LTC Loeffke's giving me the chance, he only remarked, "He's not doing you any favors." Jim's experience as both platoon leader and company commander made him more aware than I of what I was getting myself into.

Jim's statement did not bother me. For the next six days I intended to forget about the war and think of nothing past R&R. Later, while holding the phone receiver as the operator put through a call to Linda's parents, I learned the war would be impossible to set aside for six days, or perhaps, ever.

While the operator was connecting the call, a ship sailed past into view out our window. Linda snapped her fingers to gain my attention so I would not miss the beautiful craft. My reactions immediately returned me to the jungle and the recon platoon where only days before snapping fingers meant gooks in sight. I dove for the floor, frantically searching for my rifle that was not to be found. Seconds later, I sheepishly returned to Hawaii and took up the phone receiver again.

I explained to Linda what had happened with a nervous laugh. She joined my laughter and said, "Everyone told me you would be crazy—I was beginning to think they were right."

✆ 14 OCTOBER 1969
Tuesday

> Honolulu, Hawaii
>   Went to Waikiki, International market, etc—Also went to a movie—Having an absolutely wonderful time

Linda had done well in the selection of our hotel. Far from the downtown area, the Colony Surf was near Diamond Head which, along with the ocean, offered a magnificent view out our window. Our suite was complete with kitchen facilities that greatly benefitted Linda's pregnancy and my C-ration-induced lust for food of all types. The refrigerator was soon filled with ice cream, fresh fruit, and candies.

We both liked the isolation of our quarters, as neither of us was interested in the crowded beaches and night clubs of Waikiki. I had been surrounded by people at all times for the last six months. All I wanted now was to be with my wife.

I was surprised that the pregnancy seemed to have little effect on Linda beyond causing a bulge at her midriff. She was never tired nor sick, and except for a craving for banana cream pie that we could not find anywhere in the city, was her usual self.

We spent the afternoon walking the streets and seeing the

sites. We ate when hungry, stopped to see a movie when we got tired, and ignored the clocks completely.

The transition from the dangers of Vietnam to the luxuries of Honolulu was astonishingly easy. Except for being startled by sudden noises and occasionally finding myself watching the roadside for ambushes from a cab window, the war seemed far away. At times I even thought that Nam had only been a long nightmare while at others I feared that Hawaii was the dream and I would suddenly wake up back in the jungle.

15 OCTOBER 1969
Wednesday

Honolulu, Hawaii
   Back to same as yesterday—Another movie
   We stay up late and sleep late
   My wife is very pregnant and very beautiful

Across the United States this was the period of the largest organized protests against the war in Vietnam thus far. Moratorium Week extended to the islands with the streets filled with young protestors carrying signs and handing out leaflets.

At the International Market, young, long-haired men dressed in beads and tie-dyed shirts easily identified me as a soldier by my close-cut hair. They seemed to take delight in handing me fliers calling the military "baby killers," "terrorists," and "murderers for Nixon." I was more disgusted than angry with their accusations. All we wanted was to be left alone. With Linda at my side, it should have been obvious that I was much more interested in making babies than in killing them.

Linda and I talked about ourselves and our times together before the war. We spent hours discussing the baby's December due date. Yet, we never said anything about plans after Vietnam. Linda had already accepted my intent to remain in uniform. Wherever the Army sent me, we would be together and that was all we really wanted. We made no mention of the possibility of my not returning at all.

I had said little about the war other than telling Linda about the men in my platoon and about fellow officers like Loeffke, McGinnis, Little, Jong, and Sassner. She asked for more descriptions of DeForrest, Bass, Standard and others I had mentioned in letters. When she asked late that afternoon what Nam was really like, we were walking along a back street well away from the tourist spots on the beach. Country and Western music from a small bar across the street made it sound like a good place to tell Linda about the war.

The tavern was rather run-down and definitely did not cater to the tourist trade. Several locals at the bar gave us curious glances as we took seats in a back booth, but their attitude seemed to be that if we shared their taste in music, we were welcome to stay.

And stay we did. Until well after midnight, I told Linda about the paddies, jungle, fire fights, and the exhilaration and terror of combat. I took as much time describing the humor as the tragedy, and we shared more laughter than grief.

Linda understood better than I had hoped that I had done, and would return to do, what I thought was right. She did not ask nor did I have to tell her that I had no apologies nor regrets.

Today when I recall those fantastic days in Hawaii, that night in a back street bar comes to mind more vividly than the beaches, shops and other typical tourist offerings of the islands. The whole damn war seemed to make a little better sense.

✈ 16 OCTOBER 1969
Thursday

> Rented a car—'69 Mustang convertible—Took tour of island—Diamond Head, coastline, pineapple and sugarcane fields etc.
>
> At place where Captain Cook landed they had talking birds—Very interesting
>
> Hawaii is very nice but seems confining

Oahu was beautiful with great variation in terrain. However, having been raised in the vast open spaces of West Texas, I found the island to be small and limiting.

On the north beaches we stopped to watch surfers riding monstrous waves. After seeing several boards tossed high in the air while their riders tumbled in the boiling sea, I decided that all brave men were not in uniform.

Farther down the road we passed huge fields of sugarcane and pineapples. Linda and I were neither far-removed from the farm and found the island's agriculture as interesting as the beaches. The pineapple plantations brought back memories of the Delta. Signs telling us not to pick the fruit on threat of arrest were not as effective a deterrent as the skull and cross bones warnings in the booby-trapped filled pineapple fields near Fire Base Claudette. My appreciation for pineapple had been lost after daily consumption in the Delta, but Linda insisted we stop at the Dole farm headquarters so she could sample the fruit.

Our last stop was made at the landing site of Captain Cook. His voyages had been detailed in my elementary school books and had made a great impression on me. Seeing his landing place verified that the Army was fulfilling its promise of fun, travel, and adventure, though Uncle Sam surely asked a lot in return. I had been half-way around the world, completed half my war and learned many things that I really did not want to know, yet I was still young and innocent enough to be impressed by talking birds.

✈ **17 OCTOBER 1969**
Friday

> Drove around more in car—Bought some things for folks at home
> Artist drew our pictures—Very good
> Time getting short
> Linda and I stayed up till 0500, daylight, talking—Mostly about when we were living in College Station

Linda and I did our best to cheat the clock by staying awake till sun-up and sleeping only briefly before beginning another day. I never tired of resting my hand on Linda's stomach to feel the baby kick as we talked of our school days and the five months we were together while I finished my last semester at A & M after our marriage.

We also talked about baby names. Being familiar with genetic studies that said a child's sex was determined by the father, we assumed Linda was carrying our son. On my side of the family, no females had been born in over seventy years. We directed most of our conversation to boys' names and decided that he would be named Lohn Michael.

As almost an after-thought, Linda asked, "What if it's a girl?"

Laughing at the very idea, I responded, "Since she would be the first Lanning female in recent times, let's call her Reveille. It would be appropriate for an Army brat anyway."

Linda joined in my laughter because she had liked the word "reveille" since living near Reveille Road in Houston before we married. The fact that it was the name of the A&M mascot only added to the humorous naming of a daughter we knew would be a son.

We debated other female names but never came to a consensus. Linda finally said, "I guess the choice will be mine since you won't be there when I sign the birth certificate. If it's a girl, we will spell it R-e-v-e-i-l-e-e so it includes your name." Because it was going to be a boy anyway, I readily agreed with her name and spelling.

The artist's sketches were good likeness although we both thought we appeared very young. Of course, we were young, but so much had happened so fast that we did not think of ever being any older than during those few days in Hawaii.

We did not mention it, but we were well aware that our time together was rapidly nearing the end.

✈ 18 OCTOBER 1969
Saturday

Last day in Hawaii
Has been a wonderful R&R
Will send this book home with Linda and start another

In every person's life there are special times that are never forgotten. Vietnam offered a year of triumph, despair, horror and other emotions burned into my memory so strongly that I can never forget them. It all happened when I was so young, inexperienced and naive that I did not thoroughly realize the impact on the rest of my life at the time. One thing that I did grasp with an intensity that has never faded was that life just does just not get any better than that week in Hawaii with Linda.

All good things must come to an end, however, and each tick of the damn clock brought me closer to reporting to the airport for the flight back to the war. We wasted no time anguishing over the fact that our time together was drawing to a close. Neither did we let sleep interfere with our last hours together. We stayed up all night, loving, talking, laughing, and being grateful for the time together.

Shortly after sunup, I gave Linda my journal. She gave me three smaller blank books that would each hold the entries for two months. By the time all three new journals were complete, I would be home.

🛩 19 OCTOBER 1969

Hawaii
     The last few hours with my wonderful wife—Saw sun come up over Diamond Head
     Hard to leave—Sad scenes at airport—No ones seems happy about returning to RVN
     Boarded Flight P207A Pan Am

In the airport waiting room, many of the wives were crying and more than a few men had tears in their eyes. Hawaii had been too wonderful to let a sad departure spoil our memories. Linda shed no tears though she told me years later that she cried all the way on her flight back to San Francisco. When I kissed her good-bye and walked up the ramp to board the airplane, I looked back to see her send me off with a smile.

When I had left Linda back in April, I could hardly wait to get to Vietnam. I had looked forward to the adventure, excitement and anticipation of finally being part of the war. Leaving

Hawaii was different. This time I knew exactly what I was going back to.

In April, Linda had been convinced she would never see me again while I was sure nothing could happen to me. My wife left Hawaii confident that we would be together again at the end of six more months. This time it was my turn; I worried that I would never see her again.

As the plane took off and turned west, my prayers about surviving until R&R and asking nothing more came to mind. It was time to see if I could renegotiate.

POST-JOURNAL

I returned to Vietnam from R&R to find command of Bravo Company awaiting me. Within hours I was back in the jungle facing new challenges and responsibilities.

The remainder of my tour would prove to be all that I had expected—and more. During the first week of December, in the midst of a month of nearly continuous combat, a crackling radio message brought word of the birth of my daughter, Reveilee Ann. She would be almost five months old before I held her in my arms. The fact that our first meeting was so long delayed bothered me little—for I was so grateful to have survived to see what my child would become.

For several years after my return, I anticipated receiving orders for a second tour in Vietnam. However, the continued reduction of US combat forces and the increased turnover of the war to the ARVNs drastically decreased the requirements for additional Infantrymen.

The Army continued to provide its promised fun, travel, and adventure. Linda and I moved frequently and adjusted fairly well to the peace-time Army. In 1972 our second daughter, Meridith, was born with her father present at the hospital rather than 11,000 miles away in the jungle.

In 1975 I was again in command of an Infantry company—this time in Germany. Shortly after the fall of Saigon, my unit was on a training mission in Berlin where we were given a tour of the Soviet-occupied sector of the city. In the main square of East Berlin we stopped to observe the continuing celebration of the communist victory in Vietnam. As we watched, one of my senior NCOs, a veteran of two Nam tours, asked me, "Was it worth it?"

I thought of magnificent responses about dedication, bravery, loyalty, and a sense of doing what was right; however, after a long pause, I replied, "It really doesn't make any difference. We did our best. After all, it was the only war we had."

It has often been said that there is at least one book in every man who goes to war. When I began writing of my experiences nearly fifteen years after my return from Vietnam, I initially thought my "one book" would be an extremely thin volume. Months, and many worn typewriter ribbons, later I discovered that the memories were so vivid and the experience so intensely recalled that one book was not sufficient to tell the entire story. The second volume, relating the remainder of my one-year tour, will soon be published as *Vietnam 1969–1970: A Company Commander's Journal*

About the Author

Michael Lee Lanning was born in Sweetwater, Texas, and is a graduate of Texas A&M University with a Bachelor of Science in Education. He also holds a Master of Science in Journalism from East Texas State University.

Lanning entered the United States Army in 1968. He is a career officer and has served throughout the United States as well as in Europe and Vietnam. Past assignments include infantry, armor, airborne, and Ranger assignments as platoon leader, company commander, and battalion executive officer. He is presently assigned to the Armed Forces Information Service in Washington, D.C., after being transferred from Fort Lewis, Washington, where he was the I Corps and Fort Lewis Public Affairs Officer.

Lieutenant Colonel Lanning is Ranger qualified, is a senior parachutist, and has been awarded the Combat Infantryman Badge, the Bronze Star for Valor with two oak leaf clusters, the Meritorious Service Medal with one oak leaf cluster, the Air Medal, the Army Commendation Medal, and other U. S. and foreign decorations.

He is married and has two teenage daughters. The Lannings now consider the Pacific Northwest home.